Pictures from Italy

CHARLES DICKENS

Pictures from Italy

with an introduction and notes by
David Paroissien

The Street of the Tombs : Pompeii

COWARD, McCANN & GEOGHEGAN
NEW YORK

Contents

Illustrations

Acknowledgements

For permission to quote from copyright material I wish to thank the following: Mr Christopher Dickens for quotations from Dickens's letters; Steven Marcus and Chatto and Windus for the quotation from *Dickens: From Pickwick to Dombey*. I would also like to thank the following: the Huntington Library, San Marino, California, for permission to quote from the letter of Basil Hall, the letter of Samuel Palmer, and Dickens's letter to Mitton; the Henry W. and Albert A. Berg Collection, The New York Public Library, Astor, Lenox and Tilden Foundations, for permission to consult and quote from Dickens's correspondence with the De la Rues; and Mr Howell J. Heaney, for drawing my attention to Dickens's letter to Lady Blessington in the Free Library of Philadelphia. I am grateful to the editor of *English Miscellany* for permission to incorporate my comments on the genesis of the text of *Pictures from Italy* into the Introduction and to the editor of *The Dickensian* for permission to include the note concerning the original illustrator, here slightly amended, in this book.

D.P.

Introduction

ON Monday 1 July 1844 'an English travelling carriage of considerable proportions, fresh from the shady halls of the Pantechnicon near Belgrave-square,' left London on the Dover road. Inside were Charles Dickens, his wife Catherine, Georgina Hogarth, his sister-in-law, five children, two nurses, and the family dog, all under the watchful eye of Louis Roche, the 'Brave Courier' of *Pictures from Italy*. Two weeks and two days later the party arrived in Albaro, a suburb of Genoa, where Dickens's friend Angus Fletcher had rented the Villa di Bella Vista on his behalf. After nearly three months of mosquitoes, fleas, and vermin, the family moved into the *piano nobile* of the Palazzo Peschiere, a fine house in Genoa, splendidly situated on a hill and surrounded by beautiful gardens, the price being one quarter of that negotiated by Fletcher for the 'Pink Jail.' For the remaining eight months the 'Palace of the Fishponds' served as the novelist's headquarters: here Dickens wrote his second Christmas book *The Chimes*, transmitted to his friend John Forster 'regular accounts of all sight-seeings and journey-ings',[1] and relaxed in the following spring in a 'shady arm-chair up among the Peschiere oranges,' as he went over in his mind all the roads he had taken on his Italian travels.[2]

When Dickens departed for Genoa in 1844 with the in-tention of writing a travel book about Italy he was acting in a manner typical of many of his fellow countrymen. Eminent writers such as Fielding, Smollett, Goldsmith, and Hazlitt, to mention a few, had popularized the idea of publishing personal accounts of their Continental travels, often in the form of familiar letters; and perhaps Dickens was consciously following their example when he formed his plan to write a series of letters to Forster which would form the basis of his book. As for the choice of location and the roads travelled, Dickens was clearly indebted to the opinions of certain of his friends. W. S. Landor recommended Genoa as preferable to Pisa and suggested renting Casa Saluzzi, Byron's former villa[3]; Lady Blessington and Count D'Orsay were also fond of Genoa and discussed their stay there with Dickens (I, 643); Leigh Hunt had found Albaro cheap and delightful during his visit in 1822[4]; finally, there was Samuel Rogers, a veteran of the Italian scene, whose opinions of the country were well known to Dickens.

The decision to take a house was in keeping with the preference for settling for several months in one place which, by the early nineteenth century, had replaced the neo-classical Grand Tour with its prescribed itinerary of best-known cities, monuments, and works of art. Interest in Pagan and Christian antiquity was giving way to curiosity about Italian life and customs; and travellers, especially in the two decades after the Napoleonic wars, found greater satisfaction in transplanting their families to less famous towns such as Livorno, Pisa, Fiesole, Genoa, and Albaro for a number of months, where they could leisurely observe the life around them. In a review of three recent books on Italy, Mary Shelley speaks in 1826 of 'a new generation' of travellers who have lately been dubbed 'Anglo-Italians.' Among the characteristics of this 'new race' are an understanding of the language, fewer complaints about being starved, upset, and robbed, more independence from guide books, and a deeper interest in the Italian people.[5]

While Dickens was not averse to complaining of the dirt, he nevertheless shares certain characteristics of this 'new race.' Dickens's visit to Italy was planned as a domestic excursion rather than as an opportunity to make a circuit of the famous sites. He studied Italian before leaving and engaged a language tutor while abroad; and he spent more time in the streets, shops, and theatres of Genoa than he did haunting the ruins of classical antiquity. As a result, *Pictures from Italy* is full of personal and eclectic sketches – of marionettes acting *St Helena, or the Death of Napoleon*, of Genoese men playing 'Mora,' of the guides, waiters and postilions who attended Dickens on his travels, of artists' models in Rome – rather than of solemn catalogues of paintings and discourses on art. For the Italian people he developed a lasting warmth and affection, saving his ridicule for the English and French tourists who inspected 'every tomb, and every church, and every ruin, and every Picture Gallery' (*PI*, p. 185) and returned home without learning anything about the life of the people around them.

The main impetus behind Dickens's decision to go abroad, however, was a personal one; and factors such as the advice of friends on locations or the prevailing fashion for Italy appear secondary, shaping the incidentals of his residence rather than the plan itself. Of greater importance was the increasing restlessness and tension that Dickens experienced as he started work on *Martin Chuzzlewit* in January 1843. Already upset by the unfavourable reviews of his *American Notes* (1842), Dickens was further agitated by the poor sales of his new serial. 'I am so irritated,' he confided to Forster on 28 June 1843, 'so rubbed in the tenderest part of my eyelids with bay-salt, by what I told you yesterday [of the sales of *Martin Chuzzlewit*] that a wrong kind of fire is burning in my head, and I don't think I *can* write' (I, 526–27). Accordingly it is not surprising to find Dickens telling Forster five months later that 'I should unquestionably fade away from the public eye for a year, and enlarge my stock of description and observation by seeing countries new to me;' a move which would perhaps alleviate his uneasiness and provide some temporary relief from the public. Secondly, the prospect of going abroad offered Dickens an opportunity to live cheaply and reorganize his finances after the losses from the sales of the novel. 'I shall take all the family, and two

servants . . . to some place which I know beforehand to be
CHEAP and in a delightful climate . . . where I shall rent some
house for six or eight months' (I, 544–45).

The other part of this project, revealed to Forster for the
first time in November, was Dickens's intention to send his
friend descriptions of his travels, exactly as he had done in
America, out of which a new travel book could be made. To
counter the objections Forster was likely to raise, Dickens
cited Scott's unfortunate trip to Italy as a warning to those
who waited too long before travelling, and put the case for a
travel book instead of another novel. The former, 'if to be
done at all, would cost me very little trouble; and surely
would go very far to pay charges, whenever published' (I,
545–46).

As Dickens's comments to Forster suggest, a year in Italy
offered him a chance to escape, while the travel book would
contribute usefully to keeping his 'whole Menagerie' abroad
with little effort. Dickens was, in fact, in a mood for relaxation: he was not going to survey the enormous stock of
information extant upon Italy, he was not going to 'expiate
at any length on famous Pictures and Statues,' and he was not
going to examine the government or misgovernment of the
country. Rather, he informs his readers in a prefatory com-
ment to *Pictures from Italy*, 'this Book is a series of faint
reflections – mere shadows in the water – of places to which
the imaginations of most people are attracted in a greater or
less degree,' adding that if 'they have ever a fanciful and idle
air, perhaps the reader will suppose them written in the shade
of a Sunny Day.'

This deliberate air of fancy and idleness – of an arm-chair
view of Italy from under the shade of the Peschiere orange
trees – is probably responsible for the general tendency to
overlook Dickens's reactions to the Italian experience.
Apart from a survey of the 'facts' by biographers, there has
been little attempt to examine the travel context to which the
book belongs, or even to consider Dickens's first impressions

of Italy with his later editorial views as represented in
Household Words and *All the Year Round.*

An obvious exception to this indifference are Mario Praz's
comments on *Pictures from Italy* in his study of the disap-
pearance of the epic and the rise of the nineteenth-century
novel.[6] For Praz, the travel book is a characteristic example
of the Victorians' bourgeois social preoccupations, which he
finds diametrically opposed to those of the more cultured
traveller of the eighteenth century, who carried with him his
library of classical authors in order to verify quotations on
the spot. Yet for all the dichotomy Praz discovers between
the reverent antiquarianism of Addison's *Remarks on Several
Parts of Italy* (1705) and Dickens's picture of Rome as a
macabre London slum in 1846, it is worth remembering that
the eighteenth-century experience of Italy was not so mono-
lithic that one can rest with Addison. Travel writers such as
Samuel Sharp, Smollett, Lady Anna Miller, the Earl of Cork,
and Mrs Piozzi all had a keen eye for social conditions and
none were so deeply immersed in humanistic pursuits as to
ignore the Italians of the present day. Accordingly, when we
turn to *Pictures from Italy,* we should bear in mind that
Victorian Dickens, with his anti-heroic point of view, was not
the first to complain about what Shelley in 1818 called 'the
other' Italy.[7] As Herbert Barrows points out in his Introduction to Mrs Piozzi's *Observations and Remarks,* 'shortly after
midpoint in the century the voice of dissidence had become so
loud . . . in its complaints about the character of the Italian
people and the discomfort and indignity to which the traveler
was subjected on the tour, that Guiseppe Baretti . . . felt
obliged to correct the picture which was being offered to
English readers, and did so in a spirited and sensible book,
An Account of the Manners of Italy' (1768).[8]

Nor is the continuity of experience between Dickens and
his eighteenth-century forerunners limited to this area. The
Dickens who likened his first view of the Eternal City, with
its mud, rain, and clouds, to London also responded to the

terrifying and savage aspects of natural scenery in the manner of Burke, Dennis, Walpole, and Gray. Struggling through snow, pierced by the cold, and almost deafened by the incessant roar of cataracts, Dickens found his night journey over the Simplon Pass, with its 'impenetrable shadows, and deep glooms . . . more and more sublime at every step' (*PI*, p. 137). Similarly, 'the gloom and grandeur' of Vesuvius inspired him to undertake a hazardous ascent to the very brim of the cone in order to 'look down, for a moment, into the Hell of boiling fire below.' 'There is something in the fire and roar,' he reflects, 'that generates an irresistible desire to get nearer to it' (*PI*, p. 251). Less frightening but equally compelling was the 'tremendous solitude', especially at night, of the Coliseum, which Dickens visited daily during his stay in Rome, in a manner reminiscent of Mme de Staël and Byron.[9]

Perhaps a more definitive shift of interest in Italy, and one to which Dickens's was no exception, was the later generation's sympathy with the awakening of Italian nationalism in the early nineteenth century. While Dickens refrained from any open or clandestine involvement with nationalists during his stay (though he did deliver letters to friends of Antonio Gallenga,[10] his exiled Italian instructor, and engaged 'a little, patient, revolutionary officer . . . to read and speak Italian' three times a week with him[11]), his championship of Italian exiles and their cause suggests how deeply he reacted to the misrule and oppression abroad. Shortly before leaving England Dickens was among those who expressed disapproval at the order of Sir James Graham, the Home Secretary, to open Mazzini's letters and communicate their contents to the Neapolitan government; upon returning he joined the Council of 'The People's International League,' founded in April 1847 to 'enlighten the British public as to the political condition and relations of foreign countries; to disseminate the principles of national freedom and progress; to embody and manifest an efficient public opinion in favour of the right of every people to self-government and the maintenance of their own nationality; to promote a good understanding between peoples of every country.'[12] Later, he became a member of the committee formed in London to raise funds for Italian refugees who left Rome after the French captured the city in 1849.[13]

Dickens's most prominent role, however, was probably the part he played in educating public opinion about the Italian cause through his journalistic and editorial work. From his short-lived editorship of the *Daily News* (from November 1845 to February 1846), to his successful direction of the weekly miscellanies *Household Words* (March 1850 to May 1859) and *All the Year Round* (April 1859 to his death in 1870), Dickens strove to overcome the insularity of his British audience by providing thorough coverage of foreign affairs. In addition to numerous travel pieces and colourful descriptions of places and local customs from a variety of contributors, both journals paid close attention to Italy. *Household Words* sent a special correspondent to interview Francesco and Rosa Madiai, two harmless citizens imprisoned by the Tuscan authorities for possessing a Bible, and ran a series of first-hand accounts of the abuse of political prisoners, the tyranny of censorship, and the prevalence of legal corruption in the Kingdom of the Two Sicilies. Later, reports of the battles of Magenta and Solferino and Garibaldi's campaigns in Sicily and Naples, together with reviews of books on Italy and scholarly articles on Italian history, filled many pages of *All the Year Round*.

Although most of the pieces were the work of individual correspondents, they nevertheless reflect Dickens's views: 'the statements and opinions of this journal generally are, of course, to be received,' he told his *All the Year Round* readers, 'as the statements and opinions of its conductor,' a practice which was equally true of *Household Words*. Consequently, one finds the same warm regard for the Italian people and impatient desire for their liberty, progress, social welfare and happiness, together with a strong antipathy towards the Church of Rome and its papal bulls – 'enemies of the human race,' declares one article in *Household Words* – that one would expect from the author of *Pictures from Italy*. The only difference between Dickens's earlier and later writings is that in the travel book he avoided, either in deference to the Italians or in a wish not to provoke the hostile reaction that his *American Notes* had caused, any overt comments on the country's internal affairs. However, by the 1850s foreign policy had engaged an increasing share of public attention in Britain and it is not surprising to see Dickens both leading and reflecting this development in the pages of his two weekly magazines.

*

It is one of the ironies of Dickens's wish to escape to 'some delicious nook' that the very scenes – 'Italian Castles, bright in sunny days, and pale in moonlight nights' (I, 580) – he fancied would provide relief accelerated the development of his ideas about the relationship of the past to social change. In May 1843 Dickens had told his friend Douglas Jerrold: 'if I ever destroy myself, it will be in the bitterness of hearing those infernal and damnably good old times extolled' (I, 517); and once amidst the slums of Naples Dickens confronted in the *lazzaroni* living evidence of the oppressive conditions from the past. As Steven Marcus observes, 'it was Italy, the country more evocative of a sense of the historic past than any other, which affected him most. To Dickens the Continent often seemed a monument to a past which, no matter how familiar he became with it, never ceased to horrify him. He passes from one *Salle de la Question* to another without ever failing to be shaken, without ever losing his innocence and outrage over the tales of inhumanity they told. This innocence and outrage preserved him, as they preserved Blake, from the indifference and complacency which frequently accompany what we call the wisdom of history and the wisdom of tradition.'[14]

Two years later, while staying in Switzerland, Dickens visited Chillon and described to Forster 'the insupportable solitude and dreariness' he felt upon inspecting the towers and lonely ramparts. Inside was a courtyard surrounded 'by prisons, oubliettes, and old chambers of torture; so terrifically sad, that death itself is not more sorrowful.' 'Good God,' Dickens continued, 'the greatest mystery in all the earth, to me, is how or why the world was tolerated by its Creator, through the good old times, and wasn't dashed to fragments' (I, 777–78).

The natural beauty of the Italian countryside and the stunning panoramas of the bay of Genoa from the Palazzo Peschiere had little effect upon such perceptions as they began to stir in Dickens in 1844. After an initial period of inactivity and idleness, he set to work on *The Chimes*, a story which reflects his deepening awareness that the causes of crime and misery were legacies of ingrained historical and economic injustices rather the consequences of individual villainy. As Dickens soon discovered, the 'distractions' of travel were ambiguous and his search for peace more elusive than perhaps he had imagined.

The truth of this is borne out when we examine the way in which Dickens spent his leisure time while in Italy. He had no sooner completed *The Chimes* when he determined to rush to England in the face of approaching winter, in order to spend a few nights in London and read aloud his story to a group of friends. On 6 November he set off with the Brave Courier on a whirlwind tour across northern Italy to Venice and back to Milan. After two days sightseeing in Milan, he started at six in the morning and travelled all day and night across the Alps without pause, before stopping at Strasbourg. Off again after a night's rest, he completed the Strasbourg–Paris leg of his journey in fifty hours of continuous coach travel. Later, in the comparative calm of the Peschiere,

Dickens noted the effect upon the mind of travelling with little rest at night and none in the day: 'the rapid and unbroken succession of novelties that had passed before me, came back like half-formed dreams: and a crowd of objects wandered in the greatest confusion through my mind . . . At intervals, some one among them would stop, as it were, in its restless flitting to and fro . . . After a few moments, it would dissolve, like a view in a magic-lantern' (*PI*, p. 107).

The loneliness and hallucinatory effect produced by such frenzied travelling is similar to the confusion James Carker experiences on his haunted flight across France in Dickens's next novel, *Dombey and Son* (1846–48). As critics have previously suggested, he put a good deal of himself into Carker, and without doubt his introspection and personal acquaintance with a similar state of mind is largely responsible for the immediacy with which he renders Carker's tormented, self-destroying psyche. Carker's flight begins as he steals out of Dijon, in an attempt to elude Mr Dombey, who has finally learned of his manager's plot to overthrow him and elope with his wife. Once on the open road, the journey begins: 'nothing clear without, and nothing clear within. Objects flitting past, merging into one another, dimly descried, confusedly lost sight of, gone! . . . The lamps, gleaming on the medley of horses' heads, jumbled with the shadowy driver, and the fluttering of his cloak made a thousand indistinct shapes, answering to his thoughts. Shadows of familiar people, stooping at their desks and books, in their remembered attitudes; strange apparitions of the man he was flying from, or of Edith; repetitions in the ringing bells and rolling wheels, of words that he had spoken; confusions of time and place, making last night a month ago, a month ago last night – home now distant beyond hope, now easily accessible' (*Dombey and Son*, ch. 55).

Further manifestations of what Dickens's biographer, Edgar Johnson, terms the 'progressive and underlying disturbance'[15] at work in this stage of Dickens's career are symptoms of his deteriorating relationship with his wife Catherine. Not long before departing for Italy Dickens became infatuated with a young pianist called Christiana Weller; once in Genoa there was Mme De la Rue, "a most affectionate and excellent little woman" (I, 708), who suffered from a severe nervous disorder. Feeling sorry for her, Dickens, with the agreement of Mme De la Rue's husband, tried to banish her afflictions by mesmerism. To Catherine's concern, the ensuing therapy sessions occupied a considerable amount of Dickens's time, and her antagonism to the experiment increased until she refused to speak to the De la Rues. Finally, after trying to excuse Catherine's conduct as a nervous breakdown, Dickens was forced to make a 'painful declaration of her state of mind' to his friends.[16] So determined was Mrs Dickens to avoid further trouble, that she resisted her husband's wish to return to Genoa the following summer and forced him 'to take a middle course for the present,' as Dickens told Mme De la Rue, by going no closer than the Lake of Geneva (I, 745).

In spite of these domestic and intellectual tensions, there were interludes in which Dickens managed to relax and, on balance, the twelve months in Italy were a success. For a brief period he had lived anonymously, far from the public eye: no hostile press, no women snipping off fragments of his clothing for souvenirs, no pressing mobs. Instead, he delighted in 'the beautiful Italian manners, the sweet language, the quick recognition of a pleasant look or cheerful word; the captivating expression of a desire to oblige in everything' (I, 683); and when Dickens took his leave of the country, he did so with affection.

In view of the unquestionably greater importance of Dickens's novels, it is not surprising to find that the text of *Pictures from Italy* has been neglected along with Dickens's reaction to the Italian experience. Yet the genesis of the travel book and Dickens's method of composition are not without interest;

and there is sufficient existing confusion to justify an attempt to straighten the record by tracing *Pictures from Italy* from its inception through the various stages of the text.

Dickens's first reference to his proposed travel book was, as we have seen, in his letter to Forster of 1 November 1843. No further mention of the project survives until the following February when, after a meeting with Andrew Doyle, the editor of the *Morning Chronicle*, Dickens told Forster how the idea of contributing a weekly letter to the newspaper from abroad emerged. 'Then said the editor,' wrote Dickens to Forster, '– and this I particularly want you to turn over in your mind, at leisure – supposing me to go abroad, could I contemplate such a thing as the writing of a letter a week under any signature I chose, with such scraps of descriptions and impressions as suggested themselves to my mind? If so, would I do it for *The Chronicle*? . . . He thought for such contributions Easthope [the proprietor of *The Chronicle*] would pay anything' (I, 577).

Doyle's suggestion was a practical one and it could easily have been adapted to Dicken's original plan. Instead of sending descriptions to Forster, with the intention of expanding them when he returned home, Dickens now had the option of sending his letters directly to the *Morning Chronicle*. This latter was surely an attractive possibility for Dickens, used to this serial type of publication and anxious for some means to add to his income while in Italy.

Nevertheless, Dickens was unwilling to commit himself until he had explored the pros and cons with both Forster and his publishers, Bradbury and Evans. He was also unsure of the value of his contributions from abroad, and while Doyle had encouraged Dickens to expect a good price, the amount had to be ratified by Sir John Easthope. As it turned out, Doyle's enthusiasm was not shared by Easthope, who evidently did not place a high value on the idea of Dickens's letters. When informed of this, Dickens became impatient, declaring that he refused to dally with that 'damned screw'

Easthope and reporting to his solicitor, Thomas Mitton, in a letter that he had said to Doyle: '"I won't make any bargain with him [Easthope] at all, or haggle like a pedlar, but I'll write a leader now and then, and leave him, in June, to send me a cheque for the whole."... He would pay *anything* [underlined twice] he says for letters from Italy. But that won't do. I have no doubt he would pay 20 guineas a week. But it wouldn't do.'[17]

There was, however, more to Dickens's rejection of this potentially lucrative engagement than his passing annoyance with Easthope suggests. The council with Forster and his publishers had led to the 'germ of another newspaper enterprise' (*Life*, p. 325), and for the next twenty-eight months Dickens was concerned with the fortunes of the *Daily News*.[18] His role in the launching of the paper was an important one, and from the start Dickens's loyalties must have become involved. Consequently, it is not surprising that he showed so little patience in his negotiations with Easthope.

It is difficult to say in the absence of any extant evidence whether or not the idea of using Dickens's letters from abroad in the *Daily News* was discussed at this time. Since the possibility of newspaper publication of travelling letters, first suggested by Easthope, was fresh in Dickens's mind, it is feasible that Dickens did broach the subject, though his uncertainty about the publication of his Italian sketches continued until November 1845. Evidently he abandoned the idea of the immediate publication of his travelling sketches and returned to his original scheme of sending his letters to Forster, as he had done on his American trip. The question of publication was presumably postponed until the plans for the *Daily News* had matured.

Once settled in Albaro, Forster began to receive the 'first sprightly runnings' of the personal letters which were later revised for publication in the *Daily News* and then as *Pictures from Italy*. Initially, Dickens was determined to keep to his proposal to send Forster regular accounts of Italian scenes

(I, 612); but with no immediate public outlet he laid aside any systematic approach to this task and reserved his energy for the Christmas book, to which he was definitely committed. As Forster comments on the scheme for the travel book, Dickens 'had no settled plan from the first' (*Life*, p. 333).

With *The Chimes* completed and safely delivered to his publishers in London, Dickens returned to Genoa on 20 December and remained at the Palazzo Peschiere until 19 January 1845.[19] This month of comparative calm may well have given him the opportunity to consider more thoroughly his next project and plan the opening section on France, as well as the four letters on Albaro and Genoa which appeared in the *Daily News* as 'A Retreat at Albaro;' 'First Sketch of Genoa. The Streets, Shops, and Houses;' 'In Genoa,' and 'In Genoa, and out of it.' A reference by Dickens in a letter to M. Emile De la Rue suggests that he was regularly at work on some literary business prior to his departure to Rome and Naples. Eight days after leaving Genoa, Dickens mentioned in his letter to De la Rue how he missed his company, adding 'and I heartily wish you were "crackling" your very loudest in your own Palazzo, and I were writing it [the letter] in my accustomed literary station in your drawing-room.'[20] Dickens's intimacy with the De la Rues began after his return from London when, with *The Chimes* out of the way, he had more opportunity to visit his new friends. Furthermore, as we can infer from the letter, it was during this interval that Dickens began to write regularly at the De la Rues; and perhaps it was some aspect of the projected book on Italy that kept him busy at that 'literary station'.

Between 19 January and 9 April 1845, Dickens was again 'upon the Wing' (I, 671). He and his wife spent a week in Rome before going to Naples on 14 February,[21] to meet Georgina Hogarth, who arrived by sea from Genoa. Soon afterwards, the party returned to Rome to join the De la Rues for the ceremonies of Holy Week. After the festivities, they left Rome on 25 March and arrived back in Genoa on 9 April (I, 668).

Despite the demands of the itinerary, Dickens's literary plans were not postponed as they had been during his November trip. Instead, he kept to his original intention and managed to supply Forster with running accounts of his journeyings and sightseeings between Genoa and Naples. Four days after he returned from the south, Dickens wrote to Forster that he was pleased he and D'Orsay liked the 'shadows in the water' which he had sketched along the route. 'Writing at such odd places, and in such odd seasons,' Dickens continued, 'I have been half savage with myself, very often, for not doing better' (I, 670).

If we assume the accuracy of this remark, it provides some help in establishing the date of the outline of the later chapters of *Pictures from Italy*. Evidently the letters which ultimately became the chapters on Rome, the Carnival, and Naples were composed between 19 January and 9 April, while Dickens was on the road. Furthermore, Dickens's reply to Forster reinforces the case because he could not have sent the letters from the Peschiere and received Forster's compliment within four days.

For the remaining two months of his Italian holiday, Dickens relaxed after his travels, enjoyed his circle of friends, and at regular intervals sent Forster what he called his 'rambling talk.' According to Forster, these letters ranged over the whole panorama of Dickens's travels, 'while the more important scenes and cities, such as Venice, Rome, and Naples, received such rich filling-in to the first outlines sent, as fairly justified the title of *Pictures* finally chosen for them' (*Life*, p. 372).

It is clear from the evidence extant that the establishment of specific dates for the composition of each of these sections is impossible. One can only make a reasonable guess on the basis of the surviving information and even then the conjectural nature of the conclusions must be stressed. A more profitable approach is to view Dickens's involvement with *Pictures from Italy* in its perspective, for by doing this the particular chronological stages are more easily discernible.

As we have seen, the germ of the book goes back to somewhere in 1843, when the idea first occurred to Dickens of going abroad and utilizing his travel experiences. This plan was stored in his mind until he left for Italy and began his letters to Forster in July 1844. Dickens continued to correspond for nearly eleven months and this interval may be defined as the first period of composition. The completeness of the descriptions cannot be determined, but with the exception of the presumed time of the writing of the chapters on France and Genoa and the interval in which Dickens travelled but wrote no letters, we may assume an almost one-to-one relationship between the date of Dickens's arrival in a particular place and the scenes described.

Nevertheless, while Dickens continued to write to Forster, his intentions about publication remained uncertain and there is no denying the vagueness of his ideas during the primary stage of composition. In his last letter to Forster from Genoa, Dickens returned to the problem again: 'I am in as great doubt as you about the letters I have written you with these Italian experiences. I cannot for the life of me devise any plan of using them to my own satisfaction, and yet think entirely with you that in some form I ought to use them' (I, 682).

Apparently the dilemma continued and little was said during the next four months. Upon his return to London in June 1845, Dickens threw himself into a number of tasks and the Italian letters passed into the background. His time was spent with rehearsals for Ben Jonson's *Every Man in His Humour*, planning the launching of the *Daily News*, and writing *The Cricket on the Hearth*, which he began in the middle of October (I, 709). No extant mention of the proposed travel book was made until 3 November 1845, when Dickens accepted the post of editor of the *Daily News* and agreed to the 'Publication of the series of Italian letters' (I, 714) in its pages. Without doubt, this decision must have been a relief, and it is from here that we may date the beginning of the second period, which extends to 11 March 1846, when the last letter was published in the *Daily News*.

Yet once the arrangements had been settled, there is no evidence to suggest that Dickens set to work immediately on the shaping of the Italian letters. Already, heavy commitments had compelled him to give up an article on capital punishment which he had promised the *Edinburgh Review*; and he told Macvey Napier that never in his life had so many obstacles crowded in the way of his pursuits. 'Everything I have had to do, has been interfered with, and cast aside' (I, 719). In all likelihood, Dickens did not prepare the 'Travelling Letters' for publication more than a week before their respective appearances in print, and had it not been for his speed of writing and ability to meet deadlines, it seems improbable that they would have been published in the *Daily News*. On 30 January 1846, for example, Dickens explained to Forster why it had been impossible to meet him: 'I was obliged to come down here in a hurry to give out a travelling letter I meant to have given out last night, and could not call upon you' (I, 735). There is no proof that the letter in question was number three, which appeared the following day, but Dickens's urgency makes it seem likely, especially as the next letter was not published until 9 February.

In any case, there is no doubt that Dickens was under considerable pressure, and it is not surprising that he resigned the editorship of the *Daily News* on 9 February, after only seventeen issues had appeared. As soon as he was freed from his editorial responsibilities, the remaining letters followed at a more leisurely pace, with a week or so between each one: 'First Sketch of Genoa. The Streets, Shops, and Houses,' 16 February; 'In Genoa,' 26 February; 'In Genoa, and out of it,' 22 March; and 'Piacenza to Bologna,' 11 March.[22] With the termination of the appearance of Dickens's sketches of his Italian experiences in the *Daily News*, the second period ended and the Italian letters passed into their third and final stage of composition.

The actual date of this transition is difficult to establish, and once again we can only suggest what must have taken place. According to Dickens's own interpretation, the break with the newspaper was rather dramatic. Over a month after the event, he told Mme De la Rue that 'I straightway stopped my Letters and walked bodily out of the concern' (I, 744), a remark which is more notable for its bravado than its accuracy, in view of the four letters which appeared in the *Daily News* after 9 February.

There is, of course, the possibility that Dickens did not mean he literally stopped the letters, but that he arranged to stop supplying them after he had fulfilled his prior agreement to write a certain number. In support of this alternative, there is the testimony of Forster, whose opinion Dickens freely consulted upon the entire *Daily News* business. While Forster agreed with Dickens's decision to leave the paper as soon as possible, he did not think it should absolve Dickens of all his responsibilities.[23] According to Forster's account, 'as the letters descriptive of his Italian travel (turned afterwards into *Pictures from Italy*) had begun with its first number, his name could not at once be withdrawn; and, for the time during which they were still to appear, he consented to contribute other occasional letters on important social questions' (*Life*, p. 387). Likewise, as Edgar Johnson observes, 'Both personal loyalty and principle suggested that he should act as if it has always been his intention merely to give the new paper a start and then step out' (Johnson, II, 589).

But while Dickens may have agreed to continue his 'Travelling Letters' in the *Daily News* for reasons of personal loyalty, his conduct does not explain why the series was terminated. Perhaps the most convincing explanation is that Dickens's interests began to change soon after he resigned from the editorship of the newspaper. Evidently the idea for a new novel had begun to take shape early in March, and by April Dickens had arranged with his publishers, Bradbury and Evans, to write the novel in twenty monthly parts. Before concentrating his energies on this novel, however, his first task was to prepare his travel book for publication, and it is to this aspect of *Pictures from Italy* that we now turn our attention.

Having reconstructed the three stages in the genesis of the book, it remains to clarify the general assumption that it was composed from letters addressed to Forster and that similar use was not made of letters to other friends. In 'The Reader's Passport', which constitutes an introduction to the book, Dickens simply mentions that the greater part of the descriptions were 'written on the spot, and sent home, from time to time, in private letters' (*PI*, p. 2), but he offers no identification of his correspondents. Had all these 'private letters' survived their incorporation into the manuscript, the identity of the correspondents would not, of course, be a problem.

Fortunately, in spite of the unavailability of the complete manuscript, there is sufficient evidence to confirm that it was Forster who received the bulk of the letters. As Dickens's closest friend and literary confidant, he was the obvious recipient of most of them. When Dickens assembled his letters upon his return to London, the majority must have come from this source, as had been the case with the composition of *American Notes*. Writing of the latter, Forster remarks that the letters he received from the United States 'were lent to assist in its composition' (*Life*, p. 244), a procedure in all probability repeated in the composition of *Pictures from Italy*.

Furthermore, it had been Dickens's intention from the beginning to send regular accounts of his journeyings to Forster (I, 545), and there is no evidence to suggest that he departed far from this plan. As he told Mme De la Rue shortly before the publication of *Pictures from Italy*, 'the greater part of the descriptions were written in letters to Forster' (I, 745). Also, from what Forster says in his biography about receiving Dickens's 'rambling talk' and the latter's rifling his letters prior to publishing his Italian experiences, there is no reason to question Dickens's statement (*Life*, pp. 372 and 333).

This does not exclude the possibility of Dickens's having consulted letters to other friends, though in the absence of a complete edition of letters for the years 1844 to 1846 it is difficult to establish the identity of other possible sources. So little attention has been given to this problem that J. Fitzgerald Molloy seems to be alone in mentioning that Dickens borrowed his letters to Lady Blessington when he was composing his travel book on Italy.[24] But Molloy was not concerned with Dickens's use of Lady Blessington's letters and he did not expand his remarks about *Pictures from Italy*. That he was correct, however, is revealed in a previously unpublished letter to Lady Blessington[25]:

DEVONSHIRE TERRACE
SUNDAY FIRST MARCH 1846

My Dear Lady Blessington

Do you or Count D'Orsay happen to have, in any unransacked corner, any letter I wrote you from Italy? I don't think it at all likely; but as drowning men catch at straws, I grasp at scraps of paper, to keep myself on in my travelling recollections.

I have a vague remembrance of something I wrote you about Bologna (I think) and Verona – and of something I wrote to Count D'Orsay about the Models at Rome – both of which fragments I should like to recall more distinctly, if you could help me to a better remembrance of them.

Always My Dear Lady Blessington

Faithfully yours
Charles Dickens

THE COUNTESS OF BLESSINGTON

Lady Blessington apparently responded immediately, for the following day Dickens acknowledged his receipt of the letters: 'I will take the greatest care of them,' he wrote, 'though I blush to find how little they deserve it' (I, 739). Of the letters requested by Dickens, only two appear to have survived: one he had written from Milan and another from Genoa.[26]

The 'scraps of paper' which Dickens grasped at did indeed help him on with his travelling recollections, as a comparison with the text of *Pictures from Italy* shows. Not only did they jog his memory, but some paragraphs were transcribed almost word for word into the text. A description of an equestrian company at Modena (*PI*, pp. 93–95) and a caricature of tourists in Rome (*PI*, pp. 185–86) appear with only minor alterations. The paragraphs in *Pictures from Italy* about Verona and its Roman amphitheatre are considerably more detailed than the account in the Blessington letter, but many of the descriptive phrases from the letter appear in the text. Only the sections relating to personal matters remained completely unused.

In addition to proving that Dickens used letters other than Forster's, the Blessington letters provide an insight into the method of composition used for *Pictures from Italy*. A comparison of both texts reveals how Dickens relied upon the Blessington letters to recapture the mood of dimly remembered scenes and used the letters as a travel diary or journal. Evidently his missing letters to Forster were employed in the same way, until he had extracted a sufficient number of scenes of Italian life to form the nucleus of *Pictures from Italy*.

At first sight, his method of composition appears unnecessarily complicated, involving both the recovery of the letters and the piecing together and moulding of them into a larger unit. Presumably it would have been simpler had he confined his comments on Italy to a journal reserved for that purpose. Nevertheless, the letter method had been proved reliable by no less an experienced travel-book writer than Captain Basil Hall, who had introduced Dickens to this technique. It was upon Hall's recommendation that Dickens used the method in the composition of his *American Notes*, and having apparently found it satisfactory, was prepared to use it again. Hall and Dickens had been friends since 1839 and both shared an enthusiasm for travel literature. Not long before Hall's death he had written to Dickens in 1841 from the Mediterranean, where he was apparently collecting material for a book which he did not live to publish, explaining 'a plan which, so far as I know, is rather new.' Hall asked Dickens if he would mind returning a letter he had sent him from Trafalgar, or a copy of the same, 'if it be not long ago consigned to the back of the fire.' He then went on to say that

heretofore I have written my Journals chiefly for my friends – or for myself – and when I came to make out of them a book of travels, I had to select much purely as seemed suitable for the public eye. This, however, was a difficult and rather dangerous task – dangerous, I mean, to the unity of the texture of the work, and very often fatal to that sustained interest without which a book of travels is the dullest of dull reading. Besides, I have often had reason to fear that in thus taking detached facts of a Journal, much of the simplicity of truth was lost. The whole, indeed, might be written in perfect good faith but when sundry omissions came to be made, it often struck me that a false impression might remain.[27]

Hall's aim was, in fact, to write his book on the road. The first draft would be the descriptive letters addressed to a friend at home. Upon his return, Hall planned to recover the letters and then expand them into a book rather than cut down extensive notes from a personal journal which were written with no public audience in mind.

Evidently the experiment proved successful, and Hall found that he was able to write at a faster rate than usual. Dickens must have been impressed with the idea, and although he never acknowledged a debt to Hall, his own method for *American Notes* and *Pictures from Italy* is similar enough to suggest that he adapted it to suit his own purposes. For example, in the surviving autograph pages of the seventh and eighth 'Travelling Letters' for the *Daily News*, there are two instances where Dickens makes extensive use of letters he wrote while in Italy. Following a break in the text, there are vertical lines indicating that the narrative is to continue in one of the incorporated letters. In both cases the pages thus used are in the hand of an unidentified amanuensis (doubtlessly a member of his family and perhaps Georgina Hogarth), whom Dickens employed to copy letters pertinent to the travel book as they were returned to Devonshire Terrace.

Where Dickens has made use of such pages to help him with his travelling recollections, it was necessary for him on both occasions to cancel those parts of the copied letters which did not belong in the manuscript. Generally these passages contained references to personal matters or Dickens's family and were, of course, of no public concern. One of the copied passages which Dickens wanted to incorporate into his seventh 'Travelling Letter' contained a description of the ceremony of a nun taking the black veil, but also made reference to his wife and sister-in-law. Thus in order to use the letter, Dickens removed the reference to 'Kate and Georgy' and substituted the less personal 'my ladies.'

Following Basil Hall's apparently revolutionary advice of using personal letters rather than a journal as the rough draft of a travel book, Dickens evidently made good progress; though the task of putting 'them together, and making additions to them, and touching them up,' as he admitted to Mme De la Rue, was 'rather a long job' (I, 745). Throughout March and April he continued with this final stage of composition, enlarging the sections which dealt with his November travels, those to Venice, Rome, and Naples, and the closing 'Rapid Diorama.' The book was finished by early May, the proofs corrected, and the first edition of *Pictures from Italy* made its appearance by mid-May, thus bringing to a close a chain of events that reaches back almost three years.

1. Walter Dexter, ed., *The Letters of Charles Dickens*, 3 vols., The Nonesuch Dickens (Bloomsbury: Nonesuch Press, 1938), I, 612. Hereafter cited in the text by volume and page number.

2. John Forster, *The Life of Charles Dickens*, edited and annotated by J. W. T. Ley (London: Cecil Palmer, 1928), p. 372. Hereafter cited as *Life*.

3. Una Pope-Hennessy, *Charles Dickens* (London: Chatto & Windus, 1945), p. 208.

4. Thornton Hunt, *The Correspondence of Leigh Hunt, Edited by His Eldest Son*, 2 vols. (London: Smith, Elder, & Co., 1862), I, 192–93.

5. Anon [Mary Shelley], 'The English in Italy', *Westminster Review*, VI (October 1826), 325–41.

6. Mario Praz, Appendix II, 'Rome and the Victorians,' *The Hero in Eclipse in Victorian Fiction*, translated by Angus Davidson (London: Oxford University Press, 1969), pp. 444–67.

7. Roger Ingpen, ed., *The Letters of Percy Bysshe Shelley*, 2 vols. (London: Pitman & Sons, 1909), II, 649.

8. Hester Lynch Piozzi, *Observations and Reflections Made in the Course of a Journey Through France, Italy, and Germany*, ed. Herbert Barrows (Ann Arbor: University of Michigan Press, 1967), p. xv.

9. *Little Dorrit* (1855–57) is the only novel in which Dickens makes use of his vivid sketches of Italy. Book II opens with the arrival of the Dorrit family at the Convent of the St Bernard Pass; afterwards they travel to Venice and Rome. For the use of the motif of Rome, with its 'melancholy and morally suggestive debris,' as a literary formula in nineteenth-century fiction, see Q. D. Leavis, 'A Note on Literary Indebtedness: Dickens, George Eliot, Henry James', *The Hudson Review*, 8 (Autumn 1955), 423–28.

10. Antonio Gallenga, *Episodes of My Second Life*, 2 vols. (London: Chapman & Hall, 1884), II, 372–73.

11. Dickens, letter to Samuel Rogers, 1 September 1844, in P. W. Clayden, *Rogers and his Contemporaries*, 2 vols (London: Smith, Elder, & Co., 1889), II, 248–52.

12. 'The People's International League,' *Lowe's Edinburgh Magazine*, n.s., I (April 1847), 177–79; on Dickens's joining the Council,

see Mazzini, letter to his mother, 11 November 1847, *Scritti Editi ed Inediti di Guiseppe Mazzini,* vol. 33 (Imola, 1921), 72.

13. William J. Carlton, 'Dickens Studies Italian', *Dickensian,* 61 (May 1965), 101–8.

14. Steven Marcus, *Dickens: From Pickwick to Dombey* (New York: Basic Books, Inc., 1965), pp. 303–4, *et passim.*

15. Edgar Johnson, *Charles Dickens: His Tragedy and Triumph,* 2 vols. (New York: Simon and Schuster, 1952), II, 606. Hereafter cited as Johnson.

16. Walter Dexter, ed., *Mr and Mrs Charles Dickens: His Letters to Her* (London: Constable, 1935), p. 237.

17. Dickens, letter to Thomas Mitton, 10 March 1844, Huntington Library, HM 17797. This letter is published in *The Dickensian,* 33 (December 1936), 20, and in the Nonesuch Letters, I, 578, but in both cases there are inaccuracies in the transcription.

18. The clearest account of Dickens's role in the origin of the *Daily News* is by Gerald G. Grubb in 'Dickens and the *Daily News*: The Origin of the Idea,' *Booker Memorial Studies: Eight Essays on Victorian Literature In Memory of John Manning Booker, 1881– 1948,* ed. Hill Shine (Chapel Hill: University of North Carolina Press, 1950), pp. 60–77.

19. For Dickens's arrival in Genoa, see letter to T. Yeats Brown, 20 December 1844, MS in Free Library of Philadelphia; concerning his departure, Dickens had originally planned to leave on 20 January (cf. *Life,* p. 367), but agreed to start a day earlier in deference to Mme De la Rue, who urged Dickens: "'Don't go away upon a Monday. . . . It is not he [the bad spirit of her hallucinations] who says that. I say it,'" quoted by Dickens in a letter to M. De la Rue, 15 January 1845, MS in Berg Collection.

20. Dickens, letter to M. De la Rue, 27 January 1845, Berg MS.

21. Dickens, letter to M. De la Rue, 14 February 1845, Berg MS. This letter clearly establishes the date of Georgina's arrival as 14 February. Cf. Arthur A. Adrian, who gives 9 February as the date in his *Georgina Hogarth and the Dickens Circle* (London: Oxford University Press, 1957), p. 18.

22. For full details of the 'Travelling Letters' published in the *Daily News,* see A Note on the Text, p. 224.

23. For a more exhaustive analysis of Dickens's break with the *Daily News,* see Gerald G. Grubb, 'Dickens and the "Daily News:" Resignation', *Nineteenth-Century Fiction,* 7 (June 1952), 19–38.

24. J. Fitzgerald Molloy, *The Gorgeous Lady Blessington,* 2 vols. (London: Downey & Co., 1896), II, 244.

25. MS in Free Library of Philadelphia.
26. See I, 642–44 and I, 674–76. Walter Dexter based his transcription in the Nonesuch Letters on the two letters as they appear in the National Edition, 1908. A comparison with the originals, now in the Free Library of Philadelphia, reveals that those portions of the two letters paralleling the text of *Pictures from Italy* were omitted.
27. Basil Hall, letter to Dickens, 3 and 27 September 1841, Huntington Library, HM 18510.

The Reader's Passport

I F the readers of this volume
will be so kind as to take their
credentials for the different places
which are the subject of its
author's reminiscences, from the
Author himself, perhaps they may
visit them, in fancy, the more
agreeably, and with a better
understanding of what they are
to expect.

Many books have been written
upon Italy, affording many means
of studying the history of that
interesting country, and the innumerable associations entwined
about it. I make but little reference
to that stock of information; not
at all regarding it as a necessary
consequence of my having had

The Villa d'Este at Tivoli from the Cypress Avenue

recourse to the storehouse for my own benefit, that I should reproduce its easily accessible contents before the eyes of my readers.

Neither will there be found, in these pages, any grave examination into the government or misgovernment of any portion of the country. No visiter of that beautiful land can fail to have a strong conviction on the subject; but as I chose when residing there, a Foreigner, to abstain from the discussion of any such questions with any order of Italians, so I would rather not enter on the inquiry now. During my twelve months' occupation of a house at Genoa, I never found that authorities constitutionally jealous, were distrustful of me; and I should be sorry to give them occasion to regret their free courtesy, either to myself or any of my countrymen.

There is, probably, not a famous Picture or Statue in all Italy, but could be easily buried under a mountain of printed paper devoted to dissertations on it. I do not, therefore, though an earnest admirer of Painting and Sculpture, expatiate at any length on famous Pictures and Statues.

This Book is a series of faint reflections – mere shadows in the water – of places to which the imaginations of most people are attracted in a greater or less degree, on which mine had dwelt for years, and which have some interest for all. The greater part of the descriptions were written on the spot, and sent home, from time to time, in private letters. I do not mention the circumstance as an excuse for any defects they may present, for it would be none; but as a guarantee to the Reader that they were at least penned in the fulness of the subject, and with the liveliest impressions of novelty and freshness.

If they have ever a fanciful and idle air, perhaps the reader will suppose them written in the shade of a Sunny Day, in the midst of the objects of which they treat, and will like them none the worse for having such influences of the country upon them.

I hope I am not likely to be misunderstood by Professors

of the Roman Catholic faith, on account of anything contained in these pages. I have done my best, in one of my former productions, to do justice to them; and I trust, in this, they will do justice to me. When I mention any exhibition that impressed me as absurd or disagreeable, I do not seek to connect it, or recognise it as necessarily connected with, any essentials of their creed. When I treat of the ceremonies of the Holy Week, I merely treat of their effect, and do not challenge the good and learned Dr. Wiseman's interpretation[1] of their meaning. When I hint a dislike of nunneries for young girls who abjure the world before they have ever proved or known it; or doubt the *ex officio* sanctity of all Priests and Friars; I do no more than many conscientious Catholics both abroad and at home.

I have likened these Pictures to shadows in the water, and would fain hope that I have, nowhere, stirred the water so roughly, as to mar the shadows. I could never desire to be on better terms with all my friends than now, when distant mountains rise, once more, in my path. For I need not hesitate to avow, that, bent on correcting a brief mistake I made not long ago, in disturbing the old relations between myself and my readers, and departing for a moment from my old pursuits, I am about to resume them, joyfully, in Switzerland[2]: where, during another year of absence, I can at once work out the themes I have now in my mind, without interruption: and, while I keep my English audience within speaking distance, extend my knowledge of a noble country, inexpressibly attractive to me.

This book is made as accessible as possible, because it would be a great pleasure to me if I could hope, through its means, to compare impressions with some among the multitudes who will hereafter visit the scenes described, with interest and delight.

And I have only now, in passport wise, to sketch my reader's portrait, which I hope may be thus supposititiously traced for either sex:—

Complexion	Fair.
Eyes	Very cheerful.
Nose	Not supercilious.
Mouth	Smiling.
Visage	Beaming.
General Expression	Extremely agreeable.

The Colosseum of Rome

Going through France

O N a fine Sunday morning in the Midsummer time and
weather of eighteen hundred and forty-four, it was, my
good friend, when – don't be alarmed; not when two travellers might have been observed slowly making their way over
that picturesque and broken ground by which the first chapter
of a 'Middle Aged' novel is usually attained – but when an
English travelling carriage of considerable proportions, fresh

from the shady halls of the Pantechnicon³ near Belgrave-Square, London, was observed (by a very small French soldier; for I saw him look at it) to issue from the gate of the Hôtel Meurice in the Rue Rivoli at Paris.

I am no more bound to explain why the English family travelling by this carriage, inside and out, should be starting for Italy on a Sunday morning, of all good days in the week, than I am to assign a reason for all the little men in France being soldiers, and all the big men postilions: which is the invariable rule. But, they had some sort of reason for what they did, I have no doubt; and their reason for being there at all, was, as you know, that they were going to live in fair Genoa for a year; and that the head of the family purposed, in that space of time, to stroll about, wherever his restless humour carried him.

And it would have been small comfort to me to have explained to the population of Paris generally, that I was that Head and Chief; and not the radiant embodiment of good-humour who sat beside me in the person of a French Courier – best of servants and most beaming of men! Truth to say, he looked a great deal more patriarchal than I, who, in the shadow of his portly presence, dwindled down to no account at all.

There was, of course, very little in the aspect of Paris – as we rattled near the dismal Morgue and over the Pont Neuf – to reproach us for our Sunday travelling. The wine-shops (every second house) were driving a roaring trade; awnings were spreading, and chairs and tables arranging, outside the cafés, preparatory to the eating of ices, and drinking of cool liquids, later in the day; shoe-blacks were busy on the bridges; shops were open; carts and waggons clattered to and fro; the narrow, up-hill, funnel-like streets across the River, were so many dense perspectives of crowd and bustle, parti-coloured night-caps, tobacco-pipes, blouses, large boots, and shaggy heads of hair; nothing at that hour denoted a day of rest, unless it were the appearance, here and there, of a family pleasure-party, crammed into a bulky old lumbering cab; or of some contemplative holiday maker in the freest and easiest dishabille, leaning out of a low garret window, watching the drying of his newly polished shoes on the little parapet outside (if a gentleman), or the airing of her stockings in the sun (if a lady), with calm anticipation.

Once clear of the never-to-be-forgotten-or-forgiven pavement which surrounds Paris, the first three days of travelling towards Marseilles, are quiet and monotonous enough. To Sens. To Avallon. To Chalons. A sketch of one day's proceedings is a sketch of all three; and here it is.

We have four horses, and one postilion, who has a very long whip, and drives his team, something like the Courier of Saint Petersburgh in the circle at Astley's or Franconi's[4]: only he sits his own horse instead of standing on him. The immense jack-boots worn by these postilions, are sometimes a century or two old; and are so ludicrously disproportionate to the wearer's foot, that the spur, which is put where his own heel comes, is generally halfway up the leg of the boots. The man often comes out of the stable-yard, with his whip in his hand and his shoes on, and brings out, in both hands, one boot at a time, which he plants on the ground by the side of his horse, with great gravity, until everything is ready. When it is – and oh Heaven! the noise they make about it! – he gets into the boots, shoes and all, or is hoisted into them by a couple of friends; adjusts the rope-harness, embossed by the labours of innumerable pigeons in the stables; makes all the horses kick and plunge; cracks his whip like a madman; shouts 'En route – Hi!' and away we go. He is sure to have a contest with his horse before we have gone very far; and then he calls him a Thief, and a Brigand, and a Pig, and what not; and beats him about the head as if he were made of wood.

There is little more than one variety in the appearance of the country, for the first two days. From a dreary plain, to an interminable avenue; and from an interminable avenue, to a dreary plain again. Plenty of vines there are, in the open fields, but of a short low kind, and not trained in festoons, but about straight sticks. Beggars innumerable there are, everywhere; but an extraordinarily scanty population, and fewer children than I ever encountered. I don't believe we saw a hundred children between Paris and Chalons. Queer old towns, draw-bridged and walled: with odd little towers at the angles, like grotesque faces, as if the wall had put a mask on, and were staring, down into the moat; other strange little towers, in gardens and fields, and down lanes, and in farm-yards: all alone, and always round, with a peaked roof, and never used for any purpose at all; ruinous buildings of all sorts: sometimes an hôtel de ville, sometimes a guard-house, sometimes a dwelling-house, sometimes a château with a rank garden, prolific in dandelion, and watched over by extinguisher-topped turrets, and blink-eyed little casements; are the standard objects, repeated over and over again. Sometimes, we pass a village inn, with a crumbling wall belonging to it, and a perfect town of out-houses: and painted over the gateway, 'Stabling for Sixty Horses;' as indeed there might be stabling for sixty score, were there any horses to be stabled there, or anybody resting there, or anything stirring about the place but a dangling bush, indicative of the wine inside: which flutters idly in the wind, in lazy keeping with everything else, and certainly is never in a green old age, though always so old as to be dropping to pieces. And all day long, strange little narrow waggons, in strings of six or eight, bringing cheese from Switzerland, and frequently in charge, the whole line, of one man or even boy – and he very often asleep in the foremost cart – come jingling past: the horses drowsily ringing the bells upon their harness, and looking as if they thought (no doubt they do) their great blue woolly furniture, of immense weight and thickness, with a pair of grotesque horns growing out of the collar very much too warm for the Midsummer weather.

Then, there is the Diligence, twice or thrice a-day; with the dusty outsides in blue frocks, like butchers; and the insides in white nightcaps; and its cabriolet head on the roof, nodding and shaking, like an idiot's head; and its Young-France passengers staring out of window, with beards down to their waists, and blue spectacles awfully shading their warlike eyes, and very big sticks clenched in their National grasp. Also the Malle Poste, with only a couple of passengers, tearing along at a real good dare-devil pace, and out of sight in no time. Steady old Curés come jolting past, now and then, in such ramshackle, rusty, musty, clattering coaches as no Englishman would believe in; and bony women daudle about in solitary places, holding cows by ropes while they feed, or digging and hoeing, or doing field-work of a more laborious kind, or representing real shepherdesses with their flocks – to obtain an adequate idea of which pursuit and its followers, in any country, it is only necessary to take any pastoral poem, or picture, and imagine to yourself whatever is most exquisitely and widely unlike the descriptions therein contained.

You have been travelling along, stupidly enough, as you generally do in the last stage of the day; and the ninety-six bells upon the horses – twenty-four apiece – have been ringing sleepily in your ears for half an hour or so; and it has become a very jog-trot, monotonous, tiresome sort of business; and you have been thinking deeply about the dinner you will have at the next stage; when, down at the end of the long avenue of trees through which you are travelling, the first indication of a town appears, in the shape of some straggling cottages: and the carriage begins to rattle and roll over a horribly uneven pavement. As if the equipage were a great firework, and the mere sight of a smoking cottage chimney had lighted it, instantly it begins to crack and splutter, as if the very devil were in it. Crack, crack, crack, crack. Crack-crack-crack. Crick-crack. Crick-crack. Helo! Hola! Vite! Voleur! Brigand! Hi hi hi! En r-r-r-r-route! Whip, wheels, driver, stones, beggars, children; crack, crack, crack; helo! hola! charité pour l'amour de Dieu! crick-crack-crick-crack; crick, crick, crick; bump, jolt, crack, bump, crick-crack; round the corner, up the narrow street, down the paved hill on the other side; in the gutter; bump, bump; jolt, jog; crick, crick, crick; crack, crack, crack; into the shop-windows on the left hand side of the street, preliminary to a sweeping turn into the wooden archway on the right; rumble, rumble, rumble; clatter, clatter, clatter; crick, crick, crick; and here we are in the yard of the Hôtel de l'Ecu d'Or; used up, gone out, smoking, spent, exhausted; but sometimes making a false start unexpectedly, with nothing coming of it – like a firework to the last!

The landlady of the Hôtel de l'Ecu d'Or is here; and the landlord of the Hôtel de l'Ecu is here; and the femme de chambre of the Hôtel de l'Ecu d'Or is here; and a gentleman in a glazed cap, with a red beard like a bosom friend, who is staying at the Hôtel de l'Ecu d'Or is here; and Monsieur le Curé is walking up and down in a corner of the yard by himself, with a shovel hat upon his head, and black gown on his back, and a book in one hand, and an umbrella in the other; and everybody, except Monsieur le Curé, is open-mouthed and open-eyed, for the opening of the carriage-door. The landlord of the Hôtel de l'Ecu d'Or, dotes to that extent upon the Courier, that he can hardly wait for his coming down from the box, but embraces his very legs and boot-heels as he descends. 'My Courier! My brave Courier! My friend! My brother!' The landlady loves him, the femme de chambre blesses him, the garçon worships him. The Courier asks if his letter has been received? It has, it has. Are the rooms prepared? They are, they are. The best rooms for my noble Courier. The rooms of state for my gallant Courier; the whole house is at the service of my best of friends! He keeps his hand upon the carriage-door, and asks some other question to enhance the expectation. He carries a green leathern purse outside his coat, suspended by a belt. The idlers look at it; one touches it. It is full of five-franc pieces. Murmurs of admiration are heard among the boys. The landlord falls upon the Courier's neck, and folds him to his breast. He is so much fatter than he was, he says! He looks so rosy and so well!

The door is opened. Breathless expectation. The lady of the family gets out. Ah sweet lady! Beautiful lady! The sister of the lady of the family gets out. Great Heaven, Ma'amselle is charming! First little boy gets out. Ah, what a beautiful little boy! First little girl gets out. Oh, but this is an enchanting child! Second little girl gets out. The landlady, yielding to the finest impulse of our common nature, catches her up in her arms! Second little boy gets out. Oh, the sweet boy! Oh, the tender little family! The baby is handed out. Angelic baby! The baby has topped everything. All the rapture is expended on the baby! Then the two nurses tumble out; and the enthusiasm swelling into madness, the whole family are swept up stairs as on a cloud; while the idlers press about the carriage, and look into it, and walk round it, and touch it. For it is something to touch a carriage that has held so many people. It is a legacy to leave one's children.

The rooms are on the first floor, except the nursery for the night, which is a great rambling chamber, with four or five beds in it: through a dark passage, up two steps, down four, past a pump, across a balcony, and next door to the stable. The other sleeping apartments are large and lofty; each with two small bedsteads, tastefully hung, like the windows, with red and white drapery. The sitting-room is famous. Dinner is already laid in it for three; and the napkins are folded in cocked-hat fashion. The floors are of red tile. There are no carpets, and not much furniture to speak of; but there is abundance of looking-glass, and there are large vases under glass shades, filled with artificial flowers; and there are plenty of clocks. The whole party are in motion. The Brave Courier, in particular, is everywhere: looking after the beds; having wine poured down his throat by his dear brother the landlord, and picking up green cucumbers – always cucumbers; Heaven knows where he gets them – with which he walks about, one in each hand, like truncheons.

Dinner is announced. There is very thin soup; there are very large loaves – one apiece; a fish; four dishes afterwards; some poultry afterwards; a dessert afterwards; and no lack of wine. There is not much in the dishes; but they are very good, and always ready instantly. When it is nearly dark, the brave Courier, having eaten the two cucumbers, sliced up in the contents of a pretty large decanter of oil, and another of vinegar, emerges from his retreat below, and proposes a visit to the Cathedral, whose massive tower frowns down upon the court-yard of the inn. Off we go; and very solemn and grand it is, in the dim light: so dim at last, that the polite, old, lanthorn-jawed Sacristan has a feeble little bit of candle in his hand, to grope among the tombs with – and looks among the grim columns, very like a lost ghost who is searching for his own.

Underneath the balcony, when we return, the inferior servants of the inn are supping in the open air, at a great table; the dish, a stew of meat and vegetables, smoking hot: and served in the iron cauldron it was boiled in. They have a pitcher of thin wine, and are very merry; merrier than the gentleman with the red beard, who is playing billiards in the light room on the left of the yard, where shadows, with cues in their hands, and cigars in their mouths, cross and recross the window, constantly. Still the thin Curé walks up and down alone, with his book and umbrella. And there he walks, and there the billiard-balls rattle, long after we are fast asleep.

We are astir at six next morning. It is a delightful day; shaming yesterday's mud upon the carriage, if anything could shame a carriage, in a land where carriages are never cleaned. Everybody is brisk; and as we finish breakfast, the horses come jingling into the yard from the Post-house. Everything taken out of the carriage is put back again. The brave Courier announces that all is ready, after walking into every room, and looking all round it, to be certain that nothing is left behind. Everybody gets in. Everybody connected with the Hôtel de l'Ecu d'Or is again enchanted. The

Brave Courier runs into the house for a parcel containing cold fowl, sliced ham, bread, and biscuits, for lunch; hands it into the coach; and runs back again.

What has he got in his hand now? More cucumbers? No. A long strip of paper. It's the bill.

The Brave Courier has two belts on, this morning: one supporting the purse: another, a mighty good sort of leathern bottle, filled to the throat with the best light Bordeaux wine in the house. He never pays the bill till this bottle is full. Then he disputes it.

He disputes it now, violently. He is still the landlord's brother, but by another father or mother. He is not so nearly related to him as he was last night. The landlord scratches his head. The Brave Courier points to certain figures in the bill, and intimates that if they remain there, the Hôtel de l'Ecu d'Or is thenceforth and for ever an hôtel de l'Ecu de cuivre. The landlord goes into a little counting-house. The Brave Courier follows, forces the bill and a pen into his hand; and talks more rapidly than ever. The landlord takes the pen. The Courier smiles. The landlord makes an alteration. The Courier cuts a joke. The landlord is affectionate, but not weakly so. He bears it like a man. He shakes hands with his brave brother, but he don't hug him. Still, he loves his brother; for he knows that he will be returning that way, one of these fine days, with another family, and he foresees that his heart will yearn towards him again. The brave Courier traverses all round the carriage once, looks at the drag, inspects the wheels, jumps up, gives the word, and away we go!

It is market morning. The market is held in the little square outside, in front of the Cathedral. It is crowded with men and women, in blue, in red, in green, in white; with canvassed stalls; and fluttering merchandise. The country people are grouped about, with their clean baskets before them. Here, the lace-sellers; there, the butter and egg-sellers; there, the fruit-sellers; there, the shoe-makers. The whole place looks as if it were the stage of some great theatre, and the curtain had just run up, for a picturesque ballet. And there is the Cathedral to boot: scene-like: all grim, and swarthy, and mouldering, and cold: just splashing the pavement in one place with faint purple drops, as the morning sun, entering by a little window on the eastern side, struggles through some stained glass panes, on the western.

In five minutes we have passed the iron cross, with a little ragged kneeling-place of turf before it, in the outskirts of the town; and are again upon the road.

Lyons, the Rhone, and the Goblin of Avignon

CHALONS is a fair resting place, in right of its good inn on the bank of the river, and the little steam-boats, gay with green and red paint, that come and go upon it: which make up a pleasant and refreshing scene, after the dusty roads. But, unless you would like to dwell on an enormous plain, with jagged rows of irregular poplars on it, that look in the distance like so many combs with broken teeth: and unless you would like to pass your life without the possibility of going up-hill, or going up anything but stairs: you would hardly approve of Chalons as a place of residence.

You would probably like it better, however, than Lyons: which you may reach, if you will, in one of the before-mentioned steam-boats, in eight hours.

What a city Lyons is! Talk about people feeling, at certain unlucky times, as if they had tumbled from the clouds! Here is a whole town that has tumbled, anyhow, out of the sky; having been first caught up, like other stones that tumble down from that region, out of fens and barren places, dismal to behold! The two great streets through which the two great rivers dash, and all the little streets whose name is Legion, were scorching, blistering, and sweltering. The houses, high and vast, dirty to excess, rotten as old cheeses, and as thickly peopled. All up the hills that hem the city in, these houses swarm; and the mites inside were lolling out of the windows, and drying their ragged clothes on poles, and crawling in and out at the doors, and coming out to pant and gasp upon the pavement, and creeping in and out among huge

49

piles and bales of fusty, musty, stifling goods; and living, or rather not dying till their time should come, in an exhausted receiver. Every manufacturing town, melted into one, would hardly convey an impression of Lyons as it presented itself to me: for all the undrained, unscavengered, qualities of a foreign town, seemed grafted, there, upon the native miseries of a manufacturing one; and it bears such fruit as I would go some miles out of my way to avoid encountering again.

In the cool of the evening: or rather in the faded heat of the day: we went to see the Cathedral, where divers old women, and a few dogs, were engaged in contemplation. There was no difference, in point of cleanliness, between its stone pavement and that of the streets; and there was a wax saint, in a little box like a berth aboard ship, with a glass front to it, whom Madame Tussaud[5] would have nothing to say to, on any terms, and which even Westminster Abbey might be ashamed of. If you would know all about the architecture of this church, or any other, its dates, dimensions, endowments, and history, is it not written in Mr. Murray's 'Guide-Book', and may you not read it there, with thanks to him, as I did!

For this reason, I should abstain from mentioning the curious clock in Lyons Cathedral, if it were not for a small mistake I made, in connexion with that piece of mechanism. The keeper of the church was very anxious it should be shown; partly for the honour of the establishment and the town; and partly, perhaps, because of his deriving a percentage from the additional consideration. However that may be, it was set in motion, and thereupon a host of little doors flew open, and innumerable little figures staggered out of them, and jerked themselves back again, with that special unsteadiness of purpose, and hitching in the gait, which usually attaches to figures that are moved by clock-work. Meanwhile, the Sacristan stood explaining these wonders, and pointing them out, severally, with a wand. There was a centre puppet of the Virgin Mary; and close to her, a small pigeon-hole, out of which another and a very ill-looking puppet made one of the most sudden plunges I ever saw accomplished: instantly flopping back again at sight of her, and banging his little door, violently, after him. Taking this to be emblematic of the victory over Sin and Death, and not at all unwilling to shew that I perfectly understood the subject, in anticipation of the showman, I rashly said, 'Aha! The Evil Spirit. To be sure. He is very soon disposed of.' 'Pardon, Monsieur,' said the Sacristan, with a polite motion of his hand towards the little door, as if introducing somebody – 'The Angel Gabriel!'

Soon after day-break next morning, we were steaming down the arrowy Rhone, at the rate of twenty miles an hour, in a very dirty vessel full of merchandise, and with only three or four other passengers for our companions: among whom, the most remarkable was a silly, old, meek-faced, garlic-eating, immeasurably-polite Chevalier, with a dirty scrap of red ribbon hanging at his button-hole, as if he had tied it there, to remind himself of something: as Tom Noddy[6] in the farce ties knots in his pocket-handkerchief.

For the last two days, we had seen great sullen hills, the first indications of the Alps, lowering in the distance. Now, we were rushing on beside them: sometimes close beside them: sometimes with an intervening slope, covered with vineyards. Villages and small towns hanging in mid-air, with great woods of olives seen through the light open towers of their churches, and clouds moving slowly on, upon the steep acclivity behind them; ruined castles perched on every emi-nence; and scattered houses in the clefts and gullies of the hills; made it very beautiful. The great height of these, too, making the buildings look so tiny, that they had all the charm of elegant models; their excessive whiteness, as contrasted with the brown rocks, or the sombre, deep, dull, heavy green of the olive-tree; and the puny size, and little slow walk of the Lilliputian men and women on the bank; made a charming picture. There were ferries out of number too; bridges; the famous Pont d'Esprit, with I don't know how many arches; towns where memorable wines are made; Vallence, where Napoleon studied; and the noble river, bringing at every winding turn new beauties into view.

There lay before us, that same afternoon, the broken bridge of Avignon, and all the city baking in the sun; yet with an under-done-pie-crust, battlemented wall, that never will be brown, though it bake for centuries.

The grapes were hanging in clusters in the streets, and the brilliant Oleander was in full bloom everywhere. The streets are old and very narrow, but tolerably clean, and shaded by awnings stretched from house to house. Bright stuffs and handkerchiefs: curiosities, ancient frames of carved wood, old chairs, ghostly tables, saints, virgins, angels, and staring daubs of portraits, being exposed for sale beneath, it was very quaint and lively. All this was much set off, too, by the glimpses one caught, through rusty gates standing ajar, of quiet sleepy courtyards, having stately old houses within, as silent as tombs. It was all very like one of the descriptions in the 'Arabian Nights.'[7] The three one-eyed Calenders might have knocked at any one of those doors till the street rang again, and the porter who persisted in asking questions – the man who had the delicious purchases put into his basket in the morning – might have opened it quite naturally.

After breakfast next morning, we sallied forth to see the lions. Such a delicious breeze was blowing in, from the north, as made the walk delightful: though the pavement-stones, and stones of the walls and houses, were far too hot to have a hand laid on them comfortably.

We went, first of all, up a rocky height, to the Cathedral: where Mass was performing to an auditory very like that of Lyons, namely, several old women, a baby, and a very self-possessed dog, who had marked out for himself a little course or platform for exercise, beginning at the altar-rails and ending at the door, up and down which constitutional walk, he trotted, during the service, as methodically and calmly, as any old gentleman out of doors. It is a bare old church, and the paintings in the roof are sadly defaced by time and damp weather; but the sun was shining in, splendidly, through the red curtains of the windows, and glittering on the altar furniture; and it looked as bright and cheerful as need be.

Going apart, in this Church, to see some painting which was being executed in fresco by a French artist and his pupil, I was led to observe more closely than I might otherwise have done, a great number of votive offerings with which the walls of the different chapels were profusely hung. I will not say decorated, for they were very roughly and comically got up: most likely by poor sign-painters, who eke out their living in that way. They were all little pictures: each representing some sickness or calamity from which the person placing it there, had escaped, through the interposition of his or her patron saint, or of the Madonna; and I may refer to them as good specimens of the class generally. They are abundant in Italy.

In a grotesque squareness of outline, and impossibility of perspective, they were not unlike the woodcuts in old books: but they were oil-paintings, and the artist, like the painter of the Primrose family,[8] had not been sparing of his colours. In one, a lady was having a toe amputated – an operation which a saintly personage had sailed into the room, upon a cloud, to superintend. In another, a lady was lying in bed, tucked up very tight and prim, and staring with much composure at a tripod, with a slop-basin on it: the usual form of washing-stand, and the only piece of furniture, besides the bedstead, in her chamber. One would never have supposed her to be labouring under any complaint, beyond the inconvenience of being miraculously wide awake, if the painter had not hit upon the idea of putting all her family on their knees in one corner, with their legs sticking out behind them on the floor, like boot-trees. Above whom, the Virgin, on a kind of blue divan, promised to restore the patient. In another case, a lady was in the very act of being run over, immediately outside the city walls, by a sort of piano-forte van. But the Madonna was there again. Whether the supernatural appearance had startled the horse (a bay griffin), or whether it was invisible to him, I don't know; but he was galloping away, ding-dong, without the smallest reverence or compunction. On every picture 'Ex voto' was painted in yellow capitals in the sky.

Though votive offerings were not unknown in Pagan Temples, and are evidently among the many compromises made between the false religion and the true, when the true was in its infancy, I could wish that all the other compromises were as harmless. Gratitude and Devotion are Christian qualities; and a grateful, humble, Christian spirit may dictate the observance.

Hard by the Cathedral, stands the ancient Palace of the Popes, of which one portion is now a common jail, and another a noisy barrack: while gloomy suites of state apartments, shut up and deserted, mock their own old state and glory, like the embalmed bodies of kings. But we neither went there, to see state-rooms, nor soldiers' quarters, nor a common jail, though we dropped some money into a prisoners' box outside, whilst the prisoners, themselves, looked through the iron bars, high up, and watched us eagerly. We went to see the ruins of the dreadful rooms in which the Inquisition used to sit.

A little, old, swarthy woman, with a pair of flashing black eyes, – proof that the world hadn't conjured down the devil within her, though it had had between sixty and seventy years to do it in, – came out of the Barrack Cabaret, of which she was the keeper, with some large keys in her hands, and marshalled us the way that we should go. How she told us, on the way, that she was a Government Officer (*concierge du palais apostolique*), and had been, for I don't know how many years; and how she had shown these dungeons to princes; and how she was the best of dungeon demonstrators; and how she had resided in the palace from an infant, – had been born

there, if I recollect right, – I needn't relate. But such a
fierce, little, rapid, sparkling, energetic, she-devil I never
beheld. She was alight and flaming, all the time. Her action
was violent in the extreme. She never spoke, without stopping
expressly for the purpose. She stamped her feet, clutched us
by the arms, flung herself into attitudes, hammered against
walls with her keys, for mere emphasis: now whispered as if
the Inquisition were there still: now shrieked as if she were
on the rack herself; and had a mysterious, hag-like way with
her forefinger, when approaching the remains of some new
horror – looking back and walking stealthily, and making
horrible grimaces – that might alone have qualified her to
walk up and down a sick man's counterpane, to the exclusion
of all other figures, through a whole fever.

Passing through the court-yard, among groups of idle
soldiers, we turned off by a gate, which this She-Goblin
unlocked for our admission, and locked again behind us: and
entered a narrow court, rendered narrower by fallen stones
and heaps of rubbish; part of it choking up the mouth of a
ruined subterranean passage, that once communicated (or is
said to have done so) with another castle on the opposite
bank of the river. Close to this court-yard, is a dungeon – we
stood within it, in another minute – in the dismal tower *des
oubliettes*, where Rienzi[9] was imprisoned, fastened by an iron
chain to the very wall that stands there now, but shut out
from the sky which now looks down into it. A few steps
brought us to the Cachots, in which the prisoners of the
Inquisition were confined for forty-eight hours after their
capture, without food or drink, that their constancy might be
shaken, even before they were confronted with their gloomy
judges. The day has not got in there yet. They are still small
cells, shut in by four unyielding, close, hard walls; still profoundly dark; still massively doored and fastened, as of old.

Goblin, looking back as I have described, went softly on,
into a vaulted chamber, now used as a store-room: once the
Chapel of the Holy Office. The place where the tribunal sat,

was plain. The platform might have been removed but yesterday. Conceive the parable of the Good Samaritan having been painted on the wall of one of these Inquisition chambers! But it was, and may be traced there yet.

High up in the jealous wall, are niches where the faltering replies of the accused were heard and noted down. Many of them had been brought out of the very cell we had just looked into, so awfully; along the same stone passage. We had trodden in their very footsteps.

I am gazing round me, with the horror that the place inspires, when Goblin clutches me by the wrist, and lays, not her skinny finger, but the handle of a key, upon her lip. She invites me, with a jerk, to follow her. I do so. She leads me out into a room adjoining – a rugged room, with a funnel-shaped, contracting roof, open at the top, to the bright day. I ask her what it is. She folds her arms, leers hideously, and stares. I ask again. She glances round, to see that all the little company are there; sits down upon a mound of stones; throws up her arms, and yells out, like a fiend, 'La Salle de la Question!'

The Chamber of Torture! And the roof was made of that shape to stifle the victim's cries! Oh Goblin, Goblin, let us think of this awhile, in silence. Peace, Goblin! Sit with your short arms crossed on your short legs, upon that heap of stones, for only five minutes, and then flame out again.

Minutes! Seconds are not marked upon the Palace clock, when, with her eyes flashing fire, Goblin is up, in the middle of the chamber, describing, with her sun-burnt arms, a wheel of heavy blows. Thus it ran round! cries Goblin. Mash, mash, mash! An endless routine of heavy hammers. Mash, mash, mash! upon the sufferer's limbs. See the stone trough! says Goblin. For the water torture! Gurgle, swill, bloat, burst, for the Redeemer's honour! Suck the bloody rag, deep down into your unbelieving body, Heretic, at every breath you draw! And when the executioner plucks it out, reeking with the smaller mysteries of God's own Image,[10] know us for His chosen servants ; true believers in the Sermon on the Mount; elect disciples of Him who never did a miracle but to heal: who never struck a man with palsy, blindness, deafness, dumbness, madness, any one affliction of mankind; and never stretched His blessed hand out, but to give relief and ease!

See! cries Goblin. There the furnace was. There they made the irons red-hot. Those holes supported the sharp stake, on which the tortured persons hung poised: dangling with their whole weight from the roof. 'But;' and Goblin whispers this; 'Monsieur has heard of this tower? Yes? Let Monsieur look down, then!'

A cold air, laden with an earthy smell, falls upon the face of Monsieur; for she has opened, while speaking, a trap-door in the wall. Monsieur looks in. Downward to the bottom, upward to the top, of a steep, dark, lofty tower: very dismal, very dark, very cold. The Executioner of the Inquisition, says Goblin, edging in her head to look down also, flung those who were past all further torturing, down here. 'But look! does Monsieur see the black stains on the wall?' A glance, over his shoulder, at Goblin's keen eye, shows Monsieur – and would without the aid of the directing-key – where they are. 'What are they?' 'Blood!'

In October, 1791, when the Revolution was at its height here, sixty persons: men and women ('and priests,' says Goblin, 'priests'): were murdered, and hurled, the dying and the dead, into this dreadful pit, where a quantity of quick-lime was tumbled down upon their bodies. Those ghastly tokens of the massacre were soon no more; but while one stone of the strong building in which the deed was done, remains upon another, there they will lie in the memories of men, as plain to see as the splashing of their blood upon the wall is now.

Was it a portion of the great scheme of Retribution, that the cruel deed should be committed in this place? That a part of the atrocities and monstrous institutions, which had been, for scores of years, at work to change men's nature, should in its last service, tempt them with the ready means of gratifying their furious and beastly rage! Should enable them to show themselves, in the height of their frenzy, no worse than a great, solemn, legal establishment, in the height of its power! No worse! Much better. They used the Tower of the Forgotten, in the name of Liberty – their liberty; an earth-born creature, nursed in the black mud of the Bastille moats and dungeons, and necessarily betraying many evidences of its unwholesome bringing-up – but the Inquisition used it in the name of Heaven.

Goblin's finger is lifted; and she steals out again, into the Chapel of the Holy Office. She stops at a certain part of the flooring. Her great effect is at hand. She waits for the rest. She darts at the brave Courier, who is explaining something; hits him a sounding rap on the hat with the largest key; and bids him be silent. She assembles us all, round a little trap-door in the floor, as round a grave. 'Voilà!' she darts down at the ring, and flings the door open with a crash, in her goblin energy, though it is no light weight. 'Voilà les oubliettes! Voilà les oubliettes! Subterranean! Frightful! Black! Terrible! Deadly! Les oubliettes de l'Inquisition!'

My blood ran cold, as I looked from Goblin, down into the vaults, where these forgotten creatures, with recollections of the world outside: of wives, friends, children, brothers: starved to death, and made the stones ring with their unavailing groans. But, the thrill I felt on seeing the accursed wall below, decayed and broken through, and the sun shining in through its gaping wounds, was like a sense of victory and triumph. I felt exalted with the proud delight of living, in these degenerate times, to see it. As if I were the hero of some high achievement! The light in the doleful vaults was typical of the light that has streamed in, on all persecution in God's name, but which is not yet at its noon! It cannot look more lovely to a blind man newly restored to sight, than to a traveller who sees it, calmly and majestically, treading down the darkness of that Infernal Well.

Avignon to Genoa

G OBLIN, having shown *les oubliettes*, felt that her great
coup was struck. She let the door fall with a crash, and
stood upon it with her arms a-kimbo, sniffing prodigiously.

When we left the place, I accompanied her into her house,
under the outer gateway of the fortress, to buy a little history
of the building. Her cabaret, a dark low room, lighted by
small windows, sunk in the thick wall – in the softened light,
and with its forge-like chimney; its little counter by the door,
with bottles, jars, and glasses on it; its household implements
and scraps of dress against the walls; and a sober-looking
woman (she must have a congenial life of it, with Goblin),
knitting at the door – looked exactly like a picture by
OSTADE.[11]

I walked round the building on the outside, in a sort of
dream, and yet with the delightful sense of having awakened
from it, of which the light, down in the vaults, had given me
the assurance. The immense thickness and giddy height of
the walls, the enormous strength of the massive towers, the
great extent of the building, its gigantic proportions, frowning aspect, and barbarous irregularity, awaken awe and
wonder. The recollection of its opposite old uses: an im-
pregnable fortress, a luxurious palace, a horrible prison, a
place of torture, the court of the Inquisition: at one and the
same time, a house of feasting, fighting, religion, and blood:
gives to every stone in its huge form a fearful interest, and
imparts new meaning to its incongruities. I could think of
little, however, then, or long afterwards, but the sun in the
dungeons. The palace coming down to be the lounging-place
of noisy soldiers, and being forced to echo their rough talk

and common oaths, and to have their garments fluttering from its dirty windows, was some reduction of its state, and something to rejoice at; but the day in its cells, and the sky for the roof of its chambers of cruelty – that was its desolation and defeat! If I had seen it in a blaze from ditch to rampart, I should have felt that not that light, nor all the light in all the fire that burns, could waste it, like the sunbeams in its secret council-chamber, and its prisons.

Before I quit this Palace of the Popes,[12] let me translate from the little history I mentioned just now, a short anecdote, quite appropriate to itself, connected with its adventures.

'An ancient tradition relates, that in 1441, a nephew of Pierre de Lude, the Pope's legate, seriously insulted some distinguished ladies of Avignon, whose relations, in revenge, seized the young man, and horribly mutilated him. For several years the legate kept *his* revenge within his own breast, but he was not the less resolved upon its gratification at last. He even made, in the fulness of time, advances towards a complete reconciliation; and when their apparent sincerity had prevailed, he invited to a splendid banquet, in this palace, certain families, whole families, whom he sought to exterminate. The utmost gaiety animated the repast; but the measures of the legate were well taken. When the dessert was on the board, a Swiss presented himself, with the announcement that a strange ambassador solicited an extraordinary audience. The legate, excusing himself, for the moment, to his guests, retired, followed by his officers. Within a few moments afterwards, five hundred persons were reduced to ashes: the whole of that wing of the building having been blown into the air with a terrible explosion!'

After seeing the churches (I will not trouble you with churches just now), we left Avignon that afternoon. The heat being very great, the roads outside the walls were strewn with people fast asleep in every little slip of shade, and with lazy groups, half asleep and half awake, who were waiting until the sun should be low enough to admit of their playing bowls among the burnt-up trees, and on the dusty road. The harvest here, was already gathered in, and mules and horses were treading out the corn in the fields. We came, at dusk, upon a wild and hilly country, once famous for brigands: and travelled slowly up a steep ascent. So we went on, until eleven at night, when we halted at the town of Aix (within two stages of Marseilles) to sleep.

The hotel, with all the blinds and shutters closed to keep the light and heat out, was comfortable and airy next morning and the town was very clean; but so hot, and so intensely light, that when I walked out at noon it was like coming suddenly from the darkened room into crisp blue fire. The air was so very clear, that distant hills and rocky points appeared within an hour's walk: while the town immediately at hand – with a kind of blue wind between me and it – seemed to be white hot, and to be throwing off a fiery air from its surface.

We left this town towards evening, and took the road to Marseilles. A dusty road it was; the houses shut up close; and the vines powdered white. At nearly all the cottage doors, women were peeling and slicing onions into earthen bowls for supper. So they had been doing last night all the way from Avignon. We passed one or two shady dark châteaux, surrounded by trees, and embellished with cool basins of water: which were the more refreshing to behold, from the great scarcity of such residences on the road we had travelled. As we approached Marseilles, the road began to be covered with holiday people. Outside the public houses were parties smoking, drinking, playing draughts and cards, and (once) dancing. But dust, dust, dust, everywhere. We went on, through a long, straggling, dirty suburb, thronged with people; having on our left a dreary slope of land, on which the country-houses of the Marseilles merchants, always staring white, are jumbled and heaped without the slightest order: backs, fronts, sides, and gables towards all points of the compass; until, at last, we entered the town.

I was there, twice or thrice afterwards, in fair weather and foul; and I am afraid there is no doubt that it is a dirty and disagreeable place. But the prospect, from the fortified heights, of the beautiful Mediterranean, with its lovely rocks and islands, is most delightful. These heights are a desirable retreat, for less picturesque reasons – as an escape from a compound of vile smells perpetually arising from a great harbour full of stagnant water, and befouled by the refuse of innumerable ships with all sorts of cargoes: which, in hot weather, is dreadful in the last degree.

There were foreign sailors, of all nations, in the streets; with red shirts, blue shirts, buff shirts, tawny shirts, and shirts of orange colour; with red caps, blue caps, green caps, great beards, and no beards; in Turkish turbans, glazed English hats, and Neapolitan head-dresses. There were the townspeople sitting in clusters on the pavement, or airing themselves on the tops of their houses, or walking up and down the closest and least airy of Boulevards; and there were crowds of fierce-looking people of the lower sort, blocking up the way, constantly. In the very heart of all this stir and uproar, was the common madhouse; a low, contracted, miserable building, looking straight upon the street, without the smallest screen or court-yard; where chattering madmen and mad-women were peeping out, through rusty bars, at the staring faces below, while the sun, darting fiercely aslant into their little cells, seemed to dry up their brains, and worry them, as if they were baited by a pack of dogs.

We were pretty well accommodated at the Hôtel du Paradis, situated in a narrow street of very high houses, with a hairdresser's shop opposite, exhibiting in one of its windows two full-length waxen ladies, twirling round and round: which so enchanted the hairdresser himself, that he and his family sat in arm-chairs, and in cool undresses, on the pavement outside, enjoying the gratification of the passers-by, with lazy dignity. The family had retired to rest when we went to bed, at midnight; but the hairdresser (a corpulent man, in drab slippers) was still sitting there, with his legs stretched out before him, and evidently couldn't bear to have the shutters put up.

Next day we went down to the harbour, where the sailors of all nations were discharging and taking in cargoes of all kinds: fruits, wines, oils, silks, stuffs, velvets, and every manner of merchandise. Taking one of a great number of lively little boats with gay-striped awnings, we rowed away; under the sterns of great ships; under tow-ropes and cables; against and among other boats; and very much too near the sides of vessels that were faint with oranges, to the *Marie Antoinette*, a handsome steamer bound for Genoa, lying near the mouth of the harbour. By-and-by, the carriage, that un-wieldy 'trifle from the Pantechnicon,' on a flat barge, bumping against everything, and giving occasion for a prodigious quantity of oaths and grimaces, came stupidly alongside; and by five o'clock we were steaming out in the open sea. The vessel was beautifully clean; the meals were served under an awning on deck; the night was calm and clear; the quiet beauty of the sea and sky, unspeakable.

We were off Nice, early next morning, and coasted along, within a few miles of the Cornice road (of which more in its place) nearly all day. We could see Genoa before three; and watching it as it gradually developed its splendid amphi-theatre, terrace rising above terrace, garden above garden, palace above palace, height upon height, was ample occupa-tion for us, till we ran into the stately harbour. Having been duly astonished, here, by the sight of a few Cappuccíni monks, who were watching the fair-weighing of some wood upon the wharf, we drove off to Albaro, two miles distant, where we had engaged a house.

The way lay through the main streets, but not through the Strada Nuova, or the Strada Balbi, which are the famous streets of palaces. I never, in my life, was so dismayed! The wonderful novelty of everything, the unusual smells, the unaccountable filth (though it is reckoned the cleanest of

Italian towns), the disorderly jumbling of dirty houses, one upon the roof of another; the passages more squalid and more close than any in Saint Giles's,[13] or old Paris: in and out of which, not vagabonds, but well-dressed women, with white veils and great fans, were passing and repassing; the perfect absence of resemblance in any dwelling-house, or shop, or wall, or post, or pillar, to anything one had ever seen before; and the disheartening dirt, discomfort, and decay; perfectly confounded me. I fell into a dismal reverie. I am conscious of a feverish and bewildered vision of saints and virgins' shrines at the street corners – of great numbers of friars, monks, and soldiers – of vast red curtains, waving in the door-ways of the churches – of always going up hill, and yet seeing every other street and passage going higher up – of fruit-stalls, with fresh lemons and oranges hanging in garlands made of vine leaves – of a guard-house, and a draw-bridge – and some gateways – and vendors of iced water, sitting with little trays upon the margin of the kennel – and this is all the consciousness I had, until I was set down in a rank, dull, weedy court-yard, attached to a kind of pink jail; and was told I lived there.

I little thought, that day, that I should ever come to have an attachment for the very stones in the streets of Genoa, and to look back upon the city with affection as connected with many hours of happiness and quiet! But these are my first impressions honestly set down; and how they changed, I will set down too. At present, let us breathe after this long-winded journey.

Genoa and its Neighbourhood

THE first impressions of such a place as ALBARO, the suburb of Genoa where I am now, as my American friends would say, 'located,' can hardly fail, I should imagine, to be mournful and disappointing. It requires a little time and use to overcome the feeling of depression consequent, at first, on so much ruin and neglect. Novelty, pleasant to most people, is particularly delightful, I think, to me. I am not easily dispirited when I have the means of pursuing my own fancies and occupations; and I believe I have some natural aptitude for accommodating myself to circumstances. But, as yet, I stroll about here, in all the holes and corners of the neighbourhood, in a perpetual state of forlorn surprise; and returning to my villa; the Villa Bagnerello; (it sounds romantic, but Signor Bagnerello is a butcher hard by), have sufficient occupation in pondering over my new experiences, and comparing them, very much to my own amusement, with my expectations, until I wander out again.

The Villa Bagnerello: or the Pink Jail, a far more expressive name for the mansion: is in one of the most splendid situations imaginable. The noble bay of Genoa, with the deep blue Mediterranean, lie stretched out near at hand; monstrous old desolate houses and palaces are dotted all about; lofty hills, with their tops often hidden in the clouds, and with strong forts perched high up on their craggy sides, are close upon the left; and in front, stretching from the walls of the house, down to a ruined chapel which stands upon the bold and picturesque rocks on the sea-shore, are green vineyards, where you may wander all day long in partial shade, through interminable vistas of grapes, trained on a rough trellis work across the narrow paths.

This sequestered spot is approached by lanes so very narrow, that when we arrived at the Custom-house, we found the people here had *taken the measure* of the narrowest among them, and were waiting to apply it to the carriage; which ceremony was gravely performed in the street, while we all stood by, in breathless suspense. It was found to be a very tight fit, but just a possibility, and no more – as I am reminded every day, by the sight of various large holes which it punched in the walls on either side as it came along. We are more fortunate, I am told, than an old lady who took a house in these parts not long ago, and who stuck fast in *her* carriage in a lane; and as it was impossible to open one of the doors, she was obliged to submit to the indignity of being hauled through one of the little front windows, like a harlequin.

When you have got through these narrow lanes, you come to an archway, imperfectly stopped up by a rusty old gate – my gate. The rusty old gate has a bell to correspond, which you ring as long as you like, and which nobody answers, as it has no connexion whatever with the house. But there is a rusty old knocker, too – very loose, so that it slides round when you touch it – and if you learn the trick of it, and knock long enough, somebody comes. The Brave Courier comes, and gives you admittance. You walk into a seedy little garden, all wild and weedy, from which the vineyard opens; cross it, enter a square hall like a cellar, walk up a cracked marble staircase, and pass into a most enormous room with a vaulted roof and whitewashed walls: not unlike a great Methodist chapel. This is the *sala*. It has five windows and five doors, and is decorated with pictures which would gladden the heart of one of those picture-cleaners in London who hang up, as a sign, a picture divided, like death and the lady, at the top of the old ballad[14]: which always leaves you in a state of uncertainty whether the ingenious professor has cleaned one half or dirtied the other. The furniture of this *sala* is a sort of red brocade. All the chairs are immovable, and the sofa weighs several tons.

On the same floor, and opening out of this same chamber, are dining-room, drawing-room, and divers bed-rooms: each with a multiplicity of doors and windows. Up-stairs are divers other gaunt chambers, and a kitchen; and down-stairs is another kitchen, which, with all sorts of strange contrivances for burning charcoal, looks like an alchemical laboratory. There are also some half-dozen small sitting-rooms, where the servants, in this hot July, may escape from the heat of the fire, and where the Brave Courier plays all sorts of musical instruments of his own manufacture, all the evening long. A mighty old, wandering, ghostly, echoing, grim, bare house it is, as ever I beheld or thought of.

There is a little vine-covered terrace, opening from the drawing-room; and under this terrace, and forming one side of the little garden, is what used to be the stable. It is now a cow-house, and has three cows in it, so that we get new milk by the bucket-full. There is no pasturage near, and they never go out, but are constantly lying down and surfeiting themselves with vine-leaves – perfect Italian cows – enjoying the *dolce far' niente* all day long. They are presided over, and slept with, by an old man named Antonio, and his son: two burnt-sienna natives with naked legs and feet, who wear, each, a shirt, a pair of trousers, and a red sash, with a relic, or some sacred charm like a bonbon off a twelfth-cake, hanging round the neck. The old man is very anxious to convert me to the Catholic Faith; and exhorts me frequently. We sit upon a stone by the door, sometimes, in the evening, like Robinson Crusoe and Friday reversed; and he generally relates, towards my conversion, an abridgment of the History of Saint Peter – chiefly, I believe, from the unspeakable delight he has in his imitation of the cock.

The view, as I have said, is charming; but in the day you must keep the lattice-blinds close shut, or the sun would drive you mad; and when the sun goes down, you must shut up all the windows, or the mosquitoes would tempt you to commit suicide. So at this time of the year, you don't see much of the prospect within doors. As for the flies, you don't mind them. Nor the fleas, whose size is prodigious, and whose name is Legion, and who populate the coach-house to that extent that I daily expect to see the carriage going off bodily, drawn by myriads of industrious fleas in harness. The rats are kept away, quite comfortably, by scores of lean cats, who roam about the garden for that purpose. The lizards, of course, nobody cares for; they play in the sun, and don't bite. The little scorpions are merely curious. The beetles are rather late, and have not appeared yet. The frogs are company. There is a preserve of them in the grounds of the next villa; and after nightfall, one would think that scores upon scores of women in pattens, were going up and down a wet stone pavement without a moment's cessation. That is exactly the noise they make.

The ruined chapel, on the picturesque and beautiful seashore, was dedicated, once upon a time, to Saint John the Baptist. I believe there is a legend that Saint John's bones were received there, with various solemnities, when they were first brought to Genoa; for Genoa possesses them to this day. When there is any uncommon tempest at sea, they are brought out, and exhibited to the raging weather, which they never fail to calm. In consequence of this connexion of Saint John with the city, great numbers of the common people are christened Giovanni Baptista, which latter name is pronounced in the Genoese *patois* 'Batcheetcha,' like a sneeze. To hear everybody calling everybody else Batcheetcha, on a Sunday, or Festa-day, when there are crowds in the streets, is not a little singular and amusing to a stranger.

The narrow lanes have great villas opening into them, whose walls (outside walls, I mean), are profusely painted with all sorts of subjects, grim and holy. But time and the sea-air have nearly obliterated them; and they look like the entrance to Vauxhall Gardens[15] on a sunny day. The courtyards of these houses are overgrown with grass and weeds; all sorts of hideous patches cover the bases of the statues, as if they were afflicted with a cutaneous disorder; the outer gates are rusty; and the iron bars outside the lower windows are all tumbling down. Firewood is kept in halls where costly treasures might be heaped up, mountains high; water-falls are dry and choked; fountains, too dull to play, and too lazy to work, have just enough recollection of their identity, in their sleep, to make the neighbourhood damp; and the sirocco wind is often blowing over all these things for days together, like a gigantic oven out for a holiday.

Not long ago, there was a Festa-day, in honour of the *Virgin's mother*, when the young men of the neighbourhood, having worn green wreaths of the vine in some procession or other, bathed in them, by scores. It looked very odd and pretty. Though I am bound to confess (not knowing of the festa at that time), that I thought, and was quite satisfied, they wore them as horses do – to keep the flies off.

Soon afterwards, there was another Festa-day, in honour of a St. Nazaro. One of the Albaro young men brought two large bouquets soon after breakfast, and coming up-stairs into the great *sala*, presented them himself. This was a polite way of begging for a contribution towards the expenses of some music in the Saint's honour, so we gave him whatever it may have been, and his messenger departed: well satisfied. At six o'clock in the evening we went to the church – close at hand – a very gaudy place, hung all over with festoons and bright draperies, and filled, from the altar to the main door, with women, all seated. They wear no bonnets here, simply a long white veil – the 'mezzero;' and it was the most gauzy, ethereal-looking audience I ever saw. The young women are not generally pretty, but they walk remarkably well, and in their personal carriage and the management of their veils, display much innate grace and elegance. There were some men present: not very many: and a few of these were kneeling about the aisles, while everybody else tumbled over them. Innumerable tapers were burning in the church; the bits of silver and tin about the saints (especially in the

Virgin's necklace) sparkled brilliantly; the priests were seated about the chief altar; the organ played away, lustily, and a full band did the like; while a conductor, in a little gallery opposite to the band, hammered away on the desk before him with a scroll; and a tenor, without any voice, sang. The band played one way, the organ played another, the singer went a third, and the unfortunate conductor banged and banged, and flourished his scroll on some principle of his own: apparently well satisfied with the whole performance. I never did hear such a discordant din. The heat was intense all the time.

The men, in red caps, and with loose coats hanging on their shoulders (they never put them on), were playing bowls, and buying sweetmeats, immediately outside the church. When half-a-dozen of them finished a game, they came into the aisle, crossed themselves with the holy water, knelt on one knee for an instant, and walked off again, to play another game at bowls. They are remarkably expert at this diversion, and will play in the stony lanes and streets, and on the most uneven and disastrous ground for such a purpose, with as much nicety as on a billiard-table. But the most favourite game is the national one of Mora, which they pursue with surprising ardour, and at which they will stake everything they possess. It is a destructive kind of gambling, requiring no accessaries but the ten fingers, which are always – I intend no pun – at hand. Two men play together. One calls a number – say the extreme one, ten. He marks what portion of it he pleases by throwing out three, or four, or five fingers; and his adversary has, in the same instant, at hazard, and without seeing his hand, to throw out as many fingers as will make the exact balance. Their eyes and hands become so used to this, and act with such astonishing rapidity, that an uninitiated bystander would find it very difficult, if not impossible, to follow the progress of the game. The initiated, however, of whom there is always an eager group looking on, devour it with the most intense avidity; and they are always ready to champion one side or the other in case of a dispute, and are frequently divided in their partizanship, it is often a very noisy proceeding. It is never the quietest game in the world; for the numbers are always called in a loud sharp voice, and follow as close upon each other as they can be counted. On a holiday evening, standing at a window, or walking in a garden, or passing through the streets, or sauntering in any quiet place about the town, you will hear this game in progress in a score of wine-shops at once; and looking over any vineyard walk, or turning almost any corner, will come upon a knot of players in full cry. It is observable that most men have a propensity to throw out some particular number oftener than another; and the vigilance with which two sharp-eyed players will mutually endeavour to detect this weakness, and adapt their game to it, is very curious and entertaining. The effect is greatly heightened by the universal suddenness and vehemence of gesture; two men playing for half a farthing with an intensity as all-absorbing as if the stake were life.

Hard by here, is a large Palazzo, formerly belonging to some member of the Brignole family, but just now hired by a school of Jesuits for their summer quarters. I walked into its dismantled precincts the other evening about sunset, and couldn't help pacing up and down for a little time, drowsily taking in the aspect of the place: which is repeated hereabouts in all directions.

I loitered to and fro, under a colonnade, forming two sides of a weedy, grass-grown court-yard, whereof the house formed a third side, and a low terrace-walk, overlooking the garden and the neighbouring hills, the fourth. I don't believe there was an uncracked stone in the whole pavement. In the centre was a melancholy statue, so piebald in its decay, that it looked exactly as if it had been covered with sticking-plaster, and afterwards powdered. The stables, coach-houses, offices, were all empty, all ruinous, all utterly deserted.

Doors had lost their hinges, and were holding on by their

latches; windows were broken, painted plaster had peeled off, and was lying about in clods; fowls and cats had so taken possession of the out-buildings, that I couldn't help thinking of the fairy tales, and eyeing them with suspicion, as transformed retainers, waiting to be changed back again. One old Tom in particular: a scraggy brute, with a hungry green eye (a poor relation, in reality, I am inclined to think): came prowling round and round me, as if he half believed, for the moment, that I might be the hero come to marry the lady, and set all to rights; but discovering his mistake, he suddenly gave a grim snarl, and walked away with such a tremendous tail, that he couldn't get into the little hole where he lived, but was obliged to wait outside until his indignation and his tail had gone down together.

In a sort of summer-house, or whatever it may be, in this colonnade, some Englishmen had been living, like grubs in a nut; but the Jesuits had given them notice to go, and they had gone, and *that* was shut up too. The house: a wandering, echoing, thundering barrack of a place, with the lower windows barred up, as usual, was wide open at the door: and I have no doubt I might have gone in, and gone to bed, and gone dead, and nobody a bit the wiser. Only one suite of rooms on an upper floor was tenanted; and from one of these, the voice of a young-lady vocalist, practising bravura lustily, came flaunting out upon the silent evening.

I went down into the garden, intended to be prim and quaint, with avenues, and terraces, and orange trees, and statues, and water in stone basins; and everything was green, gaunt, weedy, straggling, under grown, or over grown, mildewy, damp, redolent of all sorts of slabby, clammy, creeping, and uncomfortable life. There was nothing bright in the whole scene but a firefly – one solitary firefly – showing against the dark bushes like the last little speck of the departed Glory of the house; and even it went flitting up and down at sudden angles, and leaving a place with a jerk, and describing an irregular circle, and returning to the same place with a twitch that startled one; as if it were looking for the rest of the Glory, and wondering (Heaven knows it might!) what had become of it.

In the course of two months, the flitting shapes and shadows of my dismal entering reverie gradually resolved themselves into familiar forms and substances; and I already began to think that when the time should come, a year hence, for closing the long holiday and turning back to England, I might part from Genoa with anything but a glad heart.

It is a place that 'grows upon you' every day. There seems to be always something to find out in it. There are the most extraordinary alleys and by-ways to walk about in. You can lose your way (what a comfort that is, when you are idle!) twenty times a day, if you like; and turn up again, under the most unexpected and surprising difficulties. It abounds in the strangest contrasts; things that are picturesque, ugly, mean, magnificent, delightful, and offensive, break upon the view at every turn.

They who would know how beautiful the country immediately surrounding Genoa is, should climb (in clear weather) to the top of Monte Faccio, or, at least, ride round the city walls: a feat more easily performed. No prospect can be more diversified and lovely than the changing views of the harbour, and the valleys of the two rivers, the Polcevera and the Bizagno, from the heights along which the strongly fortified walls are carried, like the great wall of China in little. In not the least picturesque part of this ride, there is a fair specimen of a real Genoese tavern, where the visiter may derive good entertainment from real Genoese dishes, such as Tagliarini; Ravioli; German sausages, strong of garlic, sliced and eaten with fresh green figs; cocks' combs and sheep-kidneys, chopped up with mutton chops and liver; small pieces of some unknown part of a calf, twisted into small shreds, fried, and served up in a great dish like white-bait; and other curiosities of that kind. They often get wine at these suburban Trattorie, from France and Spain and Portugal, which is brought over by small captains in little trading-vessels. They buy it at so much a bottle, without asking what it is, or caring to remember if anybody tells them, and usually divide it into two heaps; of which they label one Champagne, and the other Madeira. The various opposite flavours, qualities, countries, ages, and vintages that are comprised under these two general heads is quite extra-ordinary. The most limited range is probably from cool Gruel up to old Marsala, and down again to apple Tea.

The great majority of the streets are as narrow as any thoroughfare can well be, where people (even Italian people) are supposed to live and walk about; being mere lanes, with here, and there, a kind of well, or breathing-place. The houses are immensely high, painted in all sorts of colours, and are in every stage and state of damage, dirt, and lack of repair. They are commonly let off in floors, or flats, like the houses in the old town of Edinburgh, or many houses in Paris. There are few street doors; the entrance halls are, for the most part, looked upon as public property; and any moderately enter-prising scavenger might make a fine fortune by now and then clearing them out. As it is impossible for coaches to penetrate into these streets, there are sedan chairs, gilded and other-wise, for hire in divers places. A great many private chairs are also kept among the nobility and gentry; and at night these are trotted to and fro in all directions, preceded by bearers of great lanthorns, made of linen stretched upon a frame. The sedans and lanthorns are the legitimate successors of the long strings of patient and much-abused mules, that go jingling their little bells through these confined streets all day long. They follow them, as regularly as the stars the sun.

When shall I forget the Streets of Palaces: the Strada Nuova and the Strada Balbi! or how the former looked one summer day, when I first saw it underneath the brightest and most intensely blue of summer skies: which its narrow perspective of immense mansions, reduced to a tapering and most precious strip of brightness, looking down upon the heavy shade below! A brightness not too common, even in July and August, to be well esteemed: for, if the Truth must out, there were not eight blue skies in as many midsummer weeks, saving, sometimes, early in the morning; when, looking out to sea, the water and the firmament were one world of deep and brilliant blue. At other times, there were clouds and haze enough to make an Englishman grumble in his own climate.

The endless details of these rich Palaces: the walls of some of them, within, alive with masterpieces by Vandyke![16] The great, heavy, stone balconies, one above another, and tier over tier: with here and there, one larger than the rest, towering high up – a huge marble platform; the doorless vestibules, massively-barred lower windows, immense public staircases, thick marble pillars, strong dungeon-like arches, and dreary, dreaming, echoing vaulted chambers: among which the eye wanders again, and again, and again, as every palace is succeeded by another – the terrace gardens between house and house, with green arches of the vine, and groves of orange trees, and blushing oleander in full bloom, twenty, thirty, forty, feet above the street – the painted halls, mouldering, and blotting, and rotting in the damp corners, and still shining out in beautiful colours and voluptuous designs, where the walls are dry – the faded figures on the outsides of the houses, holding wreaths, and crowns, and flying upward, and downward, and standing in niches, and here and there looking fainter and more feeble than elsewhere, by contrast with some fresh little Cupids, who on a more recently decorated portion of the front, are stretching out what seems to be the semblance of a blanket, but is, indeed, a sun-dial – the steep, steep, uphill streets of small palaces (but very large palaces for all that), with marble terraces looking down into close by-ways – the magnificent and innumerable Churches; and the rapid passage from a street of stately edifices, into a maze of the vilest squalor, steaming with unwholesome stenches, and swarming with half-naked children and whole worlds of dirty people – make up, altogether, such a scene of wonder: so lively, and yet so dead: so noisy, and yet so quiet: so obtrusive, and yet so shy and lowering: so wide awake, and yet so fast alseep: that it is a sort of intoxication to a stranger to walk on, and on, and on, and look about him. A bewildering phantasmagoria, with all the inconsistency of a dream, and all the pain and all the pleasure of an extravagant reality!

The different uses to which some of these Palaces are applied, all at once, is characteristic. For instance, the English Banker[17] (my excellent and hospitable friend) has his office in a good-sized Palazzo in the Strada Nuova. In the hall (every inch of which is elaborately painted, but which is as dirty as a police-station in London), a hook-nosed Saracen's Head with an immense quantity of black hair (there is a man attached to it) sells walking-sticks. On the other side of the doorway, a lady with a showy handkerchief for head-dress (wife to the Saracen's Head I believe) sells articles of her own knitting; and sometimes flowers. A little further in, two or three blind men occasionally beg. Sometimes, they are visited by a man without legs, on a little go-cart, but who has such a fresh-coloured, lively face, and such a respectable, well-conditioned body, that he looks as if he had sunk into the ground up to his middle, or had come, but partially, up a flight of cellar-steps to speak to somebody. A little further in, a few men, perhaps, lie asleep in the middle of the day; or they may be chairmen waiting for their absent freight. If so, they have brought their chairs in with them, and there *they* stand also. On the left of the hall is a little room: a hatter's shop. On the first floor, is the English bank. On the first floor also, is a whole house, and a good large residence too. Heaven knows what there may be above that; but when you are there, you have only just begun to go up-stairs. And yet, coming down-stairs again, thinking of this; and passing

out at a great crazy door in the back of the hall, instead of
turning the other way, to get into the street again; it bangs
behind you, making the dismallest and most lonesome echoes,
and you stand in a yard (the yard of the same house) which
seems to have been unvisited by human foot, for a hundred
years. Not a sound disturbs its repose. Not a head, thrust
out of any of the grim, dark, jealous windows within sight,
makes the weeds in the cracked pavement faint of heart, by
suggesting the possibility of there being hands to grub them
up. Opposite to you, is a giant figure carved in stone,
reclining, with an urn, upon a lofty piece of artificial rock-
work; and out of the urn, dangles the fag end of a leaden
pipe, which, once upon a time, poured a small torrent down
the rocks. But the eye-sockets of the giant are not drier than
this channel is now. He seems to have given his urn, which is
nearly upside down, a final tilt; and after crying, like a sepul-
chral child, 'All gone!' to have lapsed into a stony silence.

In the streets of shops, the houses are much smaller, but
of great size notwithstanding, and extremely high. They are
very dirty: quite undrained, if my nose be at all reliable: and
emit a peculiar fragrance, like the smell of very bad cheese,
kept in very hot blankets. Notwithstanding the height of the
houses, there would seem to have been a lack of room in the
City, for new houses are thrust in everywhere. Wherever it
has been possible to cram a tumble-down tenement into a
crack or corner, in it has gone. If there be a nook or angle in
the wall of a church, or a crevice in any other dead wall, of
any sort, there you are sure to find some kind of habitation:
looking as if it had grown there, like a fungus. Against the
Government House, against the old Senate House, round
about any large building, little shops stick close, like parasite
vermin to the great carcase. And for all this, look where you
may: up steps, down steps, anywhere, everywhere: there are
irregular houses, receding, starting forward, tumbling
down, leaning against their neighbours, crippling themselves
or their friend, by some means or other, until one, more

irregular than the rest, choaks up the way, and you can't see any further.

One of the rottenest-looking parts of the town, I think, is down by the landing-wharf: though it may be that its being associated with a great deal of rottenness on the evening of our arrival, has stamped it deeper in my mind. Here, again, the houses are very high; and are of an infinite variety of deformed shapes; and have (as most of the houses have) something hanging out of a great many windows, and wafting its frowsy fragrance on the breeze. Sometimes it is a curtain; sometimes it is a carpet; sometimes it is a bed; sometimes a whole line-full of clothes; but there is almost always some thing. Before the basements of these houses, is an arcade over the pavement: very massive, dark, and low, like an old crypt. The stone, or plaster, of which it is made, has turned quite black; and against every one of these black piles, all sorts of filth and garbage seem to accumulate spontaneously. Beneath some of the arches, the sellers of maccaroni and polenta establish their stalls, which are by no means inviting. The offal of a fish-market, near at hand – that is to say, of a back lane, where people sit upon the ground and on various old bulk-heads and sheds, and sell fish when they have any to dispose of – and of a vegetable market, constructed on the same principle – are contributed to the decoration of this quarter; and as all the mercantile business is transacted here, and it is crowded all day, it has a very decided flavour about it. The Porto Franco, or Free Port (where goods brought in from foreign countries pay no duty until they are sold and taken out, as in a bonded warehouse in England), is down here also; and two portentous officials, in cocked hats, stand at the gate to search you if they choose, and to keep out Monks and Ladies. For, Sanctity as well as Beauty has been known to yield to the temptation of smuggling, and in the same way: that is to say, by concealing the smuggled property beneath the loose folds of its dress. So Sanctity and Beauty may, by no means, enter.

The streets of Genoa would be all the better for the importation of a few Priests of prepossessing appearance. Every fourth or fifth man in the streets is a Priest or a Monk; and there is pretty sure to be at least one itinerant ecclesiastic inside or outside every hackney carriage on the neighbouring roads. I have no knowledge, elsewhere, of more repulsive countenances than are to be found among these gentry. If Nature's handwriting be at all legible, greater varieties of sloth, deceit, and intellectual torpor, could hardly be observed among any class of men in the world.

MR. PEPYS[18] once heard a clergyman assert in his sermon, in illustration of his respect for the Priestly office, that if he could meet a Priest and angel together, he would salute the Priest first. I am rather of the opinion of PETRARCH[19] who, when his pupil BOCCACCIO[19] wrote to him in great tribulation, that he had been visited and admonished for his writings by a Carthusian Friar who claimed to be a messenger immediately commissioned by Heaven for that purpose, replied, that for his own part, he would take the liberty of testing the reality of the commission by personal observation of the Messenger's face, eyes, forehead, behaviour, and discourse. I cannot but believe myself, from similar observation, that many unaccredited celestial messengers may be seen skulking through the streets of Genoa, or droning away their lives in other Italian towns.

Perhaps the Cappuccini, though not a learned body, are, as an order, the best friends of the people. They seem to mingle with them more immediately, as their counsellors and comforters; and to go among them more, when they are sick; and to pry less than some other orders, into the secrets of families, for the purpose of establishing a baleful ascendancy over their weaker members; and to be influenced by a less fierce desire to make converts, and once made, to let them go to ruin, soul and body. They may be seen, in their coarse dress, in all parts of the town at all times, and begging in the markets early in the morning. The Jesuits too, muster strong in the streets, and go slinking noiselessly about, in pairs, like black cats.

In some of the narrow passages, distinct trades congregate. There is a street of jewellers, and there is a row of book-sellers; but even down in places where nobody even can, or ever could, penetrate in a carriage, there are mighty old palaces shut in among the gloomiest and closest walls, and almost shut out from the sun. Very few of the tradesmen have any idea of setting forth their goods, or disposing them for show. If you, a stranger, want to buy anything, you usually look round the shop till you see it; then clutch it, if it be within reach; and inquire how much. Everything is sold at the most unlikely place. If you want coffee, you go to a sweetmeat-shop; and if you want meat, you will probably find it behind an old checked curtain, down half a dozen steps, in some sequestered nook as hard to find as if the commodity were poison, and Genoa's law were death to any that uttered it.

Most of the apothecaries' shops are great lounging places. Here, grave men with sticks, sit down in the shade for hours together, passing a meagre Genoa paper from hand to hand, and talking, drowsily and sparingly, about the News. Two or three of these are poor physicians, ready to proclaim them-selves on an emergency, and tear off with any messenger who may arrive. You may know them by the way in which they stretch their necks to listen, when you enter; and by the sigh with which they fall back again into their dull corners, on finding that you only want medicine. Few people lounge in the barbers' shops; though they are very numerous, as hardly any man shaves himself. But the apothecary's has its group of loungers, who sit back among the bottles, with their hands folded over the tops of their sticks. So still and quiet, that either you don't see them in the darkened shop, or mistake them – as I did one ghostly man in bottle-green, one day, with a hat like a stopper – for Horse Medicine.

On a summer evening, the Genoese are as fond of putting themselves, as their ancestors were of putting houses, in every available inch of space within and about the town. In all the lanes and alleys, and up every little ascent, and on every dwarf wall, and on every flight of steps, they cluster like bees. Meanwhile (and especially on Festa-days) the bells of the churches ring incessantly; not in peals, or any known form of sound, but in a horrible, irregular, jerking, dingle, dingle, dingle: with a sudden stop at every fifteenth dingle or so, which is maddening. This performance is usually achieved by a boy up in the steeple, who takes hold of the clapper, or a little rope attached to it, and tries to dingle louder than every other boy similarly employed. The noise is supposed to be particularly obnoxious to Evil Spirits; but looking up into the steeples, and seeing (and hearing) these young Christians thus engaged, one might very naturally mistake them for the Enemy.

Festa-days, early in the autumn, are very numerous. All the shops were shut up, twice within a week, for these holidays; and one night, all the houses in the neighbourhood of a particular church were illuminated, while the church itself was lighted, outside, with torches; and a grove of blazing links was erected, in an open place outside one of the city gates. This part of the ceremony is prettier and more singular a little way in the country, where you can trace the illuminated cottages all the way up a steep hill side; and where you pass festoons of tapers, wasting away in the starlight night, before some lonely little house upon the road.

On these days, they always dress the church of the saint in whose honour the Festa is holden, very gaily. Gold-embroidered festoons of different colours, hang from the arches; the altar furniture is set forth; and sometimes even the lofty pillars are swathed from top to bottom in tight-fitting draperies. The cathedral is dedicated to St. Lorenzo. On St. Lorenzo's day, we went into it, just as the sun was setting. Although these decorations are usually in very indifferent taste, the effect, just then, was very superb, indeed. For the whole building was dressed in red; and the sinking sun, streaming in through a great red curtain in the chief doorway, made all the gorgeousness its own. When the sun went down, and it gradually grew quite dark inside, except for a few twinkling tapers on the principal altar, and some small dangling silverlamps, it was very mysterious and effective. But, sitting in any of the churches towards evening, is like a mild dose of opium.

With the money collected at a Festa, they usually pay for the dressing of the church, and for the hiring of the band, and for the tapers. If there be any left (which seldom happens, I believe) the souls in purgatory get the benefit of it. They are also supposed to have the benefit of the exertions of certain small boys, who shake money-boxes before some mysterious little buildings like rural turnpikes, which (usually shut up close) fly open on Red-letter days, and disclose an image and some flowers inside.

Just without the city gate, on the Albaro road, is a small house, with an altar in it, and a stationary money-box: also for the benefit of the souls in Purgatory. Still further to stimulate the charitable, there is a monstrous painting on the plaster, on either side of the grated door, representing a select party of souls, frying. One of them has a grey moustache, and an elaborate head of grey hair: as if he had been taken out of a hairdresser's window and cast into the furnace. There he is: a most grotesque and hideously comic old soul: for ever blistering in the real sun, and melting in the mimic fire, for the gratification and improvement (and the contributions) of the poorer Genoese.

They are not a very joyous people, and are seldom seen to dance on their holidays: the staple places of entertainment among the women, being the churches and the public walks. They are very good-tempered, obliging, and industrious. Industry has not made them clean, for their habitations are extremely filthy, and their usual occupation on a fine Sunday

A DOORWAY OF GENOA CATHEDRAL
James Holland

morning, is to sit at their doors, hunting in each others'
heads. But their dwellings are so close and confined that if
those parts of the city had been beaten down by Massena in
the time of the terrible Blockade,[20] it would have at least
occasioned one public benefit among many misfortunes.

The Peasant Women, with naked feet and legs, are so
constantly washing clothes, in the public tanks, and in every
stream and ditch, that one cannot help wondering, in the
midst of all this dirt, who wears them when they are clean.
The custom is to lay the wet linen which is being operated
upon, on a smooth stone, and hammer away at it, with a flat
wooden mallet. This they do, as furiously as if they were
revenging themselves on dress in general for being connected
with the Fall of Mankind.

It is not unusual to see, lying on the edge of the tank at
these times, or on another flat stone, an unfortunate baby,
tightly swathed up, arms and legs and all, in an enormous
quantity of wrapper, so that it is unable to move a toe or
finger. This custom (which we often see represented in old
pictures) is universal among the common people. A child is
left anywhere without the possibility of crawling away, or is
accidentally knocked off a shelf, or tumbled out of bed, or is
hung up to a hook now and then, and left dangling like a doll
at an English rag shop, without the least inconvenience to
anybody.

I was sitting, one Sunday, soon after my arrival, in the
little country church of San Martino, a couple of miles from
the city, while a baptism took place. I saw the priest, and an
attendant with a large taper, and a man, and a woman, and
some others; but I had no more idea, until the ceremony was
all over, that it was a baptism, or that the curious little stiff
instrument, that was passed from one to another, in the course
of the ceremony, by the handle – like a short poker – was a
child, than I had that it was my own christening. I borrowed
the child afterwards, for a minute or two (it was lying
across the font then) and found it very red in the face but

perfectly quiet, and not to be bent on any terms. The number of cripples in the streets, soon ceased to surprise me.

There are plenty of Saints' and Virgin's Shrines, of course; generally at the corners of streets. The favourite memento to the Faithful, about Genoa, is a painting representing a peasant on his knees, with a spade and some other agricultural implements beside him; and the Madonna, with the Infant Saviour in her arms, appearing to him in a cloud. This is the Legend of the Madonna della Guardia: a chapel on a mountain within a few miles, which is in high repute. It seems that this peasant lived all alone by himself, tilling some land atop of the mountain, where, being a devout man, he daily said his prayers to the Virgin in the open air; for his hut was a very poor one. Upon a certain day, the Virgin appeared to him, as in the picture, and said, 'Why do you pray in the open air, and without a priest?' The peasant explained because there was neither priest nor church at hand – a very uncommon complaint indeed in Italy. 'I should wish, then,' said the Celestial Visitor, 'to have a chapel built here, in which the prayers of the Faithful may be offered up.' 'But, Santissima Madonna,' said the peasant, 'I am a poor man; and chapels cannot be built without money. They must be supported too, Santissima; for to have a chapel and not support it liberally, is a wickedness – a deadly sin.' This sentiment gave great satisfaction to the visitor. 'Go!' said she. 'There is such a village in the valley on the left, and such another village in the valley on the right, and such another village elsewhere, that will gladly contribute to the building of a chapel. Go to them! Relate what you have seen; and do not doubt that sufficient money will be forthcoming to erect my chapel, or that it will, afterwards, be handsomely maintained.' All of which (miraculously) turned out to be quite true. And in proof of this prediction and revelation, there is the chapel of the Madonna della Guardia, rich and flourishing at this day.

The splendour and variety of the Genoese churches, can

hardly be exaggerated. The church of the Annunciata especially: built, like many of the others, at the cost of one noble family, and now in slow progress of repair: from the outer door to the utmost height of the high cupola, is so elaborately painted and set in gold, that it looks (as SIMOND[21] describes it, in his charming book on Italy) like a great enamelled snuff-box. Most of the richer churches contain some beautiful pictures, or other embellishments of great price, almost universally set, side by side, with sprawling effigies of maudlin monks, and the veriest trash and tinsel ever seen.

It may be a consequence of the frequent direction of the popular mind, and pocket, to the souls in Purgatory, but there is very little tenderness for the *bodies* of the dead here. For the very poor, there are, immediately outside one angle of the walls, and behind a jutting point of the fortification, near the sea, certain common pits – one for every day in the year – which all remain closed up, until the turn of each comes for its daily reception of dead bodies. Among the troops in the town, there are usually some Swiss: more or less. When any of these die, they are buried out of a fund maintained by such of their countrymen as are resident in Genoa. Their providing coffins for these men is matter of great astonishment to the authorities.

Certainly, the effect of this promiscuous and indecent splashing down of dead people into so many wells, is bad. It surrounds Death with revolting associations, that insensibly become connected with those whom Death is approaching. Indifference and avoidance are the natural result; and all the softening influences of the great sorrow are harshly disturbed.

There is a ceremony when an old Cavalière or the like, expires, of erecting a pile of benches in the cathedral, to represent his bier; covering them over with a pall of black velvet; putting his hat and sword on the top; making a little square of seats about the whole; and sending out formal invitations to his friends and acquaintance to come and sit there, and hear Mass: which is performed at the principal Altar, decorated with an infinity of candles for that purpose.

When the better kind of people die, or are at the point of death, their nearest relations generally walk off: retiring into the country for a little change, and leaving the body to be disposed of, without any superintendance from them. The procession is usually formed, and the coffin borne, and the funeral conducted, by a body of persons called a Confratérnita, who, as a kind of voluntary penance, undertake to perform these offices, in regular rotation, for the dead; but who, mingling something of pride with their humility, are dressed in a loose garment covering their whole person, and wear a hood concealing the face; with breathing holes and apertures for the eyes. The effect of this costume is very ghastly: especially in the case of a certain Blue Confratérnita belonging to Genoa, who, to say the least of them, are very ugly customers, and who look – suddenly encountered in their pious ministration in the streets – as if they were Ghoules or Demons, bearing off the body for themselves.

Although such a custom may be liable to the abuse attendant on many Italian customs, of being recognised as a means of establishing a current account with Heaven, on which to draw, too easily, for future bad actions, or as an expiation for past misdeeds, it must be admitted to be a good one, and a practical one, and one involving unquestionably good works. A voluntary service like this, is surely better than the imposed penance (not at all an infrequent one) of giving so many licks to such and such a stone in the pavement of the cathedral; or than a vow to the Madonna to wear nothing but blue for a year or two. This is supposed to give great delight above; blue being (as is well known) the Madonna's favourite colour. Women who have devoted themselves to this act of Faith, are very commonly seen walking in the streets.

There are three theatres in the city, besides an old one now rarely opened. The most important – the Carlo Felice: the opera-house of Genoa – is a very splendid, commodious, and beautiful theatre. A company of comedians were acting there, when we arrived: and after their departure, a second-rate opera company came. The great season is not until the carnival time – in the spring. Nothing impressed me, so much, in my visits here (which were pretty numerous) as the uncommonly hard and cruel character of the audience, who resent the slightest defect, take nothing good-humouredly, seem to be always lying in wait for an opportunity to hiss, and spare the actresses as little as the actors. But as there is nothing else of a public nature, at which they are allowed to express the least disapprobation, perhaps they are resolved to make the most of this opportunity.

There are a great number of Piedmontese Officers too, who are allowed the privilege of kicking their heels in the pit, for next to nothing: gratuitous, or cheap accommodation for these gentlemen being insisted on, by the Governor, in all public or semi-public entertainments. They are lofty critics in consequence, and infinitely more exacting than if they made the unhappy manager's fortune.

The TEATRO DIURNO, or Day Theatre, is a covered stage in the open air, where the performances take place by daylight, in the cool of the afternoon; commencing at four or five o'clock, and lasting some three hours. It is curious, sitting among the audience, to have a fine view of the neighbouring hills and houses, and to see the neighbours at their windows looking on, and to hear the bells of the churches and convents ringing at most complete cross-purposes with the scene. Beyond this, and the novelty of seeing a play in the fresh pleasant air, with the darkening evening closing in, there is nothing very exciting or characteristic in the performances. The actors are indifferent; and though they sometimes represent one of Goldoni's comedies, the staple of the Drama is French. Anything like nationality is dangerous to despotic governments, and Jesuit-beleaguered kings.

The Theatre of Puppets, or Marionetti – a famous

company from Milan – is, without any exception, the drollest exhibition I ever beheld in my life. I never saw anything so exquisitely ridiculous. They *look* between four and five feet high, but are really much smaller; for when a musician in the orchestra happens to put his hat on the stage, it becomes alarmingly gigantic, and almost blots out an actor. They usually play a comedy, and a ballet. The comic man in the comedy I saw one summer night, is a waiter at an hotel. There never was such a locomotive actor, since the world began. Great pains are taken with him. He has extra joints in his legs: and a practical eye, with which he winks at the pit, in a manner that is absolutely insupportable to a stranger, but which the initiated audience, mainly composed of the common people, receive (so they do everything else) quite as a matter of course, and as if he were a man. His spirits are prodigious. He continually shakes his legs, and winks his eye. And there is a heavy father with grey hair, who sits down on the regular conventional stage-bank, and blesses his daughter in the regular conventional way, who is tremendous. No one would suppose it possible that anything short of a real man could be so tedious. It is the triumph of art.

In the ballet, an Enchanter runs away with the Bride, in the very hour of her nuptials. He brings her to his cave, and tries to soothe her. They sit down on a sofa (the regular sofa! in the regular place, O.P. Second Entrance!) and a procession of musicians enter; one creature playing a drum, and knocking himself off his legs at every blow. These failing to delight her, dancers appear. Four first; then two; *the* two; the flesh-coloured two. The way in which they dance; the height to which they spring; the impossible and inhuman extent to which they pirouette; the revelation of their preposterous legs; the coming down with a pause, on the very tips of their toes, when the music requires it; the gentleman's retiring up, when it is the lady's turn; and the lady's retiring up, when it is the gentleman's turn; the final passion of a pas de deux;

and the going off with a bound! – I shall never see a real ballet, with a composed countenance again.

I went another night to see these Puppets act a play called 'St. Helena, or the death of Napoleon.' It began by the disclosure of Napoleon, with an immense head, seated on a sofa in his chamber at St. Helena; to whom his valet entered, with this obscure announcement:

'Sir Yew ud se on Low!'[22] (the *ow*, as in cow).

Sir Hudson (that you could have seen his regimentals!) was a perfect mammoth of a man, to Napoleon; hideously ugly; with a monstrously disproportionate face, and a great clump for the lower-jaw, to express his tyrannical and obdurate nature. He began his system of persecution, by calling his prisoner 'General Buonaparte;' to which the latter replied, with the deepest tragedy, 'Sir Yew ud se on Low, call me not thus. Repeat that phrase and leave me! I am Napoleon, Emperor of France!' Sir Yew ud se on, nothing daunted, proceeded to entertain him with an ordinance of the British Government, regulating the state he should preserve, and the furniture of his rooms: and limiting his attendants to four or five persons. 'Four or five for *me*!' said Napoleon. 'Me! One hundred thousand men were lately at my sole command; and this English officer talks of four or five for *me*!' Throughout the piece, Napoleon (who talked very like the real Napoleon, and was, for ever, having small soliloquies by himself) was very bitter on 'these English officers,' and 'these English soldiers:' to the great satisfaction of the audience, who were perfectly delighted to have Low bullied; and who, whenever Low said 'General Buonaparte' (which he always did: always receiving the same correction) quite execrated him. It would be hard to say why; for Italians have little cause to sympathise with Napoleon, Heaven knows.

There was no plot at all, except that a French officer, disguised as an Englishman, came to propound a plan of escape; and being discovered, but not before Napoleon had

magnanimously refused to steal his freedom, was immediately ordered off by Low to be hanged. In two very long
speeches, which Low made memorable, by winding up with
'Yas!' – to show that he was English – which brought down
thunders of applause. Napoleon was so affected by this
catastrophe, that he fainted away on the spot, and was
carried out by two other puppets. Judging from what followed,
it would appear that he never recovered the shock; for the
next act showed him, in a clean shirt, in his bed (curtains
crimson and white), where a lady, prematurely dressed in
mourning, brought two little children, who kneeled down by
the bed-side, while he made a decent end; the last word on
his lips being 'Vatterlo.'

It was unspeakably ludicrous. Buonaparte's boots were so
wonderfully beyond control, and did such marvellous things
of their own accord, doubling themselves up, and getting
under tables, and dangling in the air; and sometimes skating
away with him, out of all human knowledge, when he was in
full speech – mischances which were not rendered the less
absurd, by a settled melancholy depicted in his face. To put an
end to one conference with Low, he had to go to a table, and
read a book: when it was the finest spectacle I ever beheld,
to see his body bending over the volume, like a boot-jack,
and his sentimental eyes glaring obstinately into the pit. He
was prodigiously good, in bed, with an immense collar to his
shirt, and his little hands outside the coverlet. So was Dr.
Antommarchi,[23] represented by a Puppet with long lank hair,
like Mawworm's,[24] who, in consequence of some derangement
of his wires, hovered about the couch like a vulture, and gave
medical opinions in the air. He was almost as good as Low,
though the latter was great at all times – a decided brute and
villain, beyond all possibility of mistake. Low was especially
fine at the last, when, hearing the doctor and the valet say,
'The Emperor is dead!' he pulled out his watch, and wound
up the piece (not the watch) by exclaiming, with characteristic brutality, 'Ha! ha! Eleven minutes to six! The

General dead! and the spy hanged!' This brought the curtain down, triumphantly.

There is not in Italy, they say (and I believe them) a lovelier residence than the Palazzo Peschiere, or Palace of the Fishponds, whither we removed as soon as our three months' tenancy of the Pink Jail at Albaro had ceased and determined.

It stands on a height within the walls of Genoa, but aloof from the town: surrounded by beautiful gardens of its own, adorned with statues, vases, fountains, marble basins, terraces, walks of orange trees and lemon trees; groves of roses and camelias. All its spacious apartments are beautiful in their proportions and decorations; but the great hall, some fifty feet in height, with three large windows at the end, over-looking the whole town of Genoa, the harbour, and the neighbouring sea, affords one of the most fascinating and delightful prospects in the world. Any house more cheerful and habitable than the great rooms are, within, it would be difficult to conceive; and certainly nothing more delicious than the scene without, in sunshine or in moonlight, could be imagined. It is more like an enchanted Palace in an Eastern story than a grave and sober lodging.

How you may wander on, from room to room, and never tire of the wild fancies on the walls and ceilings, as bright in their fresh colouring as if they had been painted yesterday; or how one floor, or even the great hall which opens on eight other rooms, is a spacious promenade; or how there are corridors and bedchambers above, which we never use and rarely visit, and scarcely know the way through; or how there is a view of a perfectly different character on each of the four sides of the building; matters little. But that prospect from the hall, is like a vision to me. I go back to it, in fancy, as I have done in calm reality a hundred times a day; and stand there, looking out, with the sweet scents from the garden rising up about me, in a perfect dream of happiness.

There lies all Genoa, in beautiful confusion, with its many churches, monasteries, and convents, pointing up into the sunny sky; and down below me, just where the roofs begin, a solitary convent parapet, fashioned like a gallery, with an iron cross at the end, where sometimes, early in the morning, I have seen a little group of dark-veiled nuns gliding sorrowfully to and fro, and stopping now and then to peep down upon the waking world in which they have no part. Old Monte Faccio, brightest of hills in good weather, but sulkiest when storms are coming on, is here, upon the left. The Fort within the walls (the good King built it to command the town, and beat the houses of the Genoese about their ears, in case they should be discontented) commands that height upon the right. The broad sea lies beyond, in front there; and that line of coast, beginning by the lighthouse, and tapering away, a mere speck in the rosy distance, is the beautiful coast-road that leads to Nice. The garden near at hand, among the roofs and houses: all red with roses and fresh with little fountains: is the Acqua Sola – a public promenade, where the military band plays gaily, and the white veils cluster thick, and the Genoese nobility ride round, and round, and round, in stately clothes and coaches at least, if not in absolute wisdom. Within a stone's-throw, as it seems, the audience of the Day-Theatre sit: their faces turned this way. But as the stage is hidden, it is very odd, without a knowledge of the cause, to see their faces change so suddenly from earnestness to laughter; and odder still, to hear the rounds upon rounds of applause, rattling in the evening air, to which the curtain falls. But, being Sunday night, they act their best and most attractive play. And now, the sun is going down, in such magnificent array of red, and green, and golden light, as neither pen nor pencil could depict; and to the ringing of the Vesper Bells, darkness sets in at once, without a twilight. Then, lights begin to shine in Genoa, and on the country road; and the revolving lantern out at sea there, flashing, for an instant, on this Palace front and Portico, illuminates it as if there were a bright moon bursting from behind a cloud; then, merges it in deep obscurity. And this, so far as I know, is the only reason why the Genoese avoid it after dark, and think it haunted.

My memory will haunt it, many nights, in time to come; but nothing worse, I will engage. The same Ghost will occasionally sail away, as I did one pleasant Autumn evening, into the bright prospect, and snuff the morning air at Marseilles.

The corpulent hairdresser was still sitting in his slippers outside his shop-door there, but the twirling ladies in the window, with the natural inconstancy of their sex, had ceased to twirl, and were languishing, stock still, with their beautiful faces addressed to blind corners of the establishment, where it was impossible for admirers to penetrate.

The steamer had come from Genoa in a delicious run of eighteen hours, and we were going to run back again by the Cornice Road from Nice: not being satisfied to have seen only the outsides of the beautiful towns that rise in picturesque white clusters from among the olive woods, and rocks, and hills, upon the margin of the Sea.

The Boat which started for Nice that night, at eight o'clock, was very small, and so crowded with goods that there was scarcely room to move; neither was there anything to eat on board, except bread; nor to drink, except coffee. But being due at Nice at about eight or so in the morning, this was of no consequence: so when we began to wink at the bright stars, in involuntary acknowledgment of their winking at us, we turned into our berths, in a crowded, but cool little cabin, and slept soundly till morning.

The Boat, being as dull and dogged a little boat as ever was built, it was within an hour of noon when we turned into Nice Harbour, where we very little expected anything but breakfast. But we were laden with wool. Wool must not remain in the Custom House at Marseilles more than twelve months at a stretch, without paying duty. It is the custom to make fictitious removals of unsold wool to evade this law; to take it somewhere when the twelve months are nearly out; bring it straight back again; and warehouse it, as a new cargo, for nearly twelve months longer. This wool of ours, had come originally from some place in the East. It was recognised as Eastern produce, the moment we entered the harbour. Accordingly, the gay little Sunday boats, full of holiday people, which had come off to greet us, were warned away by the authorities; we were declared in quarantine;[25] and a great flag was solemnly run up to the mast-head on the wharf, to make it known to all the town.

It was a very hot day indeed. We were unshaved, unwashed, undressed, unfed, and could hardly enjoy the absurdity of lying blistering in a lazy harbour, with the town looking on from a respectful distance, all manner of whiskered men in cocked hats discussing our fate at a remote guard-house, with gestures (we looked very hard at them through telescopes) expressive of a week's detention at least: and nothing whatever the matter all the time. But even in this crisis the Brave Courier achieved a triumph. He telegraphed somebody (*I* saw nobody) either naturally connected with the hotel, or put *en rapport* with the establishment for that occasion only. The telegraph was answered, and in half an hour or less, there came a loud shout from the guard-house. The captain was wanted. Everybody helped the captain into his boat. Everybody got his luggage, and said we were going. The captain rowed away, and disappeared behind a little jutting corner of the Galley-slaves' Prison: and presently came back with something, very sulkily. The Brave Courier met him at the side, and received the something as its rightful owner. It was a wicker-basket, folded in a linen cloth; and in it were two great bottles of wine, a roast fowl, some salt fish chopped with garlic, a great loaf of bread, a dozen or so of peaches, and a few other trifles. When we had selected our own breakfast, the Brave Courier invited a chosen party to partake of these refreshments, and assured them that they

94

need not be deterred by motives of delicacy, as he would order a second basket to be furnished at their expense. Which he did – no one knew how – and by and by, the captain being again summoned, again sulkily returned with another something; over which my popular attendant presided as before: carving with a clasp-knife, his own personal property, something smaller than a Roman sword.

The whole party on board were made merry by these unexpected supplies; but none more so, than a loquacious little Frenchman, who got drunk in five minutes, and a sturdy Cappuccíno Friar, who had taken everybody's fancy mightily, and was one of the best friars in the world, I verily believe.

He had a free, open countenance; and a rich brown, flowing beard; and was a remarkably handsome man, of about fifty. He had come up to us, early in the morning, and inquired whether we were sure to be at Nice by eleven; saying that he particularly wanted to know, because if we reached it by that time he would have to perform mass, and must deal with the consecrated wafer, fasting; whereas, if there were no chance of his being in time, he would immediately breakfast. He made this communication, under the idea that the Brave Courier was the captain; and indeed he looked much more like it than anybody else on board. Being assured that we should arrive in good time, he fasted, and talked, fasting, to everybody, with the most charming good-humour; answering jokes at the expense of friars, with other jokes at the expense of laymen, and saying that friar as he was, he would engage to take up the two strongest men on board, one after the other, with his teeth, and carry them along the deck. Nobody gave him the opportunity, but I dare say he could have done it; for he was a gallant, noble figure of a man, even in the Cappuccíno dress, which is the ugliest and most ungainly that can well be.

All this had given great delight to the loquacious Frenchman, who gradually patronised the Friar very much, and seemed to commiserate him as one who might have been born a Frenchman himself, but for an unfortunate destiny. Although his patronage was such as a mouse might bestow upon a lion, he had a vast opinion of its condescension; and in the warmth of that sentiment, occasionally rose on tiptoe, to slap the Friar on the back.

When the baskets arrived: it being then too late for Mass: the Friar went to work bravely; eating prodigiously of the cold meat and bread, drinking deep draughts of the wine, smoking cigars, taking snuff, sustaining an uninterrupted conversation with all hands, and occasionally running to the boat's side and hailing somebody on shore with the intelligence that we *must* be got out of this quarantine somehow or other, as he had to take part in a great religious procession in the afternoon. After this, he would come back, laughing lustily from pure good-humour: while the Frenchman wrinkled his small face into ten thousand creases, and said how droll it was, and what a brave boy was that Friar! At length the heat of the sun without, and of the wine within, made the Frenchman sleepy. So, in the noontide of his patronage of his gigantic protegé, he lay down among the wool, and began to snore.

It was four o'clock before we were released; and the Frenchman, dirty and woolly, and snuffy, was still sleeping when the Friar went ashore. As soon as we were free, we all hurried away, to wash and dress, that we might make a decent appearance at the Procession; and I saw no more of the Frenchman until we took up our station in the main street to see it pass, when he squeezed himself into a front place, elaborately renovated; threw back his little coat, to show a broad-barred velvet waistcoat sprinkled all over with stars; and adjusted himself and his cane so as utterly to bewilder and transfix the Friar, when he should appear.

The procession was a very long one, and included an immense number of people divided into small parties; each party chaunting nasally, on its own account, without reference to any other, and producing a most dismal result. There were angels, crosses, Virgins carried on flat boards surrounded by Cupids, crowns, saints, missals, infantry, tapers, monks, nuns, relics, dignitaries of the church in green hats, walking under crimson parasols: and, here and there, a species of sacred streetlamp hoisted on a pole. We looked out anxiously for the Cappuccíni, and presently their brown robes and corded girdles were seen coming on, in a body.

I observed the little Frenchman chuckle over the idea that when the Friar saw him in the broad-barred waistcoat, he would mentally exclaim, 'Is that my Patron! *That* distinguished man!' and would be covered with confusion. Ah! never was the Frenchman so deceived. As our friend the Cappuccíno advanced, with folded arms, he looked straight into the visage of the little Frenchman, with a bland, serene, composed abstraction, not to be described. There was not the faintest trace of recognition or amusement on his features; not the smallest consciousness of bread and meat, wine, snuff, or cigars. 'C'est lui-même,' I heard the little Frenchman say, in some doubt. Oh yes, it was himself. It was not his brother or his nephew, very like him. It was he. He walked in great state: being one of the Superiors of the Order: and looked his part to admiration. There never was anything so perfect of its kind as the contemplative way in which he allowed his placid gaze to rest on us, his late companions, as if he had never seen us in his life and didn't see us then. The Frenchman, quite humbled, took off his hat at last, but the Friar still passed on, with the same imperturbable serenity; and the broad-barred waistcoat, fading into the crowd, was seen no more.

The procession wound up with a discharge of musketry that shook all the windows in the town. Next afternoon we started for Genoa, by the famed Cornice Road.

The half-French, half-Italian Vetturíno, who undertook, with his little rattling carriage and pair, to convey us thither in three days, was a careless, good-looking fellow, whose light-heartedness and singing propensities knew no bounds as long as we went on smoothly. So long, he had a word and a smile and a flick of his whip, for all the peasant girls, and odds and ends of the Somnambula for all the echoes. So long, he went jingling through every little village, with bells on his horses and rings in his ears: a very meteor of gallantry and cheerfulness. But, it was highly characteristic to see him under a slight reverse of circumstances, when, in one part of the journey, we came to a narrow place where a waggon had broken down and stopped up the road. His hands were twined in his hair immediately, as if a combination of all the direst accidents in life had suddenly fallen on his devoted head. He swore in French, prayed in Italian, and went up and down, beating his feet on the ground in a very ecstasy of despair. There were various carters and mule-drivers assembled round the broken waggon, and at last some man, of an original turn of mind, proposed that a general and joint effort should be made to get things to-rights again, and clear the way – an idea which I verily believe would never have presented itself to our friend, though we had remained there until now. It was done at no great cost of labour; but at every pause in the doing, his hands were wound in his hair again, as if there were no ray of hope to lighten his misery. The moment he was on his box once more, and clattering briskly down hill, he returned to the Somnambula and the Peasant girls, as if it were not in the power of misfortune to depress him.

Much of the romance of the beautiful towns and villages on this beautiful road, disappears when they are entered, for many of them are very miserable. The streets are narrow, dark, and dirty; the inhabitants lean and squalid; and the withered old women, with their wiry grey hair twisted up into a knot on the top of the head, like a pad to carry loads on, are so intensely ugly, both along the Riviera, and in Genoa too, that, seen straggling about in dim door-ways with their spindles, or crooning together in by corners, they are like a population of Witches – except that they certainly are not to be suspected of brooms or any other instrument of cleanliness. Neither are the pig-skins, in common use to hold wine, and hung out in the sun in all directions, by any means ornamental, as they always preserve the form of very bloated pigs, with their heads and legs cut off, dangling upside-down by their own tails.

These towns, as they are seen in the approach, however: nestling, with their clustering roofs and towers, among trees on steep hill-sides, or built upon the brink of noble bays: are charming. The vegetation is, everywhere, luxuriant and beautiful, and the Palm tree makes a novel feature in the novel scenery. In one town, San Remo – a most extraordinary place, built on gloomy open arches, so that one might ramble underneath the whole town – there are pretty terrace gardens; in other towns, there is the clang of shipwrights' hammers, and the building of small vessels on the beach. In some of the broad bays, the fleets of Europe might ride at anchor. In every case, each little group of houses presents, in the distance some enchanting confusion of picturesque and fanciful shapes.

The road itself – now high above the glittering sea, which breaks against the foot of the precipice: now turning inland to sweep the shore of a bay: now crossing the stony bed of a mountain stream: now low down on the beach: now winding among riven rocks of many forms and colours: now chequered by a solitary ruined tower, one of a chain of towers built, in old time, to protect the coast from the invasions of the Barbary Corsairs[26] – presents new beauties every moment. When its own striking scenery is passed, and it trails on through a long line of suburb, lying on the flat sea-shore, to Genoa, then, the changing glimpses of that noble city and its harbour, awaken a new source of interest; freshened by every huge, unwieldy, half-inhabited old house in its outskirts; and coming to its climax when the city gate is reached, and all Genoa with its beautiful harbour, and neighbouring hills, bursts proudly on the view.

To Parma, Modena, and Bologna

I STROLLED away from Genoa on the 6th of November, bound for a good many places (England among them), but first for Piacenza; for which town I started in the *coupé* of a machine something like a travelling caravan, in company with the Brave Courier, and a lady with a large dog, who howled dolefully, at intervals, all night. It was very wet, and very cold; very dark, and very dismal; we travelled at the rate of barely four miles an hour, and stopped nowhere for refreshment. At ten o'clock next morning, we changed coaches at Alessandria, where we were packed up in another coach (the body whereof would have been small for a fly), in company with a very old priest; a young Jesuit, his companion, who carried their breviaries and other books, and who, in the exertion of getting into the coach, had made a gash of pink leg between his black stocking and his black knee-shorts, that reminded one of Hamlet in Ophelia's closet,[27] only it was visible on both legs; a provincial Avvocáto; and a gentleman with a red nose that had an uncommon and singular sheen upon it, which I never observed in the human subject before. In this way we travelled on, until four o'clock in the afternoon; the roads being still very heavy, and the coach very slow. To mend the matter, the old priest was troubled with cramps in his legs, so that he had to give a terrible yell every ten minutes or so, and be hoisted out by the united efforts of the company; the coach always stopping for him, with great gravity. This disorder, and the roads, formed the main subject of conversation. Finding, in the afternoon, that the *coupé* had discharged two people, and had only one passenger inside – a monstrous ugly Tuscan, with a great

purple moustache, of which no man could see the ends when
he had his hat on – I took advantage of its better accommodation, and in company with this gentleman (who was very
conversational and good-humoured) travelled on, until
nearly eleven o'clock at night, when the driver reported that
he couldn't think of going any farther, and we accordingly
made a halt at a place called Stradella.

The inn was a series of strange galleries surrounding a
yard; where our coach, and a waggon or two, and a lot of
fowls, and firewood, were all heaped up together, higgledy-
piggledy; so that you didn't know, and couldn't have taken
your oath, which was a fowl and which was a cart. We
followed a sleepy man with a flaring torch, into a great, cold
room, where there were two immensely broad beds, on what
looked like two immensely broad deal dining-tables; another
deal table of similar dimensions in the middle of the bare
floor; four windows; and two chairs. Somebody said it was
my room; and I walked up and down it, for half an hour or so,
staring at the Tuscan, the old priest, the young priest, and
the Avvocáto (Red-Nose lived in the town, and had gone
home), who sat upon the beds, and stared at me in return.

The rather dreary whimsicality of this stage of the proceedings, is interrupted by an announcement from the Brave
(he has been cooking) that supper is ready; and to the priest's
chamber (the next room and the counterpart of mine) we
all adjourn. The first dish is a cabbage, boiled with a great
quantity of rice in a tureen full of water, and flavoured with
cheese. It is so hot, and we are so cold, that it appears almost
jolly. The second dish is some little bits of pork, fried with
pigs' kidneys. The third, two red fowls. The fourth, two
little red turkeys. The fifth, a huge stew of garlic and truffles,
and I don't know what else; and this concludes the entertainment.

Before I can sit down in my own chamber, and think it of
the dampest, the door opens, and the Brave comes moving in,
in the middle of such a quantity of fuel that he looks like

Birnam Wood[28] taking a winter walk. He kindles this heap in a twinkling, and produces a jorum of hot brandy and water; for that bottle of his keeps company with the seasons, and now holds nothing but the purest *eau de vie*. When he has accomplished this feat, he retires for the night; and I hear him, for an hour afterwards, and indeed until I fall asleep, making jokes in some out-house (apparently under the pillow), where he is smoking cigars with a party of confidential friends. He never was in the house in his life before; but he knows everybody everywhere, before he has been anywhere five minutes; and is certain to have attracted to himself, in the meantime, the enthusiastic devotion of the whole establishment.

This is at twelve o'clock at night. At four o'clock next morning, he is up again, fresher than a new-blown rose; making blazing fires without the least authority from the landlord; producing mugs of scalding coffee when nobody else can get anything but cold water; and going out into the dark streets, and roaring for fresh milk, on the chance of somebody with a cow getting up to supply it. While the horses are 'coming,' I stumble out into the town too. It seems to be all one little Piazza, with a cold damp wind blowing in and out of the arches, alternately, in a sort of pattern. But it is profoundly dark, and raining heavily; and I shouldn't know it to-morrow, if I were taken there to try. Which Heaven forbid!

The horses arrive in about an hour. In the interval, the driver swears: sometimes Christian oaths, sometimes Pagan oaths. Sometimes, when it is a long, compound oath, he begins with Christianity and merges into Paganism. Various messengers are despatched; not so much after the horses, as after each other; for the first messenger never comes back, and all the rest imitate him. At length the horses appear, surrounded by all the messengers; some kicking them, and some dragging them, and all shouting abuse to them. Then, the old priest, the young priest, the Avvocáto, the Tuscan, and all of us, take our places; and sleepy voices proceeding from the doors of extraordinary hutches in divers parts of the yard, cry out 'Addio corrière mio! Buon' viággio, corrière!' Salutations which the courier, with his face one monstrous grin, returns in like manner as we go jolting and wallowing away, through the mud.

At Piacenza, which was four or five hours' journey from the Inn at Stradella, we broke up our little company before the hotel door, with divers manifestations of friendly feeling on all sides. The old priest was taken with the cramp again before he had got halfway down the street; and the young priest laid the bundle of books on a door step, while he dutifully rubbed the old gentleman's legs. The client of the Avvocáto was waiting for him at the yard-gate, and kissed him on each cheek, with such a resounding smack, that I am afraid he had either a very bad case, or a scantily-furnished purse. The Tuscan, with a cigar in his mouth, went loitering off, carrying his hat in his hand that he might the better trail up the ends of his dishevelled moustache. And the Brave Courier, as he and I strolled away to look about us, began immediately to entertain me with the private histories and family affairs of the whole party.

A brown, decayed, old town, Piacenza is. A deserted, solitary, grass-grown place, with ruined ramparts; half filled-up trenches, which afford a frowsy pasturage to the lean kine that wander about them; and streets of stern houses, moodily frowning at the other houses over the way. The sleepiest and shabbiest of soldiery go wandering about, with the double curse of laziness and poverty, uncouthly wrinkling their misfitting regimentals; the dirtiest of children play with their impromptu toys (pigs and mud) in the feeblest of gutters; and the gauntest of dogs trot in and out of the dullest of archways, in perpetual search of something to eat, which they never seem to find. A mysterious and solemn Palace, guarded by two colossal statues, twin Genii of the place, stands gravely in the midst of the idle town; and the king with the marble legs, who flourished in the time of the thousand and one Nights, might live contentedly inside of it, and never have the energy, in his upper half of flesh and blood to want to come out.

What a strange, half-sorrowful and half-delicious doze it is, to ramble through these places gone to sleep and basking in the sun! Each, in its turn, appears to be, of all the mouldy, dreary, God-forgotten towns in the wide world, the chief. Sitting on this hillock where a bastion used to be, and where a noisy fortress was, in the time of the old Roman Station here, I become aware that I have never known till now, what it is to be lazy. A dormouse must surely be in very much the same condition before he retires under the wool in his cage; or a tortoise before he buries himself. I feel that I am getting rusty. That any attempt to think, would be accompanied with a creaking noise. That there is nothing, anywhere, to be done, or needing to be done. That there is no more human progress, motion, effort, or advancement, of any kind beyond this. That the whole scheme stopped here centuries ago, and lay down to rest until the Day of Judgment.

Never while the Brave Courier lives! Behold him jingling out of Piacenza, and staggering this way, in the tallest posting chaise ever seen, so that he looks out of the front window as if he were peeping over a garden wall: while the postilion, concentrated essence of all the shabbiness of Italy, pauses for a moment in his animated conversation, to touch his hat to a blunt-nosed little Virgin, hardly less shabby than himself, enshrined in a plaster Punch's show outside the town.

In Genoa, and thereabouts, they train the vines on trellis work, supported on square clumsy pillars, which, in themselves, are anything but picturesque. But, here, they twine them around trees, and let them trail among the hedges; and the vineyards are full of trees, regularly planted for this purpose, each with its own vine twining and clustering about it. Their leaves are now of the brightest gold and

deepest red; and never was anything so enchantingly graceful and full of beauty. Through miles of these delightful
forms and colours, the road winds its way. The wild festoons;
the elegent wreaths, and crowns, and garlands of all shapes;
the fairy nets flung over great trees, and making them
prisoners in sport; the tumbled heaps and mounds of exquisite shapes upon the ground; how rich and beautiful they
are! And every now and then, a long, long line of trees, will
be all bound and garlanded together: as if they had taken
hold of one another, and were coming dancing down the
field!

Parma has cheerful, stirring streets, for an Italian Town;
and consequently is not so characteristic as many places of
less note. Always excepting the retired Piazza, where the
Cathedral, Baptistery, and Campanile – ancient buildings, of
a sombre brown, embellished with innumerable grotesque
monsters and dreamy-looking creatures carved in marble and
red stone – are clustered in a noble and magnificent repose.
Their silent presence was only invaded, when I saw them, by
the twittering of the many birds that were flying in and out
of the crevices in the stones and little nooks in the architecture, where they had made their nests. They were busy,
rising from the cold shade of Temples made with hands, into
the sunny air of Heaven. Not so the worshippers within, who
were listening to the same drowsy chaunt, or kneeling before
the same kinds of images and tapers, or whispering, with
their heads bowed down, in the very salf-same dark con-
fessionals, as I had left in Genoa and everywhere else.

The decayed and mutilated paintings with which this
church is covered, have, to my thinking, a remarkably mournful and depressing influence. It is miserable to see great
works of art – something of the Souls of Painters – perishing
and fading away, like human forms. This Cathedral is odorous[29]
with the rotting of Correggio's frescoes in the Cupola.
Heaven knows how beautiful they may have been at one time.
Connoisseurs fall into raptures with them now; but such a

labyrinth of arms and legs: such heaps of foreshortened
limbs, entangled and involved and jumbled together: no
operative surgeon, gone mad, could imagine in his wildest
delirium.

There is a very interesting subterranean church here; the
roof supported by marble pillars, behind each of which there
seemed to be at least one beggar in ambush: to say nothing
of the tombs and secluded altars. From every one of these
lurking-places, such crowds of phantom-looking men and
women, leading other men and women with twisted limbs, or
chattering jaws, or paralytic gestures, or idiotic heads, or
some other sad infirmity, came hobbling out to beg, that if
the ruined frescoes in the cathedral above, had been suddenly
animated, and had retired to this lower church, they could
hardly have made a greater confusion, or exhibited a more
confounding display of arms and legs.

There is Petrarch's Monument, too; and there is the
Baptistery, with its beautiful arches and immense font; and
there is a gallery containing some very remarkable pictures,
whereof a few were being copied by hairy-faced artists, with
little velvet caps more off their heads than on. There is the
Farnese Palace, too; and in it one of the dreariest spectacles
of decay that ever was seen – a grand, old, gloomy theatre,
mouldering away.

It is a large wooden structure, of the horse-shoe shape; the
lower seats arranged upon the Roman plan, but above them,
great heavy chambers rather than boxes, where the Nobles
sat, remote, in their proud state. Such desolation as has fallen
on this theatre, enhanced in the spectator's fancy by its gay
intention and design, none but worms can be familiar with.
A hundred and ten years have passed since any play was
acted here. The sky shines in through the gashes in the
roof; the boxes are dropping down, wasting away, and only
tenanted by rats; damp and mildew smear the faded colours,
and make spectral maps upon the panels; lean rags are
dangling down where there were gay festoons on the

Proscenium; the stage has rotted so, that a narrow wooden gallery is thrown across it, or it would sink beneath the tread, and bury the visitor in the gloomy depth beneath. The desolation and decay impress themselves on all the senses. The air has a mouldering smell, and an earthy taste; any stray outer sounds that straggle in with some lost sunbeam, are muffled and heavy; and the worm, the maggot, and the rot have changed the surface of the wood beneath the touch, as time will seam and roughen a smooth hand. If ever Ghosts act plays, they act them on this ghostly stage.

It was most delicious weather, when we came into Modena, where the darkness of the sombre colonnades over the footways skirting the main street on either side, was made refreshing and agreeable by the bright sky, so wonderfully blue. I passed, from all the glory of the day, into a dim cathedral, where high mass was performing, feeble tapers were burning, people were kneeling in all directions before all manner of shrines, and officiating priests were crooning the usual chaunt, in the usual low, dull, drawling, melancholy tone.

Thinking how strange it was, to find, in every stagnant town, this same Heart beating with the same monotonous pulsation, the centre of the same torpid, listless system, I came out by another door, and was suddenly scared to death by a blast from the shrillest trumpet that ever was blown. Immediately, came tearing round the corner, an equestrian company from Paris: marshalling themselves under the walls of the church, and flouting, with their horses' heels, the griffins, lions, tigers, and other monsters in stone and marble, decorating its exterior. First, there came a stately nobleman with a great deal of hair, and no hat, bearing an enormous banner, on which was inscribed, MAZEPPA! TO-NIGHT![30] Then, a Mexican chief, with a great pear-shaped club on his shoulder, like Hercules. Then, six or eight Roman chariots: each with a beautiful lady in extremely short petticoats, and unnaturally pink tights, erect within: shedding beaming looks upon the crowd, in which there was a latent expression of discomposure and anxiety, for which I couldn't account, until, as the open back of each chariot presented itself, I saw the immense difficulty with which the pink legs maintained their perpendicular, over the uneven pavement of the town: which gave me quite a new idea of the ancient Romans and Britons. The procession was brought to a close, by some dozen indomitable warriors of different nations, riding two and two, and haughtily surveying the tame population of Modena: among whom, however, they occasionally condescended to scatter largesse in the form of a few handbills. After caracolling among the lions and tigers, and proclaiming that evening's entertainments with blast of trumpet, it then filed off, by the other end of the square, and left a new and greatly increased dulness behind.

When the procession had so entirely passed away, that the shrill trumpet was mild in the distance, and the tail of the last horse was hopelessly round the corner, the people who had come out of the church to stare at it, went back again. But, one old lady, kneeling on the pavement within, near the door, had seen it all, and had been immensely interested, without getting up; and this old lady's eye, at that juncture, I happened to catch: to our mutual confusion. She cut our embarrassment very short, however, by crossing herself devoutly, and going down, at full length, on her face, before a figure in a fancy petticoat and a gilt crown; which was so like one of the Procession-figures, that perhaps at this hour she may think the whole appearance a celestial vision. Anyhow, I must certainly have forgiven her her interest in the Circus, though I had been her Father Confessor.

There was a little fiery-eyed old man with a crooked shoulder, in the cathedral, who took it very ill that I made no effort to see the bucket (kept in an old tower) which the people of Modena took away from the people of Bologna in the fourteenth century, and about which there was war made and a mock-heroic poem by TASSONI,[31] too. Being quite content, however, to look at the outside of the Tower, and feast, in imagination, on the bucket within; and preferring to loiter in the shade of the tall Campanile, and about the Cathedral; I have no personal knowledge of this bucket, even at the present time.

Indeed, we were at Bologna, before the little old man (or the Guide-Book) would have considered that we had half done justice to the wonders of Modena. But it is such a delight to me to leave new scenes behind, and still go on, encountering newer scenes – and, moreover I have such a perverse disposition in respect of sights that are cut, and dried, and dictated – that I fear I sin against similar authorities in every place I visit.

Be this as it may, in the pleasant Cemetery at Bologna I found myself walking next Sunday morning, among the stately marble tombs and colonnades, in company with a crowd of Peasants, and escorted by a little Cicerone of that town, who was excessively anxious for the honour of the place, and most solicitous to divert my attention from the bad monuments: whereas he was never tired of extolling the good ones. Seeing this little man (a good-humoured little man he was, who seemed to have nothing in his face, but shining teeth and eyes) looking, wistfully, at a certain plot of grass, I asked him who was buried there. 'The poor people, Signore,' he said with a shrug and a smile, and stopping to look back at me – for he always went on a little before, and took off his hat to introduce every new monument. 'Only the poor, Signore! It's very cheerful. It's very lively. How green it is, how cool! It's like a meadow! There are five,' – holding up all the fingers of his right hand to express the number, which an Italian Peasant will always do, if it be within the compass of his ten fingers, – 'there are five of my little children buried there, Signore; just there; a little to the right. Well! Thanks to God! It's very cheerful. How green it is, how cool it is! It's quite a meadow!'

He looked me very hard in the face, and seeing I was

sorry for him, took a pinch of snuff (every Cicerone takes snuff), and made a little bow; partly in deprecation of his having alluded to such a subject, and partly in memory of the children and of his favourite Saint. It was as unaffected and as perfectly natural a little bow, as ever man made. Immediately afterwards, he took his hat off altogether, and begged to introduce me to the next monument; and his eyes and his teeth shone brighter than before.

Through Bologna and Ferrara

THERE was such a very smart official in attendance at the Cemetery where the little Cicerone had buried his children, that when the little Cicerone suggested to me, in a whisper, that there would be no offence in presenting this officer, in return for some slight extra service, with a couple of pauls (about tenpence, English money), I looked incredulously at his cocked hat, wash-leather gloves, well-made uniform, and dazzling buttons, and rebuked the little Cicerone with a grave shake of the head. For, in splendour of appearance, he was at least equal to the Deputy Usher of the Black Rod;[32] and the idea of his carrying, as Jeremy Diddler would say,[33] 'such a thing as tenpence' away with him, seemed monstrous. He took it in excellent part, however, when I made bold to give it him, and pulled off his cocked hat with a flourish that would have been a bargain at double the money.

It seemed to be his duty to describe the monuments to the people – at all events he was doing so; and when I compared him, like Gulliver in Brobdingnag, 'with the Institutions of my own beloved country, I could not refrain from tears of pride and exultation.' He had no pace at all; no more than a tortoise. He loitered as the people loitered, that they might gratify their curiosity; and positively allowed them, now and then, to read the inscriptions on the tombs. He was neither shabby, nor insolent, nor churlish, nor ignorant. He spoke his own language with perfect propriety, and seemed to consider himself, in his way, a kind of teacher of the people, and to entertain a just respect both for himself and them. They would no more have such a man for a Verger in Westminster Abbey, than they would let the people in (as they do at Bologna) to see the monuments for nothing.

111

Again, an ancient sombre town, under the brilliant sky; with heavy arcades over the footways of the older streets, and lighter and more cheerful archways in the newer portions of the town. Again, brown piles of sacred buildings, with more birds flying in and out of chinks in the stones; and more snarling monsters for the bases of the pillars. Again, rich churches, drowsy masses, curling incense, tinkling bells, priests in bright vestments: pictures, tapers, laced altar cloths, crosses, images, and artificial flowers.

There is a grave and learned air about the city, and a pleasant gloom upon it, that would leave it, a distinct and separate impression in the mind, among a crowd of cities, though it were not still further marked in the traveller's remembrance by the two brick leaning towers (sufficiently unsightly in themselves, it must be acknowledged), inclining cross-wise as if they were bowing stiffly to each other – a most extraordinary termination to the perspective of some of the narrow streets. The colleges, and churches too, and palaces: and above all the academy of Fine Arts, where there are a host of interesting pictures, especially by GUIDO, DOMENICHINO, and LUDOVICO CARCACCI[34]: give it a place of its own in the memory. Even though these were not, and there were nothing else to remember it by, the great Meridian on the pavement of the church of San Petronio, where the sunbeams mark the time among the kneeling people, would give it a fanciful and pleasant interest.

Bologna being very full of tourists, detained there by an inundation which rendered the road to Florence impassable, I was quartered up at the top of an Hotel, in an out-of-the-way room which I never could find: containing a bed, big enough for a boarding-school, which I couldn't fall asleep in. The chief among the waiters who visited this lonely retreat, where there was no other company but the swallows in the broad eaves over the window, was a man of one idea in connexion with the English; and the subject of his harmless monomania, was Lord Byron.[35] I made the discovery by accidentally re-

THE LEANING TOWER OF BOLOGNA
William Callow

marking to him, at breakfast, that the matting with which the floor was covered, was very comfortable at that season, when he immediately replied that Milor Beeron had been much attached to that kind of matting. Observing, at the same moment, that I took no milk, he exclaimed with enthusiasm, that Milor Beeron had never touched it. At first, I took it for granted, in my innocence, that he had been one of the Beeron servants; but no, he said no, he was in the habit of speaking about my Lord, to English gentlemen; that was all. He knew all about him, he said. In proof of it, he connected him with every possible topic, from the Monte Pulciano wine at dinner (which was grown on an estate he had owned), to the big bed itself, which was the very model of his. When I left the inn, he coupled with his final bow in the yard, a parting assurance that the road by which I was going, had been Milor Beeron's favourite ride; and before the horse's feet had well begun to clatter on the pavement, he ran briskly up-stairs again, I dare say to tell some other Englishman in some other solitary room that the guest who had just departed, was Lord Beeron's living image.

I had entered Bologna by night – almost midnight – and all along the road thither, after our entrance into the Papal territory: which is not, in any part, supremely well governed, Saint Peter's keys being rather rusty now: the driver had so worried about the danger of robbers in travelling after dark, and had so infected the Brave Courier, and the two had been so constantly stopping and getting up and down to look after a portmanteau which was tied on behind, that I should have felt almost obliged to any one who would have had the goodness to take it away. Hence it was stipulated, that, whenever we left Bologna, we should start so as not to arrive at Ferrara later than eight at night; and a delightful afternoon and evening journey it was, albeit through a flat district which gradually became more marshy from the overflow of brooks and rivers in the recent heavy rains.

At sunset, when I was walking on alone, while the horses

rested, I arrived upon a little scene, which, by one of those singular mental operations of which we are all conscious, seemed perfectly familiar to me, and which I see distinctly now. There was not much in it. In the blood-red light, there was a mournful sheet of water, just stirred by the evening wind; upon its margin a few trees. In the foreground was a group of silent peasant-girls leaning over the parapet of a little bridge, and looking, now up at the sky, now down into the water; in the distance, a deep bell; the shadow of approaching night on everything. If I had been murdered there, in some former life, I could not have seemed to remember the place more thoroughly, or with a more emphatic chilling of the blood; and the real remembrance of it acquired in that minute, is so strengthened by the imaginary recollection, that I hardly think I could forget it.

More solitary, more depopulated, more deserted, old Ferrara, than any city of the solemn brotherhood! The grass so grows up in the silent streets, that anyone might make hay there, literally, while the sun shines. But the sun shines with diminished cheerfulness in grim Ferrara; and the people are so few who pass and repass through the public places, that the flesh of its inhabitants might be grass indeed, and growing in the squares.

I wonder why the head coppersmith in an Italian town, always lives next door to the Hotel, or opposite: making the visiter feel as if the beating hammers were his own heart, palpitating with a deadly energy! I wonder why jealous corridors surround the bedroom on all sides, and fill it with unnecessary doors that can't be shut, and will not open, and abut on pitchy darkness! I wonder why it is not enough that these distrustful genii stand agape at one's dreams all night, but there must also be round open portholes, high in the wall, suggestive, when a mouse or rat is heard behind the wainscot, of a somebody scraping the wall with his toes, in his endeavours to reach one of these portholes and look in! I wonder why the faggots are so constructed, as to know of no effect but an agony of heat when they are lighted and replenished, and an agony of cold and suffocation at all other times! I wonder, above all, why it is the great feature of domestic architecture in Italian inns, that all the fire goes up the chimney, except the smoke!

The answer matters little. Coppersmiths, doors, portholes, smoke, and faggots, are welcome to me. Give me the smiling face of the attendant, man or woman; the courteous manner; the amiable desire to please and to be pleased; the light-hearted, pleasant, simple air – so many jewels set in dirt – and I am theirs again to-morrow!

ARIOSTO's house, TASSO's[36] prison, a rare old Gothic cathedral, and more churches of course, are the sights of Ferrara. But the long silent streets, and the dismantled palaces, where ivy waves in lieu of banners, and where rank weeds are slowly creeping up the long-untrodden stairs, are the best sights of all.

The aspect of this dreary town, half an hour before sunrise one fine morning, when I left it, was as picturesque as it seemed unreal and spectral. It was no matter that the people were not yet out of bed; for if they had all been up and busy, they would have made but little difference in that desert of a place. It was best to see it, without a single figure in the picture; a city of the dead, without one solitary survivor. Pestilence might have ravaged streets, squares, and market-places; and sack and siege have ruined the old houses, battered down their doors and windows, and made breaches in their roofs. In one part, a great tower rose into the air; the only landmark in the melancholy view. In another, a prodigious Castle, with a moat about it, stood aloof: a sullen city in itself. In the black dungeons of this castle, Parisina and her lover[37] were beheaded in the dead of night. The red light, beginning to shine when I looked back upon it, stained its walls without, as they have, many a time, been stained within, in old days; but for any sign of life they gave, the castle and the city might have been avoided by all human creatures, from the moment when the axe went down upon the last of the two lovers: and might have never vibrated to another sound

> Beyond the blow that to the block
> Pierced through with forced and sullen shock.

Coming to the Po, which was greatly swollen, and running fiercely, we crossed it by a floating bridge of boats, and so came into the Austrian territory, and resumed our journey: through a country of which, for some miles, a great part was under water. The Brave Courier and the soldiery had first quarrelled, for half an hour or more, over our eternal passport. But this was a daily relaxation with the Brave, who was always stricken deaf when shabby functionaries in uniform came, as they constantly did come, plunging out of wooden boxes to look at it – or in other words to beg – and who, stone deaf to my entreaties that the man might have a trifle given him, and we resume our journey in peace, was wont to sit reviling the functionary in broken English: while the unfortunate man's face was a portrait of mental agony framed in the coach window, from his perfect ignorance of what was being said to his disparagement.

There was a Postilion, in the course of this day's journey, as wild and savagely good-looking a vagabond as you would desire to see. He was a tall, stout-made, dark-complexioned fellow, with a profusion of shaggy black hair hanging all over his face, and great black whiskers stretching down his throat. His dress was a torn suit of rifle green, garnished here and there with red; a steeple-crowned hat, innocent of nap, with a broken and bedraggled feather stuck in the band; and a flaming red neck-kerchief hanging on his shoulders. He was not in the saddle, but reposed, quite at his ease, on a sort of low footboard in front of the postchaise, down among the horses' tails – convenient for having his brains kicked out, at any moment. To this Brigand, the Brave Courier, when we were at a reasonable trot, happened to suggest the practicability of going faster. He received the proposal with a perfect yell of derision; brandished his whip about his head (such a whip! it was more like a home-made bow); flung up his heels, much higher than the horses; and disappeared, in a paroxysm, somewhere in the neighbourhood of the axle-tree. I fully expected to see him lying in the road, a hundred yards behind, but up came the steeple-crowned hat again, next minute, and he was seen reposing, as on a sofa, entertaining himself with the idea, and crying, 'Ha ha! what next. Oh the devil! Faster too! Shoo—hoo—o—o!' (This last ejaculation, an inexpressibly defiant hoot). Being anxious to reach our immediate destination that night, I ventured, by and by, to repeat the experiment on my own account. It produced exactly the same effect. Round flew the whip with the same scornful flourish, up came the heels, down went the steeple-crowned hat, and presently he reappeared, reposing as before and saying to himself, 'Ha ha! what next! Faster too. Oh the devil! Shoo—hoo—o—o!'

An Italian Dream

I HAD been travelling, for some days; resting very little in the night, and never in the day. The rapid and unbroken succession of novelties that had passed before me, came back like half-formed dreams: and a crowd of objects wandered in the greatest confusion through my mind, as I travelled on, by a solitary road. At intervals, some one among them would stop, as it were, in its restless flitting to and fro, and enable me to look at it, quite steadily, and behold it in full distinctness. After a few moments, it would dissolve, like a view in a magic-lantern; and while I saw some part of it quite plainly, and some faintly, and some not at all, would show me another of the many places I had lately seen, lingering behind it, and coming through it. This was no sooner visible than, in its turn, it melted into something else.

At one moment, I was standing again, before the brown old rugged churches of Modena. As I recognised the curious pillars with grim monsters for their bases, I seemed to see them, standing by themselves in the quiet square at Padua, where there were the staid old University, and the figures, demurely gowned, grouped here and there in the open space about it. Then, I was strolling in the outskirts of that pleasant city, admiring the unusual neatness of the dwelling-houses, gardens, and orchards, as I had seen them a few hours before. In their stead, arose, immediately, the two towers of Bologna; and the most obstinate of all these objects, failed to hold its ground, a minute, before the monstrous moated castle of Ferrara, which, like an illustration to a wild romance, came back again in the red sunrise, lording it over the solitary, grass-grown, withered town. In short, I had that incoherent but delightful jumble in my brain, which travellers are apt to have, and are indolently willing to encourage. Every shake of the coach in which I sat, half dozing in the dark, appeared to jerk some new recollection out of its place, and to jerk some other new recollection into it; and in this state I fell asleep.

I was awakened after some time (as I thought) by the stopping of the coach. It was now quite night, and we were at the water side. There lay here, a black boat, with a little house or cabin in it of the same mournful colour. When I had taken my seat in this, the boat was paddled, by two men, towards a great light, lying in the distance on the sea.

Ever and again, there was a dismal sigh of wind. It ruffled the water, and rocked the boat, and sent the dark clouds flying before the stars. I could not but think how strange it was, to be floating away at that hour: leaving the land behind, and going on, towards this light upon the sea. It soon began to burn brighter: and from being one light became a cluster of tapers, twinkling and shining out of the water, as the boat approached towards them by a dreamy kind of track, marked out upon the sea by posts and piles.

We had floated on, five miles or so, over the dark water, when I heard it rippling, in my dream, against some obstruction near at hand. Looking out attentively, I saw, through the gloom, a something black and massive – like a shore, but lying close and flat upon the water, like a raft – which we were gliding past. The chief of the two rowers said it was a burial-place.

Full of the interest and wonder which a cemetery lying out there, in the lonely sea, inspired, I turned to gaze upon it as it should recede in our path, when it was quickly shut out from my view. Before I knew by what, or how, I found that we were gliding up a street – a phantom street; the houses rising on both sides, from the water, and the black boat gliding on beneath their windows. Lights were shining from some of these casements, plumbing the depth of the black stream with their reflected rays; but all was profoundly silent.

So we advanced into this ghostly city, continuing to hold our course through narrow streets and lanes, all filled and flowing with water. Some of the corners where our way branched off, were so acute and narrow, that it seemed impossible for the long slender boat to turn them; but the rowers, with a low melodious cry of warning, sent it skimming on, without a pause. Sometimes, the rowers of another black boat like our own, echoed the cry, and slackening their speed (as I thought we did ours) would come flitting past us, like a dark shadow. Other boats, of the same sombre hue, were lying moored, I thought, to painted pillars, near to dark mysterious doors that opened straight upon the water. Some of these were empty; in some, the rowers lay asleep; towards one, I saw some figures coming down a gloomy archway from the interior of a palace: gaily dressed, and attended by torch-bearers. It was but a glimpse I had of them; for a bridge, so low and close upon the boat that it seemed ready to fall down and crush us: one of the many bridges that perplexed the Dream: blotted them out, instantly. On we went, floating towards the heart of this strange place – with water all about us where never water was elsewhere – clusters of houses, churches, heaps of stately buildings growing out of it – and, everywhere, the same extraordinary silence. Presently, we shot across a broad and open stream; and passing, as I thought, before a spacious paved quay, where the bright lamps with which it was illuminated, shewed long rows of arches and pillars, of ponderous construction and great strength, but as light to the eye as garlands of hoar-frost or gossamer – and where, for the first time, I saw people walking – arrived at a flight of steps leading from the water to a large mansion, where, having passed through corridors and galleries innumerable, I lay down to rest; listening to the black boats stealing up and down below the window on the rippling water, till I fell asleep.

The glory of the day that broke upon me in this Dream; its freshness, motion, buoyancy; its sparkles of the sun in water; its clear blue sky and rustling air; no waking words can tell. But, from my window, I looked down on boats and barks; on masts, sails, cordage, flags; on groups of busy sailors, working at the cargoes of these vessels; on wide quays, strewn with bales, casks, merchandise of many kinds; on great ships, lying near at hand in stately indolence; on islands, crowned with gorgeous domes and turrets: and where golden crosses glittered in the light, atop of wondrous churches springing from the sea! Going down upon the margin of the green sea, rolling on before the door, and filling all the streets, I came upon a place of such surpassing beauty, and such grandeur, that all the rest was poor and faded, in comparison with its absorbing loveliness.

It was a great Piazza, as I thought; anchored, like all the rest, in the deep ocean. On its broad bosom, was a Palace, more majestic and magnificent in its old age, than all the buildings of the earth, in the high prime and fulness of their youth. Cloisters and galleries: so light, they might have been the work of fairy hands: so strong that centuries had battered them in vain: wound round and round this palace, and enfolded it with a Cathedral, gorgeous in the wild luxuriant fancies of the East. At no great distance from its porch, a lofty tower, standing by itself, and rearing its proud head, alone, into the sky, looked out upon the Adriatic sea. Near to the margin of the stream, were two ill-omened pillars of red granite; one having on its top, a figure with a sword and shield; the other, a winged lion. Not far from these again, a second tower: richest of the rich in all its decorations: even here, where all was rich: sustained aloft, a great orb, gleaming with gold and deepest blue: the Twelve Signs painted on it, and a mimic sun revolving in its course around them: while above, two bronze giants hammered out the hours upon a sounding bell. An oblong square of lofty houses of the whitest stone, surrounded by a light and beautiful arcade, formed part of this enchanted scene; and, here and there, gay masts for flags rose, tapering, from the pavement of the unsubstantial ground.

I thought I entered the Cathedral, and went in and out among its many arches: traversing its whole extent. A grand and dreamy structure, of immense proportions; golden with old mosaics; redolent of perfumes; dim with the smoke of incense; costly in treasure of precious stones and metals, glittering through iron bars; holy with the bodies of deceased saints; rainbow-hued with windows of stained glass; dark with carved woods and coloured marbles; obscure in its vast heights, and lengthened distances; shining with silver lamps and winking lights; unreal, fantastic, solemn, inconceivable throughout. I thought I entered the old palace; pacing silent galleries and council-chambers, where the old rulers of this mistress of the waters looked sternly out, in pictures, from the walls, and where her high-prowed galleys, still victorious on canvas, fought and conquered as of old. I thought I wandered through its halls of state and triumph – bare and empty now! – and musing on its pride and might, extinct: for that was past; all past: heard a voice say, 'Some tokens of its ancient rule, and some consoling reasons for its downfall, may be traced here, yet!'

I dreamed that I was led on, then, into some jealous rooms, communicating with a prison near the palace; separated from it by a lofty bridge crossing a narrow street; and called, I dreamed, The Bridge of Sighs.

But first I passed two jagged slits in a stone wall; the lion's mouths – now toothless – where, in the distempered horror of my sleep, I thought denunciations of innocent men to the old wicked Council, had been dropped through, many a time, when the night was dark. So, when I saw the council-room to which such prisoners were taken for examination, and the door by which they passed out, when they were condemned – a door that never closed upon a man with life and hope before him – my heart appeared to die within me.

It was smitten harder though, when, torch in hand, I

descended from the cheerful day into two ranges, one below another, of dismal, awful, horrible stone cells. They were quite dark. Each had a loop-hole in its massive wall, where, in the old time, every day, a torch was placed – I dreamed – to light the prisoner within, for half an hour. The captives, by the glimmering of these brief rays, had scratched and cut inscriptions in the blackened vaults. I saw them. For their labour with a rusty nail's point, had outlived their agony and them, through many generations.

One cell, I saw, in which no man remained for more than four-and-twenty hours; being marked for dead before he entered it. Hard by, another, and a dismal one, whereto, at midnight, the confessor came – a monk brown-robed, and hooded – ghastly in the day, and free bright air, but in the midnight of that murky prison, Hope's extinguisher, and Murder's herald. I had my foot upon the spot, where, at the same dread hour, the shriven prisoner was strangled; and struck my hand upon the guilty door – low browed and stealthy — through which the lumpish sack was carried out into a boat, and rowed away, and drowned where it was death to cast a net.

Around this dungeon stronghold, and above some part of it: licking the rough walls without, and smearing them with damp and slime within: stuffing dank weeds and refuse into chinks and crevices, as if the very stones and bars had mouths to stop: furnishing a smooth road for the removal of the bodies of the secret victims of the state – a road so ready that it went along with them, and ran before them, like a cruel officer – flowed the same water that filled this Dream of mine, and made it seem one, even at the time.

Descending from the palace by a staircase, called, I thought, the Giants'[38] – I had some imaginary recollection of an old man abdicating, coming, more slowly and more feebly, down it, when he heard the bell, proclaiming his successor – I glided off, in one of the dark boats, until we came to an old arsenal guarded by four marble lions. To make my Dream more monstrous and unlikely, one of these had words and sentences upon its body, inscribed there, at an unknown time, and in an unknown language; so that their purport was a mystery to all men.

There was little sound of hammers in this place for building ships, and little work in progress; for the greatness of the city was no more, as I have said. Indeed, it seemed a very wreck found drifting on the sea; a strange flag hoisted in its honourable stations, and strangers standing at its helm. A splendid barge in which its ancient chief had gone forth, pompously, at certain periods, to wed the ocean, lay here, I thought, no more; but, in its place, there was a tiny model, made from recollection like the city's greatness; and it told of what had been (so are the strong and weak confounded in the dust) almost as eloquently as the massive pillars, arches, roofs, reared to overshadow stately ships that had no other shadow now, upon the water or the earth.

An armoury was there yet. Plundered and despoiled; but an armoury. With a fierce standard taken from the Turks, drooping in the dull air of its cage. Rich suits of mail worn by great warriors were hoarded there; crossbows and bolts; quivers full of arrows; spears; swords, daggers, maces, shields, and heavy-headed axes. Plates of wrought steel and iron, to make the gallant horse a monster cased in metal scales; and one spring-weapon (easy to be carried in the breast) designed to do its office noiselessly, and made for shooting men with poisoned darts.

One press or case I saw, full of accursed instruments of torture: horribly contrived to cramp, and pinch, and grind, and crush men's bones, and tear and twist them with the torment of a thousand deaths. Before it, were two iron helmets, with breast-pieces: made to close up tight and smooth upon the heads of living sufferers; and fastened on to each, was a small knob or anvil, where the directing devil could repose his elbow at his ease, and listen, near the walled-up ear, to the lamentations and confessions of the wretch within. There was that grim resemblance in them to the human shape – they were such moulds of sweating faces, pained and cramped – that it was difficult to think them empty; and terrible distortions lingering within them, seemed to follow me, when, taking to my boat again, I rowed off to a kind of garden or public walk in the sea, where there were grass and trees. But I forgot them when I stood upon its farthest brink – I stood there, in my dream – and looked, along the ripple, to the setting sun: before me, in the sky and on the deep, a crimson flush; and behind me the whole city resolving into streaks of red and purple, on the water.

In the luxurious wonder of so rare a dream, I took but little heed of time, and had but little understanding of its flight. But there were days and nights in it; and when the sun was high, and when the rays of lamps were crooked in the running water, I was still afloat, I thought: plashing the slippery walls and houses with the cleavings of the tide, as my black boat, borne upon it, skimmed along the streets.

Sometimes, alighting at the doors of churches and vast palaces, I wandered on, from room to room, from aisle to aisle, through labyrinths of rich altars, ancient monuments; decayed apartments where the furniture, half awful, half grotesque, was mouldering away. Pictures were there, replete with such enduring beauty and expression: with such passion, truth, and power: that they seemed so many young and fresh realities among a host of spectres. I thought these, often intermingled with the old days of the city: with its beauties, tyrants, captains, patriots, merchants, courtiers, priests: nay, with its very stones, and bricks, and public places; all of which lived again, about me, on the walls. Then, coming down some marble staircase where the water lapped and oozed against the lower steps, I passed into my boat again, and went on in my dream.

Floating down narrow lanes, where carpenters, at work with plane and chisel in their shops, tossed the light shaving straight upon the water, where it lay like weed, or ebbed away before me in a tangled heap. Past open doors, decayed and rotten from long steeping in the wet, through which some scanty patch of vine shone green and bright, making unusual shadows on the pavement with its trembling leaves. Past quays and terraces, where women, gracefully veiled, were passing and repassing, and where idlers were reclining in the sunshine, on flag-stones and on flights of steps. Past bridges, where there were idlers too: loitering and looking over. Below stone balconies, erected at a giddy height, before the loftiest windows of the loftiest houses. Past plots of garden, theatres, shrines, prodigious piles of architecture – Gothic – Saracenic – fanciful with all the fancies of all times and countries. Past buildings that were high, and low, and black, and white, and straight, and crooked; mean and grand, crazy and strong. Twining among a tangled lot of boats and barges, and shooting out at last into a Grand Canal! There, in the errant fancy of my dream, I saw old Shylock passing to and fro upon a bridge, all built upon with shops and humming with the tongues of men; a form I seemed to know for Desdemona's, leaned down through a latticed blind to pluck a flower. And, in the dream, I thought that Shakespeare's spirit was abroad upon the water somewhere: stealing through the city.

At night, when two votive lamps burnt before an image of the Virgin, in a gallery outside the great Cathedral, near the roof, I fancied that the great piazza of the Winged Lion was a blaze of cheerful light, and that its whole arcade was thronged with people; while crowds were diverting themselves in splendid coffee-houses opening from it – which were never shut, I thought, but open all night long. When the bronze giants struck the hour of midnight on the bell, I thought the life and animation of the city were all centred here; and as I rowed away, abreast the silent quays, I only saw them dotted, here and there, with sleeping boatmen wrapped up in their cloaks, and lying at full length upon the stones.

But, close about the quays and churches, palaces But prisons: sucking at their walls, and welling up into the secret places of the town: crept the water always. Noiseless and watchful: coiled round and round it, in its many folds, like an old serpent: waiting for the time, I thought, when people should look down into its depths for any stone of the old city that had claimed to be its mistress.

Thus it floated me away, until I awoke in the old market-place at Verona. I have, many and many a time, thought, since, of this strange Dream upon the water: half-wondering if it lie there yet, and if its name be VENICE.

By Verona, Mantua, and Milan, across the Pass of the Simplon into Switzerland

---

I HAD been half afraid to go to Verona, lest it should at all put me out of conceit with Romeo and Juliet. But, I was no sooner come into the old Market-place, than the misgiving vanished. It is so fanciful, quaint, and picturesque a place, formed by such an extraordinary and rich variety of fantastic buildings, that there could be nothing better at the core of even this romantic town: scene of one of the most romantic and beautiful of stories.

It was natural enough, to go straight from the Market-place, to the House of the Capulets, now degenerated into a most miserable little inn. Noisy vetturíni and muddy market-carts were disputing possession of the yard, which was ankle-deep in dirt, with a brood of splashed and bespattered geese; and there was a grim-visaged dog, viciously panting in a doorway, who would certainly have had Romeo by the leg, the moment he put it over the wall, if he had existed and been at large in those times. The orchard fell into other hands, and was parted off many years ago; but there used to be one attached to the house – or at all events there may have been, – and the hat (Cappêllo) the ancient cognizance of the family, may still be seen, carved in stone, over the gateway of the yard. The geese, the market-carts, their drivers, and the dog, were somewhat in the way of the story, it must be confessed; and it would have been pleasanter to have found the house empty, and to have been able to walk through the disused rooms. But the hat was unspeakably comfortable; and the place where the garden used to be, hardly less so. Besides, the house is a distrustful, jealous-looking house as one would desire to see, though of a very moderate size. So I was quite satisfied with it, as the veritable mansion of old Capulet, and was correspondingly grateful in my acknowledgments to an extremely unsentimental middle-aged lady, the Padrona of the Hotel, who was lounging on the threshold looking at the geese; and who at least resembled the Capulets in the one particular of being very great indeed in the 'Family' way.

From Juliet's home, to Juliet's tomb, is a transition as natural to the visitor, as to fair Juliet herself, or to the proudest Juliet that ever has taught the torches to burn bright in any time. So, I went off, with a guide, to an old, old garden, once belonging to an old, old convent, I suppose; and being admitted, at a shattered gate, by a bright-eyed woman who was washing clothes, went down some walks where fresh plants and young flowers were prettily growing among fragments of old wall, and ivy-covered mounds; and was shewn a little tank, or water trough, which the bright-eyed woman – drying her arms upon her 'kerchief, called, 'La tomba di Giulietta la sfortunáta.' With the best disposition in the world to believe, I could do no more than believe that the bright-eyed woman believed; so I gave her that much credit, and her customary fee in ready money. It was a pleasure, rather than a disappointment, that Juliet's resting-place was forgotten. However consolatory it may have been to Yorick's Ghost,[39] to hear the feet upon the pavement overhead, and, twenty times a day, the repetition of his name, it is better for Juliet to lie out of the track of tourists, and to have no visiters but such as come to graves in spring-rain, and sweet air, and sunshine.

Pleasant Verona! With its beautiful old palaces, and charming country in the distance, seen from terrace walks, and stately, balustraded galleries. With its Roman gates, still spanning the fair street, and casting, on the sunlight of to-day, the shade of fifteen hundred years ago. With its marble-fitted churches, lofty towers, rich architecture, and quaint old quiet thoroughfares, where shouts of Montagues and Capulets [40] once resounded,

> And made Verona's ancient citizens
> Cast by their grave, beseeming ornaments,
> To wield old partizans.

With its fast-rushing river, picturesque old bridge, great castle, waving cypresses, and prospect so delightful, and so cheerful! Pleasant Verona!

In the midst of it, in the Piazza di Brá – a spirit of old time among the familiar realities of the passing hour – is the great Roman Amphitheatre. So well preserved, and carefully maintained, that every row of seats is there, unbroken. Over certain of the arches, the old Roman numerals may yet be seen; and there are corridors, and staircases, and subterranean passages for beasts, and winding ways, above-ground and below, as when the fierce thousands hurried in and out, intent upon the bloody shows of the arena. Nestling in some of the shadows and hollow places of the walls, now, are smiths with their forges, and a few small dealers of one kind or other; and there are green weeds, and leaves, and grass, upon the parapet. But little else is greatly changed.

When I had traversed all about it, with great interest, and had gone up to the topmost round of seats, and turning from the lovely panorama closed in by the distant Alps, looked down into the building, it seemed to lie before me like the inside of a prodigious hat of plaited straw, with an enormously broad brim and a shallow crown: the plaits being represented by the four-and-forty rows of seats. The comparison is a homely and fantastic one, in sober remembrance and on paper, but it was irresistibly suggested at the moment, nevertheless.

An equestrian troop had been there, a short time before – the same troop, I dare say, that appeared to the old lady in the church at Modena – and had scooped out a little ring at one end of the arena; where their performances had taken place, and where the marks of their horses' feet were still fresh. I could not but picture to myself, a handful of spectators gathered together on one or two of the old stone seats, and a spangled Cavalier being gallant, or a Policinello funny,[41] with the grim walls looking on. Above all, I thought how strangely those Roman mutes would gaze upon the favourite comic scene of the travelling English, where a British nobleman (Lord John), with a very loose stomach: dressed in a blue tailed coat down to his heels, bright yellow breeches, and a white hat: comes abroad, riding double on a rearing horse, with an English lady (Lady Betsey) in a straw bonnet and green veil, and a red spencer; and who always carries a gigantic reticule, and a put-up parasol.

I walked through and through the town all the rest of the day, and could have walked there until now, I think. In one place, there was a very pretty modern theatre, where they had just performed the opera (always popular in Verona) of Romeo and Juliet. In another, there was a collection, under a colonnade, of Greek, Roman, and Etruscan remains, presided over by an ancient man who might have been an Etruscan relic himself; for he was not strong enough to open the iron gate, when he had unlocked it, and had neither voice enough to be audible when he described the curiosities, nor sight enough to see them: he was so very old. In another place, there was a gallery of pictures: so abominably bad, that it was quite delightful to see them mouldering away. But anywhere: in the churches, among the palaces, in the streets, on the bridge, or down beside the river: it was always pleasant Verona, and in my remembrance always will be.

I read Romeo and Juliet in my own room at the inn that night – of course, no Englishman had ever read it there, before – and set out for Mantua next day at sunrise, repeating to myself (in the *coupé* of an omnibus, and next to the conductor, who was reading the Mysteries of Paris[42]),

There is no world without Verona's walls,
But purgatory, torture, hell itself.
Hence-banished is banish'd from the world,
And world's exile is death ——[43]

which reminded me that Romeo was only banished five-and-twenty miles after all, and rather disturbed my confidence in his energy and boldness.

Was the way to Mantua as beautiful, in his time, I wonder! Did it wind through pasture land as green, bright with the same glancing streams, and dotted with fresh clumps of graceful trees! Those purple mountains lay on the horizon, then, for certain; and the dresses of these peasant girls, who wear a great, knobbed, silver pin like an English 'life-preserver' through their hair behind, can hardly be much changed. The hopeful feeling of so bright a morning, and so exquisite a sunrise, can have been no stranger, even to an exiled lover's breast; and Mantua itself must have broken on him in the prospect, with its towers, and walls, and water, pretty much as on a common-place and matrimonial omnibus. He made the same sharp twists and turns, perhaps, over two rumbling drawbridges; passed through the like long, covered, wooden bridge; and leaving the marshy water behind, approached the rusty gate of stagnant Mantua.

If ever a man were suited to his place of residence, and his place of residence to him, the lean Apothecary and Mantua came together in a perfect fitness of things. It may have been more stirring then, perhaps. If so, the Apothecary was a man in advance of his time, and knew what Mantua would be, in eighteen hundred and forty-four. He fasted much, and that assisted him in his foreknowledge.

I put up at the Hotel of the Golden Lion, and was in my own room arranging plans with the Brave Courier, when there came a modest little tap at the door, which opened on an outer gallery surrounding a court-yard; and an intensely shabby little man looked in, to inquire if the gentleman would have a Cicerone to shew the town. His face was so very wistful and anxious, in the half-opened doorway, and there was so much poverty expressed in his faded suit and little pinched hat, and in the threadbare worsted glove with which he held it – not expressed the less, because these were evidently his genteel clothes, hastily slipped on – that I would as soon have trodden on him as dismissed him. I engaged him on the instant, and he stepped in directly.

While I finished the discussion in which I was engaged, he stood, beaming by himself in a corner, making a feint of brushing my hat with his arm. If his fee had been as many napoleons as it was francs, there could not have shot over the twilight of his shabbiness such a gleam of sun, as lighted up the whole man, now that he was hired.

'Well!' said I, when I was ready, 'shall we go out now?'

'If the gentleman pleases. It is a beautiful day. A little fresh, but charming; altogether charming. The gentleman with allow me to open the door. This is the Inn Yard. The court-yard of the Golden Lion! The gentleman will please to mind his footing on the stairs.'

We are now in the street.

'This is the street of the Golden Lion. This, the outside of the Golden Lion. The interesting window up there, on the first Piano, where the pane of glass is broken, is the window of the gentleman's chamber!'

Having viewed all these remarkable objects, I inquired if there were much to see in Mantua.

'Well! Truly, no. Not much! So, so,' he said, shrugging his shoulders apologetically.

'Many churches?'

'No. Nearly all suppressed by the French.'

'Monasteries or convents?'

'No. The French again! Nearly all suppressed by Napoleon.'

'Much business?'

'Very little business.'

'Many strangers?'

'Ah Heaven!'

I thought he would have fainted.

'Then, when we have seen the two large Churches yonder, what shall we do next?' said I.

He looked up the street, and down the street, and rubbed his chin timidly; and then said, glancing in my face as if a light had broken on his mind, yet with a humble appeal to my forbearance that was perfectly irresistible:

'We can take a little turn about the town, Signore!' (Si può far 'un píccolo gíro della citta).

It was impossible to be anything but delighted with the proposal, so we set off together in great good-humour. In the relief of his mind, he opened his heart, and gave up as much of Mantua as a Cicerone could.

'One must eat,' he said; 'but, bah! it was a dull place, without doubt!'

He made as much as possible of the Basilica of Santa Andrea – a noble church – and of an inclosed portion of the pavement, about which tapers were burning, and a few people kneeling, and under which is said to be preserved the Sangreal of the old Romances. This church disposed of, and another after it (the Cathedral of San Pietro), we went to the Museum, which was shut up. 'It was all the same,' he said; 'Bah! There was not much inside!' Then, we went to see the Piazza del Diavolo, built by the Devil (for no particular purpose) in a single night; then, the Piazza Virgiliana; then, the statue of Virgil – *our* Poet,[44] my little friend said, plucking up a spirit, for the moment, and putting his hat a little on one side. Then, we went to a dismal sort of farmyard, by which a picture-gallery was approached. The moment the gate of this retreat was opened, some five hundred geese came waddling round us, stretching out their necks, and clamouring in the most hideous manner, as if they were ejaculating, 'Oh! here's somebody come to see the Pictures! Don't go up! Don't go up!' While we went up, they waited very quietly about the door, in a crowd, cackling to one another occasionally, in a subdued tone; but the instant we appeared again, their necks came out like telescopes, and setting up a great noise, which meant, I have no doubt, 'What, you would go, would you! What do you think of it! How do you like it!' they attended us to the outer gate, and cast us forth, derisively, into Mantua.

The geese who saved the Capitol,[45] were, as compared with these, Pork to the learned Pig. What a gallery it was! I would take their opinion on a question of art, in preference to the discourses of Sir Joshua Reynolds.[46]

Now that we were standing in the street, after being thus ignominiously escorted thither, my little friend was plainly reduced to the 'piccolo giro,' or little circuit of the town, he had formerly proposed. But my suggestion that we should visit the Palazzo Te (of which I had heard a great deal, as a strange wild place) imparted new life to him, and away we went.

The secret of the length of Midas' ears,[47] would have been more extensively known, if that servant of his, who whispered it to the reeds, had lived in Mantua, where there are reeds and rushes enough to have published it to all the world. The Palazzo Te[48] stands in a swamp, among this sort of vegetation; and is, indeed, as singular a place as I ever saw.

Not for its dreariness, though it is very dreary. Nor for its dampness, though it is very damp. Nor for its desolate condition, though it is as desolate and neglected as house can be. But chiefly for the unaccountable nightmares with which its interior has been decorated (among other subjects of more delicate execution), by Giulio Romano. There is a leering Giant over a certain chimney-piece, and there are dozens of Giants (Titans warring with Jove) on the walls of another room, so inconceivably ugly and grotesque, that it is marvellous how any man can have imagined such creatures. In the chamber in which they abound, these monsters, with swollen faces and cracked cheeks, and every kind of distortion of look and limb, are depicted as staggering under the weight of falling buildings, and being overwhelmed in the ruins; upheaving masses of rock, and burying themselves beneath; vainly striving to sustain the pillars of heavy roofs that topple down upon their heads; and, in a word, undergoing and doing every kind of mad and demoniacal destruction. The figures are immensely large, and exaggerated to the utmost pitch of uncouthness; the colouring is harsh and disagreeable; and the whole effect more like (I should imagine) a violent rush of blood to the head of the spectator, than any real picture set before him by the hand of an artist. This apoplectic performance was shewn by a sickly-looking woman, whose appearance was referable, I dare say, to the bad air of the marshes; but it was difficult to help feeling as if she were too much haunted by the Giants, and they were frightening her to death, all alone in that exhausted cistern of a Palace, among the reeds and rushes, with the mists hovering about outside, and stalking round and round it continually.

Our walk through Mantua showed us, in almost every street, some suppressed church: now used for a warehouse, now for nothing at all: all as crazy and dismantled as they could be, short of tumbling down bodily. The marshy town was so intensely dull and flat, that the dirt upon it seemed not to have come there in the ordinary course, but to have settled and mantled on its surface as on standing water. And yet there were some business-dealings going on, and some profits realizing; for there were arcades full of Jews, where those extraordinary people were sitting outside their shops: contemplating their stores of stuffs, and woollens, and bright handkerchiefs, and trinkets: and looking, in all respects, as wary and business-like, as their brethren in Houndsditch, London.[49]

Having selected a Vetturíno from among the neighbouring Christians, who agreed to carry us to Milan in two days and a half, and to start, next morning, as soon as the gates were opened, I returned to the Golden Lion, and dined luxuriously in my own room, in a narrow passage between two bedsteads: confronted by a smoky fire, and backed up by a chest of drawers. At six o'clock next morning, we were jingling in the dark through the wet cold mist that enshrouded the town; and, before noon, the driver (a native of Mantua, and sixty years of age, or thereabouts), began *to ask the way* to Milan.

It lay through Bozzolo: formerly a little republic, and now one of the most deserted and poverty-stricken of towns: where the landlord of the miserable inn (God bless him! it was his weekly custom) was distributing infinitesimal coins among a clamorous herd of women and children, whose rags were fluttering in the wind and rain outside his door, where they were gathered to receive his charity. It lay through mist, and mud, and rain, and vines trained low upon the ground, all that day and the next; the first sleeping-place being Cremona, memorable for its dark brick churches, and immensely high tower, the Torrazzo – to say nothing of its violins, of which it certainly produces none in these degenerate days; and the second, Lodi. Then we went on, through more mud, mist, and rain, and marshy ground: and through such a fog, as Englishmen, strong in the faith of their own grievances, are apt to believe is nowhere to be found but in their own country: until we entered the paved streets of Milan.

The fog was so dense here, that the spire of the far-famed Cathedral might as well have been at Bombay, for anything that could be seen of it at that time. But as we halted to refresh, for a few days then, and returned to Milan again next summer, I had ample opportunities of seeing the glorious structure in all its majesty and beauty.

All Christian homage to the saint who lies within it! There are many good and true saints in the calendar, but San Carlo Borromeo has – if I may quote Mrs. Primrose [50] on such a subject – 'my warm heart.' A charitable doctor to the sick, a munificent friend to the poor, and this, not in any spirit of blind bigotry, but as the bold opponent of enormous abuses in the Romish church, I honour his memory. I honour it none the less, because he was nearly slain by a priest, suborned, by priests, to murder him at the altar: in acknowledgment of his endeavours to reform a false and hypocritical brotherhood of monks. Heaven shield all imitators of San Carlo Borromeo as it shielded him! A reforming Pope would need a little shielding, even now.

The subterranean chapel in which the body of San Carlo Borromeo is preserved, presents as striking and as ghastly a contrast, perhaps, as any place can show. The tapers which are lighted down there, flash and gleam on alti-relievi in gold and silver, delicately wrought by skilful hands, and representing the principal events in the life of the saint. Jewels, and precious metals, shine and sparkle on every side. A windlass slowly removes the front of the altar; and, within it, in a gorgeous shrine of gold and silver, is seen, through alabaster, the shrivelled mummy of a man: the pontifical robes with which it is adorned, radiant with diamonds, emeralds, rubies: every costly and magnificent gem. The shrunken heap of poor earth in the midst of this great glitter, is more pitiful than if it lay upon a dunghill. There is not a ray of imprisoned light in all the flash and fire of jewels, but seems to mock the dusty holes where eyes were, once. Every thread of silk in the rich vestments seems only a provision from the worms that spin, for the behoof of worms that propagate in sepulchres.

In the old refectory of the dilapidated Convent of Santa Maria delle Grazie, is the work of art, perhaps better known than any other in the world: the Last Supper, by Leonardo da Vinci – with a door cut through it by the intelligent Dominican friars, to facilitate their operations at dinner time.

I am not mechanically acquainted with the art of painting, and have no other means of judging of a picture than as I see it resembling and refining upon nature, and presenting graceful combinations of forms and colours. I am, therefore,

INTERIOR OF MILAN CATHEDRAL
David Roberts

no authority whatever, in reference to the 'touch' of this or
that master; though I know very well (as anybody may, who
chooses to think about the matter) that few very great
masters can possibly have painted, in the compass of their
lives, one half of the pictures that bear their names, and that
are recognised by many aspirants to a reputation for taste, as
undoubted originals. But this, by the way. Of the Last
Supper, I would simply observe, that in its beautiful composition and arrangement, there it is, at Milan, a wonderful
picture; and that, in its original colouring, or in its original
expression of any single face or feature, there it is not.
Apart from the damage it has sustained from damp, decay,
and neglect, it has been (as Barry shows[51]) so retouched upon,
and repainted, and that so clumsily, that many of the heads
are, now, positive deformities, with patches of paint and
plaster sticking upon them like wens, and utterly distorting
the expression. Where the original artist set that impress of
his genius on a face, which, almost in a line or touch, separated him from meaner painters and made him what he was,
succeeding bunglers, filling up, or painting across seams and
cracks, have been quite unable to imitate his hand; and putting in some scowls, or frowns, or wrinkles, of their own,
have botched and spoiled the work. This is so well established as a historical fact, that I should not repeat it, at the
risk of being tedious, but for having observed an English
gentleman before the picture, who was at great pains to fall
into what I may describe as mild convulsions, at certain
minute details of expression which are not left in it. Whereas,
it would be comfortable and rational for travellers and critics
to arrive at a general understanding that it cannot fail to have
been a work of extraordinary merit, once: when, with so few
of its original beauties remaining, the grandeur of the general
design is yet sufficient to sustain it, as a piece replete with
interest and dignity.

We achieved the other sights of Milan, in due course, and
a fine city it is, though not so unmistakeably Italian as to

possess the characteristic qualities of many towns far less important in themselves. The Corso, where the Milanese gentry ride up and down in carriages, and rather than not do which, they would half starve themselves at home, is a most noble public promenade, shaded by long avenues of trees. In the splendid theatre of La Scala, there was a ballet of action performed after the opera, under the title of Prometheus:[52] in the beginning of which, some hundred or two of men and women represented our mortal race before the refinements of the arts and sciences, and loves and graces, came on earth to soften them. I never saw anything more effective. Generally speaking, the pantomimic action of the Italians is more re-markable for its sudden and impetuous character than for its delicate expression; but, in this case, the drooping mono-tony: the weary, miserable, listless, moping life: the sordid passions and desires of human creatures, destitute of those elevating influences to which we owe so much, and to whose promoters we render so little: were expressed in a manner really powerful and affecting. I should have thought it almost impossible to present such an idea so strongly on the stage, without the aid of speech.

Milan soon lay behind us, at five o'clock in the morning; and before the golden statue on the summit of the Cathedral spire was lost in the blue sky, the Alps, stupendously con-fused in lofty peaks and ridges, clouds and snow, were towering in our path.

Still, we continued to advance towards them until night-fall; and, all day long, the mountain tops presented strangely shifting shapes, as the road displayed them in different points of view. The beautiful day was just declining, when we came upon the Lago Maggiore, with its lovely islands. For how-ever fanciful and fantastic the Isola Bella may be, and is, it still is beautiful. Anything springing out of that blue water, with that scenery around it, must be.

It was ten o'clock at night when we got to Domo d'Ossola, at the foot of the Pass of the Simplon. But as the moon was shining brightly, and there was not a cloud in the starlit sky, it was no time for going to bed, or going anywhere but on. So, we got a little carriage, after some delay, and began the ascent.

It was late in November; and the snow lying four or five feet thick in the beaten road on the summit (in other parts the new drift was already deep), the air was piercing cold. But, the serenity of the night, and the grandeur of the road, with its impenetrable shadows, and deep glooms, and its sudden turns into the shining of the moon, and its incessant roar of falling water, rendered the journey more and more sublime at every step.

Soon leaving the calm Italian villages below us, sleeping in the moonlight, the road began to wind among dark trees, and after a time emerged upon a barer region, very steep and toilsome, where the moon shone bright and high. By degrees, the roar of water grew louder; and the stupendous track, after crossing the torrent by a bridge, struck in between two massive perpendicular walls of rock that quite shut out the moonlight, and only left a few stars shining in the narrow strip of sky above. Then, even this was lost, in the thick darkness of a cavern in the rock, through which the way was pierced; the terrible cataract thundering and roaring close below it, and its foam and spray hanging, in a mist, about the entrance. Emerging from this cave, and coming again into the moonlight, and across a dizzy bridge, it crept and twisted upward, through the Gorge of Gondo, savage and grand beyond description, with smooth-fronted precipices, rising up on either hand, and almost meeting overhead. Thus we went, climbing on our rugged way, higher and higher, all night, without a moment's weariness: lost in the contemplation of the black rocks, the tremendous heights and depths, the fields of smooth snow lying in the clefts and hollows, and the fierce torrents thundering headlong down the deep abyss.

Towards daybreak, we came among the snow, where a keen wind was blowing fiercely. Having, with some trouble, awakened the inmates of a wooden house in this solitude: round which the wind was howling dismally, catching up the snow in wreaths and hurling it away: we got some breakfast in a room built of rough timbers, but well warmed by a stove, and well contrived (as it had need to be) for keeping out the bitter storms. A sledge being then made ready, and four horses harnessed to it, we went, ploughing, through the snow. Still upward, but now in the cold light of morning, and with the great white desert on which we travelled, plain and clear.

We were well upon the summit of the mountain: and had before us the rude cross of wood, denoting its greatest altitude above the sea: when the light of the rising sun, struck, all at once, upon the waste of snow, and turned it a deep red. The lonely grandeur of the scene, was then at its height.

As we went sledging on, there came out of the Hospice founded by Napoleon, a group of Peasant travellers, with staves and knapsacks, who had rested there last night: attended by a Monk or two, their hospitable entertainers, trudging slowly forward with them, for company's sake. It was pleasant to give them good morning, and pretty, looking back a long way after them, to see them looking back at us, and hesitating presently, when one of our horses stumbled and fell, whether or no they should return and help us. But he was soon up again, with the assistance of a rough waggoner whose team had stuck fast there too; and when we had helped him out of his difficulty, in return, we left him slowly ploughing towards them, and went softly and swiftly forward, on the brink of a steep precipice, among the mountain pines.

Taking to our wheels again, soon afterwards, we began rapidly to descend; passing under everlasting glaciers, by means of arched galleries, hung with clusters of dripping icicles; under and over foaming waterfalls; near places of refuge, and galleries of shelter against sudden danger; through caverns over whose arched roofs the avalanches slide, in spring, and bury themselves in the unknown gulf beneath. Down, over lofty bridges, and through horrible ravines: a little shifting speck in the vast desolation of ice and snow, and monstrous granite rocks: down through the deep Gorge of the Saltine, and deafened by the torrent plunging madly down, among the riven blocks of rock, into the level country, far below. Gradually down, by zig-zag roads, lying between an upward and a downward precipice, into warmer weather, calmer air, and softer scenery, until there lay before us, glittering like gold or silver in the thaw and sunshine, the metal-covered, red, green, yellow, domes and church-spires of a Swiss town.

The business of these recollections being with Italy, and my business, consequently, being to scamper back thither as fast as possible, I will not recal (though I am sorely tempted) how the Swiss villages, clustered at the feet of Giant mountains, looked like playthings; or how confusedly the houses were heaped and piled together; or how there were very narrow streets to shut the howling winds out in the winter time; and broken bridges, which the impetuous torrents, suddenly released in spring, had swept away. Or how there were peasant women here, with great round fur caps: looking, when they peeped out of casements and only their heads were seen, like a population of Sword-bearers to the Lord Mayor of London; or how the town of Vevay, lying on the smooth lake of Geneva, was beautiful to see; or how the statue of Saint Peter in the street at Fribourg, grasps the largest key that ever was beheld; or how Fribourg is illustrious for its two suspension bridges, and its grand cathedral organ.

Or how, between that town and Bâle, the road meandered among thriving villages of wooden cottages, with over-hanging thatched roofs, and low protruding windows, glazed with small round panes of glass like crown-pieces; or how, in every little Swiss homestead, with its cart or waggon carefully stowed away beside the house, its little garden, stock of poultry, and groups of red-cheeked children, there was an air of comfort, very new and very pleasant after Italy; or how the dresses of the women changed again, and there were no more sword-bearers to be seen; and fair white stomachers, and great black, fan-shaped, gauzy-looking caps, prevailed instead.

Or how the country by the Jura mountains, sprinkled with snow, and lighted by the moon, and musical with falling water, was delightful; or how, below the windows of the great hotel of the Three Kings at Bâle, the swollen Rhine ran fast and green; or how, at Strasbourg, it was quite as fast but not as green: and was said to be foggy lower down: and, at that late time of the year, was a far less certain means of progress, than the highway road to Paris.

Or how Strasbourg itself, in its magnificent old Gothic Cathedral, and its ancient houses with their peaked roofs and gables, made a little gallery of quaint and interesting views; or how a crowd was gathered inside the Cathedral at noon, to see the famous mechanical clock in motion, striking twelve. How, when it struck twelve, a whole army of puppets went through many ingenious evolutions; and, among them, a huge puppet-cock, perched on the top, crowed twelve times, loud and clear. Or how it was wonderful to see this cock at great pains to clap its wings, and strain its throat; but obviously having no connexion whatever with its own voice; which was deep within the clock, a long way down.

Or how the road to Paris, was one sea of mud; and thence to the coast, a little better for a hard frost. Or how the cliffs of Dover were a pleasant sight, and England was so wonderfully neat – though dark, and lacking colour on a winter's day, it must be conceded.

Or how, a few days afterwards, it was cool, re-crossing the channel, with ice upon the decks, and snow lying pretty deep in France. Or how the Malle Poste scrambled through the snow, headlong, drawn in the hilly parts by any number of stout horses at a canter; or how there were, outside the Post-office Yard in Paris, before daybreak, extraordinary adventurers in heaps of rags, groping in the snowy streets with little rakes, in search of odds and ends.

Or how, between Paris and Marseilles, the snow being then exceeding deep, a thaw came on, and the mail waded rather than rolled for the next three hundred miles or so; breaking springs on Sunday nights, and putting out its two passengers to warm and refresh themselves pending the repairs, in miserable billard-rooms, where hairy company, collected about stoves, were playing cards; the cards being very like themselves – extremely limp and dirty.

Or how there was detention at Marseilles from stress of weather; and steamers were advertised to go, which did not go; or how the good Steam-packet Charlemagne at length put out, and met such weather that now she threatened to run into Toulon, and now into Nice, but, the wind moderating, did neither, but ran on into Genoa harbour instead, where the familiar Bells rang sweetly in my ear. Or how there was a travelling party on board, of whom one member was very ill in the cabin next to mine, and being ill was cross, and therefore declined to give up the Dictionary, which he kept under his pillow; thereby obliging his companions to come down to him, constantly, to ask what was the Italian for a lump of sugar – a glass of brandy and water – what's o'clock? and so forth: which he always insisted on looking out, with his own sea-sick eyes, declining to entrust the book to any man alive.

Like GRUMIO,[53] I might have told you, in detail, all this and something more – but to as little purpose – were I not deterred by the remembrance that my business is with Italy. Therefore, like GRUMIO's story, it 'shall die in oblivion.'

To Rome by Pisa and Siena

THERE is nothing in Italy, more beautiful to me, than the coast-road between Genoa and Spezzia. On one side: sometimes far below, sometimes nearly on a level with the road, and often skirted by broken rocks of many shapes: there is the free blue sea, with here and there a picturesque *felúca* gliding slowly on; on the other side, are lofty hills, ravines besprinkled with white cottages, patches of dark olive woods, country churches with their light open towers, and country houses gaily painted. On every bank and knoll by the wayside, the wild cactus and aloe flourish in exuberant profusion; and the gardens of the bright villages along the road, are seen, all blushing in the summer-time with clusters of the Belladonna, and are fragrant in the autumn and winter with golden oranges and lemons.

Some of the villages are inhabited, almost exclusively, by fishermen; and it is pleasant to see their great boats hauled up on the beach, making little patches of shade, where they lie asleep, or where the women and children sit romping and looking out to sea, while they mend their nets upon the shore. There is one town, Camoglia, with its little harbour on the sea, hundreds of feet below the road: where families of mariners live, who, time out of mind, have owned coasting-vessels in that place, and have traded to Spain and elsewhere. Seen from the road above, it is like a tiny model on the margin of the dimpled water, shining in the sun. Descended into, by the winding mule-tracks, it is a perfect miniature of a primitive seafaring town; the saltiest, roughest, most piratical little place that ever was seen. Great rusty iron rings and mooring-chains, capstans, and fragments of old masts and spars, choke up the way; hardy rough-weather boats, and seamen's clothing, flutter in the little harbour or are drawn out on the sunny stones to dry; on the parapet of the rude pier, a few amphibious-looking fellows lie asleep, with their legs dangling over the wall, as though earth or water were all one to them, and if they slipped in, they would float away, dozing comfortably among the fishes; the church is bright with trophies of the sea, and votive offerings, in commemoration of escape from storm and shipwreck. The dwellings not immediately abutting on the harbour are approached by blind low archways, and by crooked steps, as if in darkness and in difficulty of access they should be like holds of ships, or inconvenient cabins under water; and everywhere, there is a smell of fish, and seaweed, and old rope.

The coast-road whence Camoglia is descried so far below, is famous, in the warm season, especially in some parts near Genoa, for fire-flies. Walking there, on a dark night, I have seen it made one sparkling firmament by these beautiful insects; so that the distant stars were pale against the flash and glitter that spangled every olive wood and hill-side, and pervaded the whole air.

It was not in such a season, however, that we traversed this road on our way to Rome. The middle of January was only just past, and it was very gloomy and dark weather; very wet besides. In crossing the fine Pass of Bracco, we encountered such a storm of mist and rain, that we travelled in a cloud the whole way. There might have been no Mediterranean in the world, for anything we saw of it there, except when a sudden gust of wind, clearing the mist before it, for a moment, showed the agitated sea at a great depth below, lashing the distant rocks, and spouting up its foam furiously. The rain was incessant; every brook and torrent was greatly swollen; and such a deafening leaping, and roaring, and thundering of water, I never heard the like of in my life.

Hence, when we came to Spezzia, we found that the Magra, an unbridged river on the high-road to Pisa, was too high to be safely crossed in the Ferry Boat, and were fain to wait until the afternoon of next day, when it had, in some degree, subsided. Spezzia, however, is a good place to tarry at; by reason, firstly, of its beautiful bay; secondly, of its ghostly Inn; thirdly, of the head-dress of the women, who wear, on one side of their head, a small doll's straw hat, stuck on to the hair; which is certainly the oddest and most roguish head-gear that ever was invented.

The Magra safely crossed in the Ferry Boat – the passage is not by any means agreeable, when the current is swollen and strong – we arrived at Carrara, within a few hours. In good time next morning, we got some ponies, and went out to see the marble quarries.

They are four or five glens, running up into a range of lofty hills, until they can run no longer, and are stopped by being abruptly strangled by Nature. The quarries, or 'caves,' as they call them there, are so many openings, high up in the hills, on either side of these passes, where they blast and excavate for marble: which may turn out good or bad: may make a man's fortune very quickly, or ruin him by the great expense of working what is worth nothing. Some of these caves were opened by the ancient Romans, and remain as they left them to this hour. Many others are being worked at this moment; others are to be begun to-morrow, next week, next month; others are unbought, unthought of; and marble enough for more ages than have passed since the place was resorted to, lies hidden everywhere: patiently awaiting its time of discovery.

As you toil and clamber up one of these steep gorges (having left your pony soddening his girths in water, a mile or two lower down) you hear, every now and then, echoing among the hills, in a low tone, more silent than the previous silence, a melancholy warning bugle, – a signal to the miners to withdraw. Then, there is a thundering, and echoing from hill to hill, and perhaps a splashing up of great fragments of rock into the air; and on you toil again until some other bugle sounds, in a new direction, and you stop directly, lest you should come within the range of the new explosion.

There were numbers of men, working high up in these hills – on the sides – clearing away, and sending down the broken masses of stone and earth, to make way for the blocks of marble that had been discovered. As these came rolling down from unseen hands into the narrow valley, I could not help thinking of the deep glen (just the same sort of glen) where the Roc left Sinbad the Sailor; and where the merchants from the heights above, flung down great pieces of meat for the diamonds to stick to. There were no eagles here, to darken the sun in their swoop, and pounce upon them; but it was as wild and fierce as if there had been hundreds.

But the road, the road down which the marble comes, however immense the blocks! The genius of the country, and the spirit of its institutions, pave that road: repair it, watch it, keep it going! Conceive a channel of water running over a rocky bed, beset with great heaps of stone of all shapes and sizes, winding down the middle of this valley; and *that* being the road – because it was the road five hundred years ago! Imagine the clumsy carts of five hundred years ago, being used to this hour, and drawn, as they used to be, five hundred years ago, by oxen, whose ancestors were worn to death five hundred years ago, as their unhappy descendants are now, in twelve months, by the suffering and agony of this cruel work! Two pair, four pair, ten pair, twenty pair, to one block, according to its size; down it must come, this way. In their struggling from stone to stone, with their enormous loads behind them, they die frequently upon the spot; and not they alone; for their passionate drivers, sometimes tumbling down in their energy, are crushed to death beneath the wheels. But it was good five hundred years ago, and it must be good now; and a railroad down one of these steeps (the easiest thing in the world) would be flat blasphemy.

When we stood aside, to see one of these cars drawn by

only a pair of oxen (for it had but one small block of marble on it), coming down, I hailed, in my heart, the man who sat upon the heavy yoke, to keep it on the neck of the poor beasts – and who faced backward: not before him – as the very Devil of true despotism. He had a great rod in his hand, with an iron point; and when they could plough and force their way through the loose bed of the torrent no longer, and came to a stop, he poked it into their bodies, beat it on their heads, screwed it round and round in their nostrils, got them on a yard or two, in the madness of intense pain; repeated all these persuasions, with increased intensity of purpose, when they stopped again; got them on, once more; forced and goaded them to an abrupter point of the descent; and when their writhing and smarting, and the weight behind them, bore them plunging down the precipice in a cloud of scattered water, whirled his rod above his head, and gave a great whoop and hallo, as if he had achieved something, and had no idea that they might shake him off, and blindly mash his brains upon the road, in the noon-tide of his triumph.

Standing in one of the many studii of Carrara that afternoon – for it is a great workshop, full of beautifully-finished copies in marble, of almost every figure, group, and bust, we know – it seemed, at first, so strange to me that those exquisite shapes, replete with grace, and thought, and delicate repose, should grow out of all this toil, and sweat, and torture! But I soon found a parallel to it, and an explanation of it, in every virtue that springs up in miserable ground, and every good thing that has its birth in sorrow and distress. And, looking out of the sculptor's great window, upon the marble mountains, all red and glowing in the decline of day, but stern and solemn to the last, I thought, my God! how many quarries of human hearts and souls, capable of far more beautiful results, are left shut up and mouldering away: while pleasure-travellers through life, avert their faces, as they pass, and shudder at the gloom and ruggedness that conceal them!

The then reigning Duke of Modena,[54] to whom this territory in part belonged, claimed the proud distinction of being the only sovereign in Europe who had not recognised Louis-Philippe as King of the French! He was not a wag, but quite in earnest. He was also much opposed to railroads; and if certain lines in contemplation by other potentates, on either side of him, had been executed, would have probably enjoyed the satisfaction of having an omnibus plying to and fro, across his not very vast dominions, to forward travellers from one terminus to another.

Carrara, shut in by great hills, is very picturesque and bold. Few tourists stay there; and the people are nearly all connected, in one way or other, with the working of marble. There are also villages among the caves, where the workmen live. It contains a beautiful little Theatre, newly-built; and it is an interesting custom there, to form the chorus of labourers in the marble quarries, who are self-taught and sing by ear. I heard them in a comic opera, and in an act of 'Norma;'[55] and they acquitted themselves very well; unlike the common people of Italy generally, who (with some exceptions among the Neapolitans) sing vilely out of tune, and have very disagreeable singing voices.

From the summit of a lofty hill beyond Carrara, the first view of the fertile plain in which the town of Pisa lies – with Leghorn, a purple spot in the flat distance – is enchanting. Nor is it only distance that lends enchantment to the view;[56] for the fruitful country, and rich woods of olive trees through which the road subsequently passes, render it delightful.

The moon was shining when we approached Pisa, and for a long time we could see, behind the wall, the leaning Tower, all awry in the uncertain light; the shadowy original of the old pictures in school-books, setting forth 'The Wonders of the World.' Like most things connected in their first associations with school-books and school-times, it was too small. I felt it keenly. It was nothing like so high above the wall as I had hoped. It was another of the many deceptions practised by Mr. Harris, Bookseller,[57] at the corner of St. Paul's Church-yard, London. *His* Tower was a fiction, but this was reality – and, by comparison, a short reality. Still, it looked very well, and very strange, and was quite as much out of the perpendicular as Harris had represented it to be. The quiet air of Pisa too; the big guard-house at the gate, with only two little soldiers in it; the streets, with scarcely any show of people in them; and the Arno, flowing quaintly through the centre of the town; were excellent. So, I bore no malice in my heart against Mr. Harris (remembering his good intentions) but forgave him before dinner, and went out, full of confidence, to see the Tower next morning.

I might have known better; but, somehow, I had expected to see it, casting its long shadow on a public street where people came and went all day. It was a surprise to me to find it in a grave retired place, apart from the general resort, and carpeted with smooth green turf. But, the group of buildings, clustered on and about this verdant carpet: comprising the Tower, the Baptistery, the Cathedral, and the Church of the Campo Santo: is perhaps the most remarkable and beautiful in the whole world; and from being clustered there, together, away from the ordinary transactions and details of the town, they have a singularly venerable and impressive character. It is the architectural essence of a rich old city, with all its common life and common habitations pressed out, and filtered away.

Simond compares the Tower to the usual pictorial representations in children's books of the Tower of Babel. It is a happy simile, and conveys a better idea of the building than chapters of laboured description. Nothing can exceed the grace and lightness of the structure; nothing can be more remarkable than its general appearance. In the course of the ascent to the top (which is by an easy staircase), the inclination is not very apparent; but, at the summit, it becomes so, and gives one the sensation of being in a ship that has heeled over, through the action of an ebb-tide. The

effect *upon the low side,* so to speak – looking over from the
gallery, and seeing the shaft recede to its base – is very
startling; and I saw a nervous traveller hold on to the Tower
involuntarily, after glancing down, as if he had some idea of
propping it up. The view within, from the ground – looking
up, as through a slanted tube – is also very curious. It certainly inclines as much as the most sanguine tourist could
desire. The natural impulse of ninety-nine people out of a
hundred, who were about to recline upon the grass below it,
to rest, and contemplate the adjacent buildings, would
probably be, not to take up their position under the leaning
side; it is so very much aslant.

The manifold beauties of the Cathedral and Baptistery
need no recapitulation from me; though in this case, as in a
hundred others, I find it difficult to separate my own delight
in recalling them, from your weariness in having them re-
recalled. There is a picture of Saint Agnes, by Andrea del
Sarto,[58] in the former, and there are a variety of rich columns
in the latter, that tempt me strongly.

It is, I hope, no breach of my resolution not to be tempted
into elaborate descriptions, to remember the Campo Santo;
where grass-grown graves are dug in earth brought more
than six hundred years ago, from the Holy Land; and where
there are, surrounding them, such cloisters, with such playing
lights and shadows falling through their delicate tracery on
the stone pavement, as surely the dullest memory could
never forget. On the walls of this solemn and lovely place,
are ancient frescoes, very much obliterated and decayed, but
very curious. As usually happens in almost any collection of
paintings, of any sort, in Italy, where there are many heads,
there is, in one of them, a striking accidental likeness of
Napoleon. At one time, I used to please my fancy with the
speculation whether these old painters, at their work, had a
foreboding knowledge of the man who would one day arise
to wreak such destruction upon art: whose soldiers would
make targets of great pictures, and stable their horses

among triumphs of architecture. But the same Corsican face is so plentiful in some parts of Italy at this day, that a more commonplace solution of the coincidence is unavoidable.

If Pisa be the seventh wonder of the world in right of its Tower, it may claim to be, at least, the second or third in right of its beggars. They waylay the unhappy visiter at every turn, escort him to every door he enters at, and lie in wait for him, with strong reinforcements, at every door by which they know he must come out. The grating of the portal on its hinges is the signal for a general shout, and the moment he appears, he is hemmed in, and fallen on, by heaps of rags and personal distortions. The beggars seem to embody all the trade and enterprise of Pisa. Nothing else is stirring, but warm air. Going through the streets, the fronts of the sleepy houses look like backs. They are all so still and quiet, and unlike houses with people in them, that the greater part of the city has the appearance of a city at daybreak, or during a general siesta of the population. Or it is yet more like those backgrounds of houses in common prints, or old engravings, where windows and doors are squarely indicated, and one figure (a beggar of course) is seen walking off by itself into illimitable perspective.

Not so Leghorn (made illustrious by SMOLLETT's [59] grave), which is a thriving, business-like, matter-of-fact place, where idleness is shouldered out of the way by commerce. The regulations observed there, in reference to trade and merchants, are very liberal and free; and the town, of course, benefits by them. Leghorn has a bad name in connexion with stabbers, and with some justice it must be allowed; for, not many years ago, there was an assassination club there, the members of which bore no ill-will to anybody in particular, but stabbed people (quite strangers to them) in the streets at night, for the pleasure and excitement of the recreation. I think the president of this amiable society, was a shoemaker. He was taken, however, and the club was broken up.

It would, probably, have disappeared in the natural course of events, before the railroad between Leghorn and Pisa, which is a good one, and has already begun to astonish Italy with a precedent of punctuality, order, plain dealing, and improvement – the most dangerous and heretical astonisher of all. There must have been a slight sensation, as of earthquake, surely, in the Vatican, when the first Italian railroad was thrown open.

Returning to Pisa, and hiring a good-tempered Vetturíno, and his four horses, to take us on to Rome, we travelled through pleasant Tuscan villages and cheerful scenery all day. The roadside crosses in this part of Italy are numerous and curious. There is seldom a figure on the cross, though there is sometimes a face; but they are remarkable for being garnished with little models in wood, of every possible object that can be connected with the Saviour's death. The cock that crowed when Peter had denied his Master thrice, is usually perched on the tip-top; and an ornithological phenomenon he generally is. Under him, is the inscription. Then, hung on to the cross-beam, are the spear, the reed with the sponge of vinegar and water at the end, the coat without seam for which the soldiers cast lots, the dice-box with which they threw for it, the hammer that drove in the nails, the pincers that pulled them out, the ladder which was set against the cross, the crown of thorns, the instrument of flagellation, the lantern with which Mary went to the tomb (I suppose), and the sword with which Peter smote the servant of the high priest, – a perfect toy-shop of little objects, repeated at every four or five miles, all along the highway.

On the evening of the second day from Pisa, we reached the beautiful old city of Siena. There was what they called a Carnival, in progress; but, as its secret lay in a score or two of melancholy people walking up and down the principal street in common toy-shop masks, and being more melancholy, if possible, than the same sort of people in England, I say no more of it. We went off, betimes next morning, to see the Cathedral, which is wonderfully picturesque inside and out, especially the latter – also the market-place, or great Piazza, which is a large square, with a great broken-nosed fountain in it: some quaint gothic houses: and a high square brick tower; *outside* the top of which – a curious feature in such views of Italy – hangs an enormous bell. It is like a bit of Venice, without the water. There are some curious old Palazzi in the town, which is very ancient; and without having (for me) the interest of Verona, or Genoa, it is very dreamy and fantastic, and most interesting.

We went on again, as soon as we had seen these things, and going over a rather bleak country (there had been nothing but vines until now: mere walking sticks at that season of the year), stopped, as usual, between one and two hours in the middle of the day, to rest the horses; that being a part of every Vetturíno contract. We then went on again, through a region gradually becoming bleaker and wilder, until it became as bare and desolate as any Scottish moors. Soon after dark, we halted for the night, at the osteria of La Scala: a perfectly lone house, where the family were sitting round a great fire in the kitchen, raised on a stone platform three or four feet high, and big enough for the roasting of an ox. On the upper, and only other floor of this hotel, there was a great wild rambling sála, with one very little window in a by-corner, and four black doors opening into four black bed-rooms in various directions. To say nothing of another large black door, opening into another large black sála, with the staircase coming abruptly through a kind of trap-door in the floor, and the rafters of the roof looming above: a suspicious little press skulking in one obscure corner: and all the knives in the house lying about in various directions. The fire-place was of the purest Italian architecture, so that it was perfectly impossible to see it for the smoke. The waitress was like a dramatic brigand's wife, and wore the same style of dress upon her head. The dogs barked like mad; the echoes returned the compliments bestowed upon them; there was not another house within twelve miles; and things had a dreary, and rather a cut-throat, appearance.

They were not improved by rumours of robbers having come out, strong and boldly, within a few nights; and of their having stopped the mail very near that place. They were known to have waylaid some travellers not long before, on Mount Vesuvius itself, and were the talk at all the roadside inns. As they were no business of ours, however (for we had very little with us to lose), we made ourselves merry on the subject, and were very soon as comfortable as need be. We had the usual dinner in this solitary house; and a very good dinner it is, when you are used to it. There is something with a vegetable or some rice in it, which is a sort of short-hand or arbitrary character for soup, and which tastes very well, when you have flavoured it with plenty of grated cheese, lots of salt, and abundance of pepper. There is the half fowl of which this soup has been made. There is a stewed pigeon, with the gizzards and livers of himself and other birds stuck all round him. There is a bit of roast beef, the size of a small French roll. There are a scrap of Parmesan cheese, and five little withered apples, all huddled together on a small plate, and crowding one upon the other, as if each were trying to save itself from the chance of being eaten. Then there is coffee; and then there is bed. You don't mind brick floors; you don't mind yawning doors, nor banging windows; you don't mind your own horses being stabled under the bed: and so close, that every time a horse coughs or sneezes, he wakes you. If you are good-humoured to the people about you, and speak pleasantly, and look cheerful, take my word for it you may be well entertained in the very worst Italian Inn, and always in the most obliging manner, and may go from one end of the country to the other (despite all stories to the contrary) without any great trial of your patience anywhere. Especially, when you get such wine in flasks, as the Orvieto, and the Monte Pulciano.

It was a bad morning when we left this place; and we went,

for twelve miles, over a country as barren, as stony, and as wild, as Cornwall in England, until we came to Radicofani, where there is a ghostly, goblin inn: once a hunting-seat, belonging to the Dukes of Tuscany. It is full of such rambling corridors, and gaunt rooms, that all the murdering and phantom tales that ever were written, might have originated in that one house. There are some horrible old Palazzi in Genoa: one in particular, not unlike it, outside: but there is a windy, creaking, wormy, rustling, door-opening, foot-on-staircase-falling character about this Radicofani Hotel, such as I never saw, anywhere else. The town, such as it is, hangs on a hill-side above the house, and in front of it. The inhabitants are all beggars; and as soon as they see a carriage coming, they swoop down upon it, like so many birds of prey.

When we got on the mountain pass, which lies beyond this place, the wind (as they had forewarned us at the inn) was so terrific, that we were obliged to take my other half out of the carriage, lest she should be blown over, carriage and all, and to hang to it, on the windy side (as well as we could for laughing) to prevent its going, Heaven knows where. For mere force of wind, this land-storm might have competed with an Atlantic gale, and had a reasonable chance of coming off victorious. The blast came sweeping down great gullies in a range of mountains on the right: so that we looked with positive awe at a great morass on the left, and saw that there was not a bush or twig to hold by. It seemed as if, once blown from our feet, we must be swept out to sea, or away into space. There was snow, and hail, and rain, and lightning, and thunder; and there were rolling mists, travelling with incredible velocity. It was dark, awful, and solitary to the last degree; there were mountains above mountains, veiled in angry clouds; and there was such a wrathful, rapid, violent, tumultuous hurry, everywhere, as rendered the scene unspeakably exciting and grand.

It was a relief to get out of it, notwithstanding; and to cross even the dismal dirty Papal Frontier. After passing through two little towns; in one of which, Acquapendente, there was also a 'Carnival' in progress: consisting of one man dressed and masked as a woman, and one woman dressed and masked as a man, walking ankle-deep, through the muddy streets, in a very melancholy manner: we came, at dusk, within sight of the Lake of Bolsena, on whose bank there is a little town of the same name, much celebrated for malaria. With the exception of this poor place, there is not a cottage on the banks of the lake, or near it (for nobody dare sleep there); not a boat upon its waters; not a stick or stake to break the dismal monotony of seven-and-twenty watery miles. We were late in getting in, the roads being very bad from heavy rains; and, after dark, the dulness of the scene was quite intolerable.

We entered on a very different, and a finer scene of desolation, next night, at sunset. We had passed through Monte-fiaschone (famous for its wine) and Viterbo (for its fountains): and after climbing up a long hill of eight or ten miles extent, came suddenly upon the margin of a solitary lake: in one part very beautiful, with a luxuriant wood; in another, very barren, and shut in by bleak volcanic hills. Where this lake flows, there stood, of old, a city. It was swallowed up one day; and in its stead, this water rose. There are ancient traditions (common to many parts of the world) of the ruined city having been seen below, when the water was clear; but however that may be, from this spot of earth it vanished. The ground came bubbling up above it; and the water too; and here they stand, like ghosts on whom the other world closed suddenly, and who have no means of getting back again. They seem to be waiting the course of ages, for the next earthquake in that place; when they will plunge below the ground, at its first yawning, and be seen no more. The unhappy city below, is not more lost and dreary, than these fire-charred hills and the stagnant water, above. The red sun looked strangely on them, as with the knowledge that they were made for caverns and darkness;

and the melancholy water oozed and sucked the mud, and crept quietly among the marshy grass and reeds, as if the overthrow of all the ancient towers and house-tops, and the death of all the ancient people born and bred there, were yet heavy on its conscience.

A short ride from this lake, brought us to Ronciglione; a little town like a large pig-sty, where we passed the night. Next morning at seven o'clock, we started for Rome.

As soon as we were out of the pig-sty, we entered on the Campagna Romana; an undulating flat (as you know) where few people can live; and where, for miles and miles, there is nothing to relieve the terrible monotony and gloom. Of all kinds of country that could, by possibility, lie outside the gates of Rome, this is the aptest and fittest burial-ground for the Dead City. So sad, so quiet, so sullen; so secret in its covering up of great masses of ruin, and hiding them; so like the waste places into which the men possessed with devils used to go and howl, and rend themselves, in the old days of Jerusalem. We had to traverse thirty miles of this Campagna; and for two-and-twenty we went on and on, seeing nothing but now and then a lonely house, or a villanous-looking shepherd: with matted hair all over his face, and himself wrapped to the chin in a frowsy brown mantle: tending his sheep. At the end of that distance, we stopped to refresh the horses, and to get some lunch, in a common malaria-shaken, despondent little public-house, whose every inch of wall and beam, inside, was (according to custom) painted and decorated in a way so miserable that every room looked like the wrong side of another room, and, with its wretched imitation of drapery, and lop-sided little daubs of lyres, seemed to have been plundered from behind the scenes of some travelling circus.

When we were fairly off again, we began, in a perfect fever, to strain our eyes for Rome; and when, after another mile or two, the Eternal City appeared, at length, in the distance; it looked like – I am half afraid to write the word –

like LONDON!!! There it lay, under a thick cloud, with innumerable towers, and steeples, and roofs of houses, rising up into the sky, and high above them all, one Dome. I swear, that keenly as I felt the seeming absurdity of the comparison, it was so like London, at that distance, that if you could have shewn it me, in a glass, I should have taken it for nothing else.

Rome

WE entered the Eternal City, at about four o'clock in the afternoon, on the thirtieth of January, by the Porta del Popolo, and came immediately – it was a dark muddy day, and there had been heavy rain – on the skirts of the Carnival. We did not, then, know that we were only looking at the fag end of the masks, who were driving slowly round and round the Piazza, until they could find a promising opportunity for falling into the stream of carriages, and getting, in good time, into the thick of the festivity; and coming among them so abruptly, all travel-stained and weary, was not coming very well prepared to enjoy the scene.

We had crossed the Tiber by the Ponte Molle, two or three miles before. It had looked as yellow as it ought to look, and hurrying on between its worn-away and miry banks, had a promising aspect of desolation and ruin. The masquerade dresses on the fringe of the Carnival, did great violence to this promise. There were no great ruins, no solemn tokens of antiquity, to be seen; – they all lie on the other side of the city. There seemed to be long streets of commonplace shops and houses, such as are to be found in any European town; there were busy people, equipages, ordinary walkers to and fro; a multitude of chattering strangers. It was no more *my* Rome: the Rome of anybody's fancy, man or boy: degraded and fallen and lying asleep in the sun among a heap of ruins: than the Place de la Concorde in Paris is. A cloudy sky, a dull cold rain, and muddy streets, I was prepared for, but not for this: and I confess to having gone to bed, that night, in a very indifferent humour, and with a very considerably quenched enthusiasm.

162

Immediately on going out next day, we hurried off to St. Peter's. It looked immense in the distance, but distinctly and decidedly small, by comparison, on a near approach. The beauty of the Piazza in which it stands, with its clusters of exquisite columns, and its gushing fountains – so fresh, so broad, and free, and beautiful – nothing can exaggerate. The first burst of the interior, in all its expansive majesty and glory: and, most of all, the looking up into the Dome: is a sensation never to be forgotten. But, there were preparations for a Festa; the pillars of stately marble were swathed in some impertinent frippery of red and yellow; the altar, and entrance to the subterranean chapel: which is before it: in the centre of the church: were like a goldsmith's shop, or one of the opening scenes in a very lavish pantomime. And though I had as high a sense of the beauty of the building (I hope) as it is possible to entertain, I felt no very strong emotion. I have been infinitely more affected in many English Cathedrals when the organ has been playing, and in many English country churches when the congregation have been singing. I had a much greater sense of mystery and wonder, in the Cathedral of San Mark at Venice.

When we came out of the church again (we stood nearly an hour staring up into the dome: and would not have 'gone over' the Cathedral then, for any money), we said to the coachman, 'Go to the Coliseum.' In a quarter of an hour or so, he stopped at the gate, and we went in.

It is no fiction, but plain, sober, honest Truth, to say: so suggestive and distinct is it at this hour: that, for a moment – actually in passing in – they who will, may have the whole great pile before them, as it used to be, with thousands of eager faces staring down into the arena, and such a whirl of strife, and blood, and dust, going on there, as no language can describe. Its solitude, its awful beauty, and its utter desolation, strike upon the stranger, the next moment, like a softened sorrow; and never in his life, perhaps, will he be so moved and overcome by any sight, not immediately connected with his own affections and afflictions.

To see it crumbling there, an inch a year; its walls and arches overgrown with green; its corridors open to the day; the long grass growing in its porches; young trees of yesterday, springing up on its ragged parapets, and bearing fruit; chance produce of the seeds dropped there by the birds who build their nests within its chinks and crannies; to see its Pit of Fight filled up with earth, and the peaceful Cross planted in the centre; to climb into its upper halls, and look down on ruin, ruin, ruin, all about it; the triumphal arches of Constantine, Septimus Severus, and Titus;[60] the Roman Forum; the Palace of the Cæsars; the temples of the old religion, fallen down and gone; is to see the ghost of old Rome, wicked wonderful old city, haunting the very ground on which its people trod. It is the most impressive, the most stately, the most solemn, grand, majestic, mournful sight, conceivable. Never, in its bloodiest prime, can the sight of the gigantic Coliseum, full and running over with the lustiest life, have moved one heart, as it must move all who look upon it now, a ruin. GOD be thanked: a ruin!

As it tops the other ruins: standing there, a mountain among graves: so do its ancient influences outlive all other remnants of the old mythology and old butchery of Rome, in the nature of the fierce and cruel Roman people. The Italian face changes as the visiter approaches the city; its beauty becomes devilish; and there is scarcely one countenance in a hundred, among the common people in the streets, that would not be at home and happy in a renovated Coliseum to-morrow.

Here was Rome indeed at last; and such a Rome as no one can imagine in its full and awful grandeur! We wandered out upon the Appian Way, and then went on, through miles of ruined tombs and broken walls, with here and there a desolate and uninhabited house: past the Circus of Romulus,[61] where the course of the chariots, the stations of the judges, competitors, and spectators, are yet as plainly to be seen as in old time: past the tomb of Cæcilia Metella [62]: past all inclosure, hedge, or stake, wall or fence: away upon the open Campagna, where on that side of Rome, nothing is to be beheld but Ruin. Except where the distant Apennines bound the view upon the left, the whole wide prospect is one field of ruin. Broken aqueducts, left in the most picturesque and beautiful clusters of arches; broken temples; broken tombs. A desert of decay, sombre and desolate beyond all expression; and with a history in every stone that strews the ground.

On Sunday, the Pope [63] assisted in the performance of High Mass at St. Peter's. The effect of the Cathedral on my mind, on that second visit, was exactly what it was at first, and what it remains after many visits. It is not religiously impressive or affecting. It is an immense edifice, with no one point for the mind to rest upon; and it tires itself with wandering round and round. The very purpose of the place, is not expressed in anything you see there, unless you examine its details – and all examination of details is incompatible with the place itself. It might be a Pantheon, or a Senate House, or a great architectural trophy, having no other object than an architectural triumph. There is a black statue of St. Peter, to be sure, under a red canopy; which is larger than life, and which is constantly having its great toe kissed by good Catholics. You cannot help seeing that: it is so very prominent and popular. But it does not heighten the effect of the temple, as a work of art; and it is not expressive – to me at least – of its high purpose.

A large space behind the altar, was fitted up with boxes, shaped like those at the Italian Opera in England, but in their decoration much more gaudy. In the centre of the kind of theatre thus railed off, was a canopied dais with the Pope's chair upon it. The pavement was covered with a carpet of the brightest green; and what with this green, and the intolerable reds and crimsons, and gold borders of the hangings, the whole concern looked like a stupendous bonbon. On either side of the altar, was a large box for lady strangers. These were filled with ladies in black dresses and black veils. The gentlemen of the Pope's guard, in red coats, leather breeches, and jack-boots, guarded all this reserved space, with drawn swords, that were very flashy in every sense; and from the altar all down the nave, a broad lane was kept clear by the Pope's Swiss guard, who wear a quaint striped surcoat, and striped tight legs, and carry halberds like those which are usually shouldered by those theatrical supernumeraries, who never *can* get off the stage fast enough, and who may be generally observed to linger in the enemy's camp after the open country, held by the opposite forces, has been split up the middle by a convulsion of Nature.

I got upon the border of the green carpet, in company with a great many other gentlemen, attired in black (no other passport is necessary), and stood there at my ease, during the performance of mass. The singers were in a crib of wire-work (like a large meat-safe or bird-cage) in one corner; and sang most atrociously. All about the green carpet, there was a slowly moving crowd of people: talking to each other: staring at the Pope through eye-glasses: defrauding one another, in moments of partial curiosity, out of precarious seats on the bases of pillars: and grinning hideously at the ladies. Dotted here and there, were little knots of friars (Francescáni, or Cappuccíni, in their coarse brown dresses and peaked hoods) making a strange contrast to the gaudy ecclesiastics of higher degree, and having their humility gratified to the utmost, by being shouldered about, and elbowed right and left, on all sides. Some of these had muddy sandals and umbrellas, and stained garments: having trudged in from the country. The faces of the greater part were as coarse and heavy as their dress; their dogged, stupid, monotonous stare at all the glory and splendour, having something in it, half miserable, and half ridiculous.

Upon the green carpet itself, and gathered round the

altar, was a perfect army of cardinals and priests, in red, gold, purple, violet, white, and fine linen. Stragglers from these, went to and fro among the crowd, conversing two and two, or giving and receiving introductions, and exchanging salutations; other functionaries in black gowns, and other functionaries in court-dresses, were similarly engaged. In the midst of all these, and stealthy Jesuits creeping in and out, and the extreme restlessness of the Youth of England, who were perpetually wandering about, some few steady persons in black cassocks, who had knelt down with their faces to the wall, and were poring over their missals, became, unintentionally a sort of humane man-traps, and with their own devout legs tripped up other people's by the dozen.

There was a great pile of candles lying down on the floor near me, which a very old man in a rusty black gown with an open-work tippet, like a summer ornament for a fireplace in tissue-paper, made himself very busy in dispensing to all the ecclesiastics: one apiece. They loitered about with these for some time, under their arms like walking-sticks, or in their hands like truncheons. At a certain period of the ceremony, however, each carried his candle up to the Pope, laid it across his two knees to be blessed, took it back again, and filed off. This was done in a very attenuated procession, as you may suppose, and occupied a long time. Not because it takes long to bless a candle through and through, but because there were so many candles to be blessed. At last they were all blessed; and then they were all lighted; and then the Pope was taken up, chair and all, and carried round the church.

I must say, that I never saw anything, out of November, so like the popular English commemoration of the fifth of that month. A bundle of matches and a lantern, would have made it perfect. Nor did the Pope, himself, at all mar the resemblance, though he has a pleasant and venerable face; for, as this part of the ceremony makes him giddy and sick, he shuts his eyes when it is performed: and having his eyes shut, and a great mitre on his head, and his head itself wagging to and fro as they shook him in carrying, he looked as if his mask were going to tumble off. The two immense fans which are always borne, one on either side of him, accompanied him, of course, on this occasion. As they carried him along, he blessed the people with the mystic sign; and as he passed them, they kneeled down. When he had made the round of the church, he was brought back again, and if I am not mistaken, this performance was repeated, in the whole, three times. There was, certainly, nothing solemn or effective in it; and certainly very much that was droll and tawdry. But this remark applies to the whole ceremony, except the raising of the Host, when every man in the guard dropped on one knee instantly, and dashed his naked sword on the ground; which had a fine effect.

The next time I saw the Cathedral, was some two or three weeks afterwards, when I climbed up into the ball; and then, the hangings being taken down, and the carpet taken up, but all the framework left, the remnants of these decorations looked like an exploded cracker.

The Friday and Saturday having been solemn Festa days, and Sunday being always a *dies non* in carnival proceedings, we had looked forward, with some impatience and curiosity, to the beginning of the new week: Monday and Tuesday being the two last and best days of the Carnival.

On the Monday afternoon at one or two o'clock, there began to be a great rattling of carriages into the courtyard of the hotel; a hurrying to and fro of all the servants in it; and, now and then, a swift shooting across some doorway or balcony, of a straggling stranger in a fancy dress: not yet sufficiently well used to the same, to wear it with confidence and defy public opinion. All the carriages were open, and had the linings carefully covered with white cotton or calico, to prevent their proper decorations from being spoiled by the incessant pelting of sugar-plums; and people were packing and cramming into every vehicle as it waited for its occupants,

enormous sacks, and baskets-full of these confétti, together
with such heaps of flowers, tied up in little nosegays, that
some carriages were not only brimful of flowers, but literally
running over: scattering, at every shake and jerk of the
springs, some of their abundance on the ground. Not to be
behind-hand in these essential particulars, we caused two
very respectable sacks of sugar-plums (each about three feet
high) and a large clothes-basket full of flowers to be conveyed into our hired barouche, with all speed. And from our
place of observation, in one of the upper balconies of the
hotel, we contemplated these arrangements with the liveliest
satisfaction. The carriages now beginning to take up their
company, and move away, we got into ours, and drove off
too, armed with little wire masks for our faces; the sugar-
plums, like Falstaff's adulterated sack, having lime in their
composition.

The Corso is a street a mile long; a street of shops, and
palaces, and private houses, sometimes opening into a broad
piazza. There are virandas and balconies, of all shapes and
sizes, to almost every house – not on one story alone, but
often to one room or another on every story – put there in
general with so little order or regularity, that if, year after
year, and season after season, it had rained balconies, hailed
balconies, snowed balconies, blown balconies, they could
scarcely have come into existence in a more disorderly
manner.

This is the great fountain-head and focus of the Carnival.
But all the streets in which the Carnival is held, being
vigilantly kept by dragoons, it is necessary for carriages, in
the first instance, to pass, in line, down another thoroughfare,
and so come into the Corso at the end remote from the
Piazza del Popolo; which is one of its terminations. Accordingly, we fell into the string of coaches, and, for some time,
jogged on quietly enough; now crawling on at a very slow
walk; now trotting half a dozen yards; now backing fifty;
and now stopping altogether: as the pressure in front obliged

us. If any impetuous carriage dashed out of the rank and clattered forward, with the wild idea of getting on faster, it was suddenly met, or overtaken, by a trooper on horseback, who, deaf as his own drawn sword to all remonstrances, immediately escorted it back to the very end of the row, and made it a dim speck in the remotest perspective. Occasionally, we interchanged a volley of conféti with the carriage next in front, or the carriage next behind; but, as yet, this capturing of stray and errant coaches by the military, was the chief amusement.

Presently, we came into a narrow street, where, besides one line of carriages going, there was another line of carriages returning. Here the sugar-plums and the nosegays began to fly about, pretty smartly; and I was fortunate enough to observe one gentleman attired as a Greek warrior, catch a light-whiskered brigand on the nose (he was in the very act of tossing up a bouquet to a young lady in a first-floor window) with a precision that was much applauded by the by-standers. As this victorious Greek was exchanging a facetious remark with a stout gentleman in a door-way – one-half black and one-half white, as if he had been peeled up the middle – who had offered him his congratulations on this achievement, he received an orange from a house-top, full on his left ear, and was much surprised, not to say discomfited. Especially, as he was standing up at the time; and in consequence of the carriage moving on suddenly, at the same moment, staggered ignominiously, and buried himself among his flowers.

Some quarter of an hour of this sort of progress, brought us to the Corso; and anything so gay, so bright, and lively as the whole scene there, it would be difficult to imagine. From all the innumerable balconies: from the remotest and highest, no less than from the lowest and nearest: hangings of bright red, bright green, bright blue, white and gold, were fluttering in the brilliant sunlight. From windows, and from parapets, and tops of houses, streamers of the richest colours, and draperies of the gaudiest and most sparkling hues, were floating out upon the street. The buildings seemed to have been literally turned inside out, and to have all their gaiety towards the highway. Shop-fronts were taken down, and the windows filled with company, like boxes at a shining theatre; doors were carried off their hinges, and long tapestried groves, hung with garlands of flowers and evergreens, displayed within; builders' scaffoldings were gorgeous temples, radiant in silver, gold, and crimson; and in every nook and corner, from the pavement to the chimney-tops, where women's eyes could glisten, there they danced, and laughed, and sparkled, like the light in water. Every sort of bewitching madness of dress was there. Little preposterous scarlet jackets; quaint old stomachers, more wicked than the smartest boddices; Polish pelisses, strained and tight as ripe gooseberries; tiny Greek caps, all awry, and clinging to the dark hair, Heaven knows how; every wild, quaint, bold, shy, pettish, madcap fancy had its illustration in a dress; and every fancy was as dead forgotten by its owner, in the tumult of merriment, as if the three old aqueducts that still remain entire, had brought Lethe into Rome, upon their sturdy arches, that morning.

The carriages were now three abreast; in broader places four; often stationary for a long time together; always one close mass of variegated brightness; showing, the whole street-full, through the storm of flowers, like flowers of a larger growth themselves. In some, the horses were richly caparisoned in magnificent trappings; in others they were decked from head to tail, with flowing ribbons. Some were driven by coachmen with enormous double faces: one face leering at the horses: the other cocking its extraordinary eyes into the carriage: and both rattling again, under the hail of sugar-plums. Other drivers were attired as women, wearing long ringlets and no bonnets, and looking more ridiculous in any real difficulty with the horses (of which, in such a concourse, there were a great many) than tongue can tell, or pen describe. Instead of sitting *in* the carriages, upon the seats, the handsome Roman women, to see and to be seen the better, sit in the heads of the barouches, at this time of general license, with their feet upon the cushions – and oh the flowing skirts and dainty waists, the blessed shapes and laughing faces, the free, good-humoured, gallant figures that they make! There were great vans, too, full of handsome girls – thirty, or more together, perhaps – and the broadsides that were poured into, and poured out of, these fairy fire-ships, splashed the air with flowers and bonbons for ten minutes at a time. Carriages, delayed long in one place, would begin a deliberate engagement with other carriages, or with people at the lower windows; and the spectators at some upper balcony or window, joining in the fray, and attacking both parties, would empty down great bags of confétti, that descended like a cloud, and in an instant made them white as millers. Still, carriages on carriages, dresses on dresses, colours on colours, crowds upon crowds, without end. Men and boys clinging to the wheels of coaches, and holding on behind, and following in their wake, and diving in among the horses' feet to pick up scattered flowers to sell again; maskers on foot (the drollest, generally) in fantastic exaggerations of court-dresses, surveying the throng through enormous eye-glasses, and always transported with an ecstasy of love, on the discovery of any particularly old lady at a window; long strings of Policinelli, laying about them with blown bladders at the ends of sticks; a waggon-full of madmen, screaming and tearing to the life; a coach-full of grave mamelukes, with their horse-tail standard set up in the midst; a party of gipsy-women engaged in terrific conflict with a shipful of sailors; a man-monkey on a pole, surrounded by strange animals with pigs' faces, and lions' tails, carried under their arms, or worn gracefully over their shoulders; carriages on carriages, dresses on dresses, colours on colours, crowds upon crowds, without end. Not many actual characters sustained, or represented, perhaps, considering the number dressed, but the main pleasure of the scene consisting in its perfect good temper; in its bright, and infinite, and flashing variety; and in its entire abandonment to the mad humour of the time – an abandonment so perfect, so contagious, so irresistible, that the steadiest foreigner fights up to his middle in flowers and sugar-plums, like the wildest Roman of them all, and thinks of nothing else till half-past four o'clock, when he is suddenly reminded (to his great regret) that this is not the whole business of his existence, by hearing the trumpets sound, and seeing the dragoons begin to clear the street.

How it ever *is* cleared for the race that takes place at five, or how the horses ever go through the race, without going over the people, is more than I can say. But the carriages get into the by-streets, or up into the Piazza del Popolo, and some people sit in temporary galleries in the latter place, and tens of thousands line the Corso on both sides, when the horses are brought out into the Piazza – to the foot of that same column which, for centuries, looked down upon the games and chariot-races in the Circus Maximus.[64]

At a given signal, they are started off. Down the live lane, the whole length of the Corso, they fly like the wind: riderless, as all the world knows: with shining ornaments upon their backs, and twisted in their plaited manes: and with heavy little balls stuck full of spikes, dangling at their sides, to goad them on. The jingling of these trappings, and the rattling of their hoofs upon the hard stones; the dash and fury of their speed along the echoing street; nay, the very cannon that are fired – these noises are nothing to the roaring of the multitude: their shouts: the clapping of their hands. But it is soon over – almost instantaneously. More cannon shake the town. The horses have plunged into the carpets put across the street to stop them; the goal is reached; the prizes are won (they are given, in part, by the poor Jews, as a compromise for not running foot-races themselves); and there is an end to that day's sport.

But if the scene be bright, and gay, and crowded, on the last day but one, it attains, on the concluding day, to such a height of glittering colour, swarming life, and frolicsome uproar, that the bare recollection of it makes me giddy at this moment. The same diversions, greatly heightened and intensified in the ardour with which they are pursued, go on until the same hour. The race is repeated; the cannon are fired; the shouting and clapping of hands are renewed; the cannon are fired again; the race is over; and the prizes are won. But the carriages: ankle-deep in sugar-plums within, and so beflowered and dusty without, as to be hardly recognisable for the same vehicles that they were, three hours ago: instead of scampering off in all directions, throng into the Corso, where they are soon wedged together in a scarcely moving mass. For the diversion of the Moccoletti, the last gay madness of the Carnival, is now at hand; and sellers of little tapers, like what are called Christmas candles in England, are shouting lustily on every side, 'Moccoli, Moccoli! Ecco Moccoli!' – a new item in the tumult; quite abolishing that other item of 'Ecco Fióri! Ecco Fior—r—r!' which has been making itself audible over all the rest, at intervals, the whole day through.

As the bright hangings and dresses are all fading into one dull, heavy, uniform colour in the decline of the day, lights begin flashing, here and there: in the windows, on the house-tops, in the balconies, in the carriages, in the hands of the foot-passengers: little by little: gradually, gradually: more and more: until the whole long street is one great glare and blaze of fire. Then, everybody present has but one engrossing object; that is, to extinguish other people's candles, and to keep his own alight; and everybody: man, woman, or child, gentleman or lady, prince or peasant, native or foreigner: yells and screams, and roars incessantly, as a taunt to the subdued, 'Senza Moccolo, Senza Moccolo!' (Without a light! Without a light!) until nothing is heard but a gigantic chorus of those two words, mingled with peals of laughter.

The spectacle, at this time, is one of the most extraordinary that can be imagined. Carriages coming slowly by, with everybody standing on the seats or on the box, holding up their lights at arms' length, for greater safety; some in paper shades; some with a bunch of undefended little tapers, kindled altogether; some with blazing torches; some with feeble little candles; men on foot, creeping along, among the wheels, watching their opportunity, to make a spring at some particular light, and dash it out; other people climbing up into carriages, to get hold of them by main force; others, chasing some unlucky wanderer, round and round his own coach, to blow out the light he has begged or stolen some-where, before he can ascend to his own company, and enable them to light their extinguished tapers; others, with their hats off, at a carriage-door, humbly beseeching some kind-hearted lady to oblige them with a light for a cigar, and when she is in the fulness of doubt whether to comply or no, blowing out the candle she is guarding so tenderly with her little hand; other people at the windows, fishing for candles with lines and hooks, or letting down long willow-wands with handkerchiefs at the end, and flapping them out, dexterously, when the bearer is at the height of his triumph; others, biding their time in corners, with immense extin-guishers like halberds, and suddenly coming down upon glorious torches; others, gathered round one coach, and sticking to it; others, raining oranges and nosegays at an obdurate little lantern, or regularly storming a pyramid of men, holding up one man among them, who carries one feeble little wick above his head, with which he defies them all! Senza Moccolo! Senza Moccolo! Beautiful women, standing up in coaches, pointing in derision at extinguished lights, and clapping their hands, as they pass on, crying, 'Senza Moccolo! Senza Moccolo!'; low balconies full of lovely faces and gay dresses, struggling with assailants in the streets; some repressing them as they climb up, some bending down, some leaning over, some shrinking back – delicate arms and bosoms – graceful figures – glowing lights, fluttering dresses, Senza Moccolo, Senza Moccolo, Senza Moc-co-lo-o-o-o! – when in the wildest enthusiasm of the cry, and fullest ecstasy of the sport, the Ave Maria rings from the church steeples, and the Carnival is over in an instant – put out like a taper, with a breath!

There was a masquerade at the theatre at night, as dull and senseless as a London one, and only remarkable for the summary way in which the house was cleared at eleven o'clock: which was done by a line of soldiers forming along the wall, at the back of the stage, and sweeping the whole company out before them, like a broad broom. The game of the Moccoletti (the word, in the singular, Moccoletto, is the diminutive of Moccolo, and means a little lamp or candle-snuff) is supposed by some to be a ceremony of burlesque mourning for the death of the Carnival: candles being indispensable to Catholic grief. But whether it be so, or be a remnant of the ancient Saturnalia, or an incorporation of both, or have its origin in anything else, I shall always remember it, and the frolic, as a brilliant and most captivating sight: no less remarkable for the unbroken good-humour of all concerned, down to the very lowest (and among those who scaled the carriages, were many of the commonest men and boys) than for its innocent vivacity. For, odd as it may seem to say so, of a sport so full of thoughtlessness and personal display, it is as free from any taint of immodesty as any general mingling of the two sexes can possibly be; and there seems to prevail, during its progress, a feeling of general, almost childish, simplicity and confidence, which one thinks of with a pang, when the Ave Maria has rung it away, for a whole year.

Availing ourselves of a part of the quiet interval between the termination of the Carnival and the beginning of the Holy Week: when everybody had run away from the one, and few people had yet begun to run back again for the other: we went conscientiously to work, to see Rome. And, by dint of going out early every morning, and coming back late every evening, and labouring hard all day, I believe we made acquaintance with every post and pillar in the city, and the country round; and, in particular, explored so many churches that I abandoned that part of the enterprise at last, before it was half finished, lest I should never, of my own accord, go to church again, as long as I lived. But, I managed, almost every day, at one time or other, to get back to the Coliseum, and out upon the open Campagna, beyond the Tomb of Cæcilia Metella.

We often encountered, in these expeditions, a company of English Tourists, with whom I had an ardent, but ungratified longing, to establish a speaking acquaintance. They were one Mr. Davis, and a small circle of friends. It was impossible not to know Mrs. Davis's name, from her being always in great request among her party, and her party being everywhere. During the Holy Week, they were in every part of every scene of every ceremony. For a fortnight or three weeks before it, they were in every tomb, and every church, and every ruin, and every Picture Gallery; and I hardly ever observed Mrs. Davis to be silent for a moment. Deep underground, high up in St. Peter's, out on the Campagna, and stifling in the Jews' quarter, Mrs. Davis turned up, all the same. I don't think she ever saw anything, or ever looked at anything; and she had always lost something out of a straw hand-basket, and was trying to find it, with all her might and main, among an immense quantity of English halfpence, which lay, like sands upon the seashore, at the bottom of it. There was a professional Cicerone always attached to the party (which had been brought over from London, fifteen or twenty strong, by contract), and if he so much as looked at Mrs. Davis, she invariably cut him short by saying, 'There, God bless the man, don't worrit me! I don't understand a word you say, and shouldn't if you was to talk 'till you was black in the face!' Mr. Davis always had a snuff-coloured great-coat on, and carried a great green umbrella in his hand, and had a slow curiosity constantly devouring him, which prompted him to do extraordinary things, such as taking the covers off urns in tombs, and looking in at the ashes as if they were pickles – and tracing out inscriptions with the ferrule of his umbrella, and saying, with intense thoughtfulness, 'Here's a B you see, and there's a R, and this is the way we goes on in; is it!' His antiquarian habits occasioned his being frequently in the rear of the rest; and one of the agonies of Mrs. Davis, and the party in general, was an ever-present fear that Davis would be lost. This caused them to scream for him, in the strangest places, and at the most improper seasons. And when he came, slowly emerging out of some Sepulchre or other, like a peaceful Ghoule, saying 'Here I am!' Mrs. Davis invariably replied, 'You'll be buried alive in a foreign country Davis, and it's no use trying to prevent you!'

Mr. and Mrs. Davis, and their party, had, probably, been brought from London in about nine or ten days. Eighteen hundred years ago, the Roman legions under Claudius,[65] protested against being led into Mr. and Mrs. Davis's country, urging that it lay beyond the limits of the world.

Among what may be called the Cubs or minor Lions of Rome, there was one that amused me mightily. It is always to be found there; and its den is on the great flight of steps that lead from the Piázza di Spágna, to the church of Trínita del Monte. In plainer words, these steps are the great place of resort for the artists' 'Models,' and there they are constantly waiting to be hired. The first time I went up there, I could not conceive why the faces seemed familiar to me; why they appeared to have beset me, for years, in every possible variety of action and costume; and how it came to pass that they started up before me, in Rome, in the broad day, like so many saddled and bridled nightmares. I soon found that we had made acquaintance, and improved it, for several years, on the walls of various Exhibition Galleries. There is one old gentleman, with long white hair and an immense beard, who, to my knowledge, has gone half through the catalogue of the Royal Academy. This is the venerable, or patriarchal model. He carries a long staff; and every knot and twist in that staff I have seen, faithfully delineated, innumerable times. There is another man in a blue cloak, who always pretends to be asleep in the sun (when there is any) and who, I need not say, is always very wide awake, and very attentive to the disposition of his legs. This is the *dolce far' niente* model. There is another man in a brown cloak, who leans against a wall, with his arms folded in his mantle, and looks out of the corners of his eyes: which are just visible beneath his broad slouched hat. This is the assassin model. There is another man, who constantly looks over his own shoulder, and is always going away, but never goes. This is the haughty or scornful model. As to Domestic Happiness, and Holy Families, they should come very cheap, for there are lumps of them, all up the steps; and the cream of the thing, is, that they are all the falsest vagabonds in the world, especially made up for the purpose, and having no counterparts in Rome or any other part of the habitable globe.

My recent mention of the Carnival, reminds me of its being said to be a mock mourning (in the ceremony with which it closes), for the gaieties and merry-makings before Lent; and this again reminds me of the real funerals and mourning processions of Rome, which, like those in most other parts of Italy, are rendered chiefly remarkable to a Foreigner, by the indifference with which the mere clay is universally regarded, after life has left it. And this is not from the survivors having had time to dissociate the memory of the dead from their well-remembered appearance and form on earth; for the interment follows too speedily after death, for that: almost always taking place within four-and-twenty hours, and, sometimes, within twelve.

At Rome, there is the same arrangement of Pits in a great bleak, open, dreary space, that I have already described as existing in Genoa. When I visited it, at noonday, I saw a solitary coffin of plain deal: uncovered by any shroud or pall, and so slightly made, that the hoof of any wandering mule would have crushed it in: carelessly tumbled down, all on one side, on the door of one of the pits – and there left, by itself, in the wind and sunshine. 'How does it come to be left here?' I asked the man who showed me the place. 'It was brought here half an hour ago, Signore,' he said. I remembered to have met the procession, on its return: straggling away at a good round pace. 'When will it be put in the pit?' I asked him. 'When the cart comes, and it is opened to-night,' he said. 'How much does it cost to be brought here in this way, instead of coming in the cart?' I asked him. 'Ten scudi,' he said (about two pounds, two-and-sixpence, English). 'The other bodies, for whom nothing is paid, are taken to the church of the Santa Maria della Consolázione,' he continued, 'and brought here, altogether, in the cart at night.' I stood, a moment, looking at the coffin, which had two initial letters scrawled upon the top; and turned away, with an expression in my face, I suppose, of not much liking its exposure in that manner: for he said, shrugging his shoulders with great vivacity, and giving a pleasant smile, 'But he's dead, Signore, he's dead. Why not?'

Among the innumerable churches, there is one I must select for separate mention. It is the church of the Ara Coeli,[66] supposed to be built on the site of the old Temple of Jupiter Feretrius; and approached, on one side, by a long steep flight of steps, which seem incomplete without some group of bearded soothsayers on the top. It is remarkable for the possession of a miraculous Bambíno, or wooden doll, representing the Infant Saviour; and I first saw this miraculous Bambíno, in legal phrase, in manner following, that is to say:

We had strolled into the church one afternoon, and were looking down its long vista of gloomy pillars (for all these ancient churches built upon the ruins of old temples, are dark and sad), when the Brave came running in, with a grin upon his face that stretched it from ear to ear, and implored us to follow him, without a moment's delay, as they were going to show the Bambíno to a select party. We accordingly hurried off to a sort of chapel, or sacristy, hard by the chief altar, but not in the church itself, where the select party: consisting of two or three Catholic gentlemen and ladies (not Italians) were already assembled: and where one hollow-cheeked young monk was lighting up divers candles, while another was putting on some clerical robes over his coarse brown habit. The candles were on a kind of altar, and above it were two delectable figures, such as you would see at any English fair, representing the Holy Virgin, and Saint Joseph, as I suppose, bending in devotion over a wooden box, or coffer; which was shut.

The hollow-cheeked monk, number One, having finished lighting the candles, went down on his knees, in a corner, before this set-piece; and the monk number Two, having put on a pair of highly ornamented and gold-bespattered gloves, lifted down the coffer, with great reverence, and set it on the altar. Then, with many genuflexions, and muttering certain prayers, he opened it, and let down the front, and took off sundry coverings of satin and lace from the inside. The ladies had been on their knees from the commencement; and the gentlemen now dropped down devoutly, as he exposed to view, a little wooden doll, in face very like General Tom Thumb,[67] the American Dwarf: gorgeously dressed in satin and gold lace, and actually blazing with rich jewels. There was scarcely a spot upon its little breast, or neck, or stomach, but was sparkling with the costly offerings of the Faithful. Presently, he lifted it out of the box, and, carrying it round among the kneelers, set its face against the forehead of every one, and tendered its clumsy foot to them to kiss – a ceremony which they all performed, down to a dirty little raga-muffin of a boy who had walked in from the street. When this was done, he laid it in the box again: and the company, rising, drew near, and commended the jewels in whispers. In good time, he replaced the coverings, shut up the box, put it back in its place, locked up the whole concern (Holy Family and all) behind a pair of folding-doors; took off his priestly vestments; and received the customary 'small charge,' while his companion, by means of an extinguisher fastened to the end of a long stick, put out the lights, one after another. The candles being all extinguished, and the money all collected, they retired, and so did the spectators.

I met this same Bambíno, in the street, a short time afterwards, going, in great state, to the house of some sick person. It is taken to all parts of Rome for this purpose, constantly; but, I understand that it is not always as successful as could be wished; for, making its appearance at the bedside of weak and nervous people in extremity, accompanied by a numerous escort, it not unfrequently frightens them to death. It is most popular in cases of child-birth, where it has done such wonders, that if a lady be longer than usual in getting through her difficulties, a messenger is despatched, with all speed, to solicit the immediate attendance of the Bambíno. It is a very valuable property, and much confided in – especially by the religious body to whom it belongs.

I am happy to know that it is not considered immaculate, by some who are good Catholics, and who are behind the scenes, from what was told me by the near relation of a Priest, himself a Catholic, and a gentleman of learning and intelligence. This Priest made my informant promise that he would, on no account, allow the Bambíno to be borne into the bedroom of a sick lady, in whom they were both interested. 'For,' said he, 'if they (the monks) trouble her with it, and intrude themselves into her room, it will certainly kill her.' My informant accordingly looked out of the window when it came; and, with many thanks, declined to open the door. He endeavoured, in another case of which he had no other knowledge than such as he gained as a passer-by at the moment, to prevent its being carried into a small unwholesome chamber, where a poor girl was dying. But, he strove against it unsuccessfully, and she expired while the crowd were pressing round her bed.

Among the people who drop into St. Peter's at their leisure, to kneel on the pavement, and say a quiet prayer, there are certain schools and seminaries, priestly and otherwise, that come in, twenty or thirty-strong. These boys, always kneel down in single file, one behind the other, with a tall grim master in a black gown, bringing up the rear: like a pack of cards arranged to be tumbled down at a touch, with a disproportionately large Knave of clubs at the end. When they have had a minute or so at the chief altar, they scramble up, and filing off to the chapel of the Madonna, or the sacrament, flop down again in the same order; so that if anybody *did* stumble against the master, a general and sudden overthrow of the whole line must inevitably ensue.

The scene in all the churches is the strangest possible. The same monotonous, heartless, drowsy chaunting, always going on; the same dark building, darker from the brightness of the street without; the same lamps dimly burning; the self-same people kneeling here and there; turned towards you, from one altar or other, the same priest's back, with the same large cross embroidered on it; however different in size, in shape, in wealth, in architecture, this church is from that, it is the same thing still. There are the same dirty beggars stopping in their muttered prayers to beg; the same miserable cripples exhibiting their deformity at the doors; the same blind men, rattling little pots like kitchen peppercastors; their depositories for alms; the same preposterous crowns of silver stuck upon the painted heads of single saints and Virgins in crowded pictures, so that a little figure on a mountain has a head-dress bigger than the temple in the foreground, or adjacent miles of landscape; the same favourite shrine or figure, smothered with little silver hearts and crosses, and the like: the staple trade and show of all the jewellers; the same odd mixture of respect and indecorum, faith and phlegm: kneeling on the stones, and spitting on them, loudly; getting up from prayers to beg a little, or to pursue some other worldly matter: and then kneeling down again, to resume the contrite supplication at the point where it was interrupted. In one church, a kneeling lady got up from her prayers, for a moment, to offer us her card, as a teacher of Music; and in another, a sedate gentleman with a very thick walking-staff, arose from his devotions to belabour his dog, who was growling at another dog: and whose yelps and howls resounded through the church, as his master quietly relapsed into his former trains of meditation – keeping his eye upon the dog, at the same time, nevertheless.

Above all, there is always a receptacle for the contributions of the Faithful, in some form or other. Sometimes, it is a money-box, set up between the worshipper, and the wooden life-size figure of the Redeemer; sometimes, it is a little chest for the maintenance of the Virgin; sometimes, an appeal on behalf of a popular Bambíno; sometimes, a bag at the end of a long stick, thrust among the people here and there, and vigilantly jingled by an active Sacristan; but there it always is, and, very often, in many shapes in the same church, and doing pretty well in all. Nor, is it wanting in the open air – the streets and roads – for, often as you are walking along, thinking about anything rather than a tin canister, that object pounces out upon you from a little house by the way-side; and on its top is painted, 'For the Souls in Purgatory;' an appeal which the bearer repeats a great many times, as he rattles it before you, much as Punch rattles the cracked bell which his sanguine disposition makes an organ of.

And this reminds me that some Roman altars of peculiar sanctity, bear the inscription, 'Every Mass performed at this altar, frees a soul from Purgatory.' I have never been able to find out the charge for one of these services, but they should needs be expensive. There are several Crosses in Rome too, the kissing of which, confers indulgences for varying terms. That in the centre of the Coliseum, is worth a hundred days;

and people may be seen kissing it, from morning to night. It is curious that some of these crosses seem to acquire an arbitrary popularity; this very one among them. In another part of the Coliseum there is a cross upon a marble slab, with the inscription, 'Who kisses this cross shall be entitled to Two hundred and forty days' indulgence.' But I saw no one person kiss it, though, day after day, I sat in the arena, and saw scores upon scores of peasants pass it, on their way to kiss the other.

To single out details from the great dream of Roman Churches, would be the wildest occupation in the world. But St. Stefano Rotondo, a damp mildewed vault of an old church in the outskirts of Rome, will always struggle uppermost in my mind, by reason of the hideous paintings with which its walls are covered. These represent the martyrdoms of saints and early Christians; and such a panorama of horror and butchery no man could imagine in his sleep, though he were to eat a whole pig, raw, for supper. Grey-bearded men being boiled, fried, grilled, crimped, singed, eaten by wild beasts, worried by dogs, buried alive, torn asunder by horses, chopped up small with hatchets: women having their breasts torn with iron pincers, their tongues cut out, their ears screwed off, their jaws broken, their bodies stretched upon the rack, or skinned upon the stake, or crackled up and melted in the fire: these are among the mildest subjects. So insisted on, and laboured at, besides, that every sufferer gives you the same occasion for wonder as poor old Duncan [68] awoke, in Lady Macbeth, when she marvelled at his having so much blood in him.

There is an upper chamber in the Mamertine prison, over what is said to have been – and very possibly may have been – the dungeon of St. Peter. This chamber is now fitted up as an oratory, dedicated to that saint; and it lives, as a distinct and separate place, in my recollection, too. It is very small and low-roofed; and the dread and gloom of the ponderous, obdurate old prison are on it, as if they had come up in a dark mist through the floor. Hanging on the walls, among the clustered votive offerings, are objects, at once strangely in keeping, and strangely at variance, with, the place – rusty daggers, knives, pistols, clubs, divers instruments of violence and murder, brought here, fresh from use, and hung up to propitiate offended Heaven: as if the blood upon them would drain off in consecrated air, and have no voice to cry with. It is all so silent and so close, and tomb-like; and the dungeons below, are so black, and stealthy, and stagnant, and naked; that this little dark spot becomes a dream within a dream: and in the vision of great churches which come rolling past me like a sea, it is a small wave by itself, that melts into no other wave, and does not flow on with the rest.

It is an awful thing to think of the enormous caverns that are entered from some Roman churches, and undermine the city. Many churches have crypts and subterranean chapels of great size, which, in the ancient time, were baths, and secret chambers of temples, and what not; but I do not speak of them. Beneath the church of St. Giovanni and St. Paolo, there are the jaws of a terrific range of caverns, hewn out of the rock, and said to have another outlet underneath the Coliseum – tremendous darknesses of vast extent, half-buried in the earth and unexplorable, where the dull torches, flashed by the attendants, glimmer down long ranges of distant vaults branching to the right and left, like streets in a city of the dead; and show the cold damp stealing down the walls, drip-drop, drip-drop, to join the pools of water that lie here and there, and never saw, and never will see, one ray of the sun. Some accounts make these the prisons of the wild beasts destined for the amphitheatre; some, the prisons of the condemned gladiators; some, both. But the legend most appalling to the fancy is, that in the upper range (for there are two stories of these caves) the Early Christians destined to be eaten at the Coliseum Shows, heard the wild beasts, hungry for them, roaring down below; until, upon the night and solitude of their captivity, there burst the sudden noon and life of the vast theatre crowded to the parapet, and of these, their dreaded neighbours, bounding in!

Below the church of San Sebastiano, two miles beyond the gate of San Sebastiano, on the Appian way, is the entrance to the catacombs of Rome – quarries in the old time, but afterwards the hiding-places of the Christians. These ghastly passages have been explored for twenty miles; and form a chain of labyrinths, sixty miles in circumference.

A gaunt Franciscan friar, with a wild bright eye, was our only guide, down into this profound and dreadful place. The narrow ways and openings hither and thither, coupled with the dead and heavy air, soon blotted out, in all of us, any recollection of the track by which we had come; and I could not help thinking, 'Good Heaven, if, in a sudden fit of madness he should dash the torches out, or if he should be seized with a fit, what would become of us!' On we wandered, among martyrs' graves: passing great subterranean vaulted roads, diverging in all directions, and choked up with heaps of stones, that thieves and murderers may not take refuge there, and form a population under Rome, even worse than that which lives between it and the sun. Graves, graves, graves; graves of men, of women, of their little children, who ran crying to the persecutors, 'We are Christians! We are Christians!' that they might be murdered with their parents; Graves with the palm of martyrdom roughly cut into their stone boundaries, and little niches, made to hold a vessel of the martyrs' blood; Graves of some who lived down here, for years together, ministering to the rest, and preaching truth, and hope, and comfort, from the rude altars, that bear witness to their fortitude at this hour; more roomy graves, but far more terrible, where hundreds, being surprised, were hemmed in and walled up: buried before Death, and killed by slow starvation.

'The Triumphs of the Faith are not above ground in our splendid churches,' said the friar, looking round upon us, as we stopped to rest in one of the low passages, with bones and dust surrounding us on every side. 'They are here! Among the Martyrs' Graves!' He was a gentle, earnest man, and said it from his heart; but when I thought how Christian men have dealt with one another; how, perverting our most merciful religion, they have hunted down and tortured, burnt and beheaded, strangled, slaughtered, and oppressed each other; I pictured to myself an agony surpassing any that this Dust had suffered with the breath of life yet lingering in it, and how these great and constant hearts would have been shaken – how they would have quailed and drooped – if a fore-knowledge of the deeds that professing Christians would commit in the Great Name for which they died, could have rent them with its own unutterable anguish, on the cruel wheel, and bitter cross, and in the fearful fire.

Such are the spots and patches in my dream of churches, that remain apart, and keep their separate identity. I have a fainter recollection, sometimes, of the relics; of the fragment of the pillar of the Temple that was rent in twain; of the portion of the table that was spread for the Last Supper; of the well at which the woman of Samaria gave water to Our Saviour; of two columns from the house of Pontius Pilate; of the stone to which the Sacred hands were bound, when the scourging was performed; of the gridiron of Saint Lawrence, and the stone below it, marked with the frying of his fat and blood; these set a shadowy mark on some cathedrals, as an old story, or a fable might, and stop them for an instant, as they flit before me. The rest is a vast wilderness of consecrated buildings of all shapes and fancies, blending one with another; of battered pillars of old Pagan temples, dug up from the ground, and forced, like giant captives, to support the roofs of Christian churches; of pictures, bad, and wonderful, and impious, and ridiculous; of kneeling people, curling incense, tinkling bells, and sometimes (but not often) of a swelling organ; of Madonne, with their breasts stuck full of swords, arranged in a half-circle like a modern fan; of actual skeletons of dead saints, hideously attired in gaudy satins,

ROME FROM THE BORGHESE GARDENS

Samuel Palmer

silks, and velvets trimmed with gold: their withered crust of
skull adorned with precious jewels, or with chaplets of
crushed flowers; sometimes, of people gathered round the
pulpit, and a monk within it stretching out the crucifix, and
preaching fiercely: the sun just streaming down through some
high window on the sail-cloth stretched above him and across
the church, to keep his high-pitched voice from being lost
among the echoes of the roof. Then my tired memory comes
out upon a flight of steps, where knots of people are asleep,
or basking in the light; and strolls away, among the rags,
and smells, and palaces, and hovels, of an old Italian street.

On one Saturday morning (the eighth of March), a man
was beheaded here. Nine or ten months before, he had waylaid a Bavarian countess, travelling as a pilgrim to Rome –
alone and on foot, of course – and performing, it is said, that
act of piety for the fourth time. He saw her change a piece of
gold at Viterbo, where he lived; followed her; bore her company on her journey for some forty miles or more, on the
treacherous pretext of protecting her; attacked her, in the
fulfilment of his unrelenting purpose, on the Campagna,
within a very short distance of Rome, near to what is called
(but what is not) the Tomb of Nero; robbed her; and beat
her to death with her own pilgrim's staff. He was newly
married, and gave some of her apparel to his wife: saying that
he had bought it at a fair. She, however, who had seen the
pilgrim-countess passing through their town, recognised
some trifle as having belonged to her. Her husband then told
her what he had done. She, in confession, told a priest; and
the man was taken, within four days after the commission
of the murder.

There are no fixed times for the administration of justice,
or its execution, in this unaccountable country; and he had
been in prison ever since. On the Friday, as he was dining
with the other prisoners, they came and told him he was to be
beheaded next morning, and took him away. It is very

unusual to execute in Lent; but his crime being a very bad one, it was deemed advisable to make an example of him at that time, when great numbers of pilgrims were coming towards Rome, from all parts, for the Holy Week. I heard of this on the Friday evening, and saw the bills up at the churches, calling on the people to pray for the criminal's soul. So, I determined to go, and see him executed.

The beheading was appointed for fourteen and a half o'clock, Roman time: or a quarter before nine in the forenoon. I had two friends with me; and as we did not know but that the crowd might be very great, we were on the spot by half-past seven. The place of execution was near the church of San Giovanni decolláto (a doubtful compliment to St. John the Baptist) in one of the impassable back streets without any footway, of which a great part of Rome is composed – a street of rotten houses, which do not seem to belong to anybody, and do not seem to have ever been inhabited, and certainly were never built on any plan, or for any particular purpose, and have no window-sashes, and are a little like deserted breweries, and might be warehouses but for having nothing in them. Opposite to one of these, a white house, the scaffold was built. An untidy, unpainted, uncouth, crazy-looking thing of course: some seven feet high, perhaps: with a tall, gallows-shaped frame rising above it, in which was the knife, charged with a ponderous mass of iron, all ready to descend, and glittering brightly in the morning-sun, whenever it looked out, now and then, from behind a cloud.

There were not many people lingering about; and these were kept at a considerable distance from the scaffold, by parties of the Pope's dragoons. Two or three hundred foot-soldiers were under arms, standing at ease in clusters here and there; and the officers were walking up and down in twos and threes, chatting together, and smoking cigars.

At the end of the street, was an open space, where there would be a dust-heap, and piles of broken crockery, and mounds of vegetable refuse, but for such things being thrown

anywhere and everywhere in Rome, and favouring no particular sort of locality. We got into a kind of wash-house,
belonging to a dwelling house on this spot; and standing
there, in an old cart, and on a heap of cart wheels piled against
the wall, looked, through a large grated window, at the
scaffold, and straight down the street beyond it, until in
consequence of its turning off abruptly to the left, our perspective was brought to a sudden termination, and had a
corpulent officer, in a cocked hat, for its crowning feature.

Nine o'clock struck, and ten o'clock struck, and nothing
happened. All the bells of all the churches rang as usual. A
little parliament of dogs assembled in the open space, and
chased each other, in and out among the soldiers. Fierce-
looking Romans of the lowest class, in blue cloaks, russet
cloaks, and rags uncloaked, came and went, and talked
together. Women and children fluttered, on the skirts of the
scanty crowd. One large muddy spot was left quite bare, like
a bald place on a man's head. A cigar-merchant, with an
earthen pot of charcoal ashes in one hand, went up and down,
crying his wares. A pastry-merchant divided his attention
between the scaffold and his customers. Boys tried to climb
up walls, and tumbled down again. Priests and monks
elbowed a passage for themselves among the people, and
stood on tiptoe for a sight of the knife: then went away.
Artists, in inconceivable hats of the middle-ages, and beards
(thank Heaven!) of no age at all, flashed picturesque scowls
about them from their stantions in the throng. One gentleman (connected with the fine arts, I presume) went up and
down in a pair of Hessian-boots, with a red beard hanging
down on his breast, and his long and bright red hair, plaited
into two tails, one on either side of his head; which fell over
his shoulders in front of him, very nearly to his waist, and
were carefully entwined and braided!

Eleven o'clock struck; and still nothing happened. A
rumour got about, among the crowd, that the criminal would
not confess; in which case, the priests would keep him until

the Ave Maria (sunset); for it is their merciful custom never finally to turn the crucifix away from a man at that pass, as one refusing to be shriven, and consequently a sinner abandoned of the Saviour, until then. People began to drop off. The officers shrugged their shoulders and looked doubtful. The dragoons, who came riding up below our window, every now and then, to order an unlucky hackney-coach or cart away, as soon as it had comfortably established itself and was covered with exulting people (but never before) became imperious, and quick-tempered. The bald place hadn't a straggling hair upon it; and the corpulent officer, crowning the perspective, took a world of snuff.

Suddenly, there was a noise of trumpets. 'Attention!' was among the foot-soldiers instantly. They were marched up to the scaffold and formed round it. The dragoons galloped to their nearer stations too. The guillotine became the centre of a wood of bristling bayonets and shining sabres. The people closed round nearer, on the flank of the soldiery. A long straggling stream of men and boys, who had accompanied the procession from the prison, came pouring into the open space. The bald spot was scarcely distinguishable from the rest. The cigar and pastry-merchants resigned all thoughts of business, for the moment, and abandoning themselves wholly to pleasure, got good situations in the crowd. The perspective ended, now, in a troop of dragoons. And the corpulent officer, sword in hand, looked hard at a church close to him, which he could see, but we, the crowd could not.

After a short delay, some monks were seen approaching to the scaffold from this church; and above their heads, coming on slowly and gloomily, the effigy of Christ upon the cross, canopied with black. This was carried round the foot of the scaffold, to the front, and turned towards the criminal, that he might see it to the last. It was hardly in its place, when he appeared on the platform, bare-footed; his hands bound; and with the collar and neck of his shirt cut away, almost to the shoulder. A young man – six-and-twenty – vigorously made, and well-shaped. Face pale; small dark moustache; and dark brown hair.

He had refused to confess, it seemed, without first having his wife brought to see him; and they had sent an escort for her, which had occasioned the delay.

He immediately kneeled down, below the knife. His neck fitting into a hole, made for the purpose, in a cross plank, was shut down, by another plank above; exactly like the pillory. Immediately below him, was a leathern bag. And into it, his head rolled instantly.

The executioner was holding it by the hair, and walking with it round the scaffold, showing it to the people, before one quite knew that the knife had fallen heavily, and with a rattling sound.

When it had travelled round the four sides of the scaffold, it was set upon a pole in front – a little patch of black and white, for the long street to stare at, and the flies to settle on. The eyes were turned upward, as if he had avoided the sight of the leathern bag, and looked to the crucifix. Every tinge and hue of life had left it in that instant. It was dull, cold, livid, wax. The body also.

There was a great deal of blood. When we left the window, and went close up to the scaffold, it was very dirty; one of the two men who were throwing water over it, turning to help the other lift the body into a shell, picked his way as through mire. A strange appearance was the apparent annihilation of the neck. The head was taken off so close, that it seemed as if the knife had narrowly escaped crushing the jaw, or shaving off the ear; and the body looked as if there were nothing left above the shoulder.

Nobody cared, or was at all affected. There was no manifestation of disgust, or pity, or indignation, or sorrow. My empty pockets were tried, several times, in the crowd immediately below the scaffold, as the corpse was being put into its coffin. It was an ugly, filthy, careless, sickening spectacle; meaning nothing but butchery beyond the momentary interest, to the one wretched actor. Yes! Such a sight has one meaning and one warning. Let me not forget it. The speculators in the lottery, station themselves at favourable points for counting the gouts of blood that spirt out, here or there; and buy that number. It is pretty sure to have a run upon it.

The body was carted away in due time, the knife cleansed, the scaffold taken down, and all the hideous apparatus removed. The executioner: an outlaw *ex officio* (what a satire on the Punishment!) who dare not, for his life, cross the Bridge of St. Angelo but to do his work: retreated to his lair, and the show was over.

At the head of the collections in the palaces of Rome, the Vatican, of course, with its treasures of art, its enormous galleries, and staircases, and suites upon suites of immense chambers, ranks highest and stands foremost. Many most noble statues, and wonderful pictures, are there; nor is it heresy to say that there is a considerable amount of rubbish there, too. When any old piece of sculpture dug out of the ground, finds a place in a gallery because it *is* old, and without any reference to its intrinsic merits: and finds admirers by the hundred, because it is there, and for no other reason on earth: there will be no lack of objects, very indifferent in the plain eyesight of any one who employs so vulgar a property, when he may wear the spectacles of Cant for less than nothing, and establish himself as a man of taste for the mere trouble of putting them on.

I unreservedly confess, for myself, that I cannot leave my natural perception of what is natural and true, at a palace-door, in Italy or elsewhere, as I should leave my shoes if I were travelling in the East. I cannot forget that there are certain expressions of face, natural to certain passions, and as unchangeable in their nature as the gait of a lion, or the flight of an eagle. I cannot dismiss from my certain knowledge, such common-place facts as the ordinary proportions of men's arms, and legs, and heads; and when I meet with performances that do violence to these experiences and recollections, no matter where they may be, I cannot honestly admire them, and think it best to say so; in spite of high critical advice that we should sometimes feign an admiration, though we have it not.

Therefore, I freely acknowledge that when I see a Jolly young Waterman [69] representing a cherubim, or a Barclay and Perkin's Drayman depicted as an Evangelist, I see nothing to commend or admire in the performance, however great its reputed Painter. Neither am I partial to libellous Angels, who play on fiddles and bassoons, for the edification of sprawling monks apparently in liquor. Nor to those Monsieur Tonsons of galleries, Saint Francis and Saint Sebastian; both of whom I submit should have very uncommon and rare merits, as works of art, to justify their compound multiplication by Italian Painters.

It seems to me, too, that the indiscriminate and determined raptures in which some critics indulge, is incompatible with the true appreciation of the really great and transcendent works. I cannot imagine, for example, how the resolute champion of undeserving pictures can soar to the amazing beauty of Titian's [70] great picture of the Assumption of the Virgin at Venice; or how the man who is truly affected by the sublimity of that exquisite production, or who is truly sensible of the beauty of Tintoretto's [70] great picture of the Assembly of the Blessed in the same place, can discern in Michael Angelo's [70] Last Judgment, in the Sistine chapel, any general idea, or one pervading thought, in harmony with the stupendous subject. He who will contemplate Raphael's [70] masterpiece, the Transfiguration, and will go away into another chamber of that same Vatican, and contemplate another design of Raphael, representing (in incredible caricature) the miraculous stopping of a great fire by Leo the Fourth [70] – and who will say that he admires them both, as works of extraordinary genius – must, as I think, be wanting in his powers of perception in one of the two instances, and, probably, in the high and lofty one.

It is easy to suggest a doubt, but I have a great doubt whether, sometimes, the rules of art are not too strictly observed, and whether it is quite well or agreeable that we should know beforehand, where this figure will be turning round, and where that figure will be lying down, and where there will be drapery in folds, and so forth. When I observe heads inferior to the subject, in pictures of merit, in Italian galleries, I do not attach that reproach to the Painter, for I have a suspicion that these great men, who were, of necessity, very much in the hands of monks and priests, painted monks and priests a great deal too often. I frequently see, in pictures of real power, heads quite below the story and the painter: and I invariably observe that those heads are of the Convent stamp, and have their counterparts among the Convent inmates of this hour; so, I have settled with myself that, in such cases, the lameness was not with the painter, but with the vanity and ignorance of certain of his employers, who would be apostles – on canvass, at all events.

The exquisite grace and beauty of Canova's.[71] statues; the wonderful gravity and repose of many of the ancient works in sculpture, both in the Capitol and the Vatican; and the strength and fire of many others; are, in their different ways, beyond all reach of words. They are especially impressive and delightful, after the works of Bernini and his disciples, in which the churches of Rome, from St. Peter's downward, abound; and which are, I verily believe, the most detestable class of productions in the wide world. I would infinitely rather (as mere works of art) look upon the three deities of the Past, the Present, and the Future, in the Chinese Collection, than upon the best of these breezy maniacs; whose every fold of drapery is blown inside-out; whose smallest vein, or artery, is as big as an ordinary forefinger; whose hair is like a nest of lively snakes; and whose attitudes put all other extravagance to shame. Insomuch that I do honestly believe, there can be no place in the world, where such intolerable abortions, begotten of the sculptor's chisel, are to be found in such profusion, as in Rome.

There is a fine collection of Egyptian antiquities, in the Vatican; and the ceilings of the rooms in which they are arranged, are painted to represent a star-light sky in the Desert. It may seem an odd idea, but it is very effective. The grim, half-human monsters from the temples, look more grim and monstrous underneath the deep dark blue; it sheds a strange uncertain gloomy air on everything – a mystery adapted to the objects; and you leave them, as you find them, shrouded in a solemn night.

In the private palaces, pictures are seen to the best advantage. There are seldom so many in one place that the attention need become distracted, or the eye confused. You see them very leisurely; and are rarely interrupted by a crowd of people. There are portraits innumerable, by Titian, and Rembrandt,[72] and Vandyke; heads by Guido, and Domenichino, and Carlo Dolci; various subjects by Correggio, and Murillo, and Raphael, and Salvator Rosa, and Spagnoletto – many of which it would be difficult, indeed, to praise too highly, or to praise enough; such is their tenderness and grace; their noble elevation, purity, and beauty.

The portrait of Beatrice di Cenci, in the Palazzo Barberini, is a picture almost impossible to be forgotten. Through the transcendent sweetness and beauty of the face, there is a something shining out, that haunts me. I see it now, as I see this paper, or my pen. The head is loosely draped in white; the light hair falling down below the linen folds. She has turned suddenly towards you; and there is an expression in the eyes – although they are very tender and gentle – as if the wildness of a momentary terror, or distraction, had been struggled with and overcome, that instant; and nothing but a celestial hope, and a beautiful sorrow, and a desolate earthly helplessness remained. Some stories say that Guido painted

it, the night before her execution; some other stories, that
he painted it from memory, after having seen her, on her
way to the scaffold. I am willing to believe that, as you see
her on his canvass, so she turned towards him, in the crowd,
from the first sight of the axe, and stamped upon his mind a
look which he has stamped on mine as though I had stood
beside him in the concourse. The guilty palace of the Cenci:
blighting a whole quarter of the town, as it stands withering
away by grains: had that face, to my fancy, in its dismal
porch, and at its black blind windows, and flitting up and
down its dreary stairs, and growing out of the darkness of its
ghostly galleries. The History is written in the Painting;
written, in the dying girl's face, by Nature's own hand. And
oh! how in that one touch she puts to flight (instead of
making kin) the puny world that claim to be related to her,
in right of poor conventional forgeries!

I saw in the Palazzo Spada, the statue of Pompey;[73] the
statue at whose base, Cæsar fell. A stern, tremendous figure!
I imagined one of greater finish: of the last refinement: full
of delicate touches: losing its distinctness, in the giddy eyes
of one whose blood was ebbing before it, and settling into
some such rigid majesty as this, as Death came creeping over
the upturned face.

The excursions in the neighbourhood of Rome are charming,
and would be full of interest were it only for the changing
views they afford, of the wild Campagna. But, every inch of
ground, in every direction, is rich in associations, and in
natural beauties. There is Albano, with its lovely lake and
wooded shore, and with its wine, that certainly has not improved since the days of Horace,[74] and in these times hardly
justifies his panegyric. There is squalid Tivoli, with the river
Anio, diverted from its course, and plunging down, headlong,
some eighty feet in search of it. With its picturesque Temple
of the Sibyl, perched high on a crag; its minor waterfalls
glancing and sparkling in the sun; and one good cavern

yawning darkly, where the river takes a fearful plunge and shoots on, low down under beetling rocks. There, too, is the Villa d'Este, deserted and decaying among groves of melancholy pine and cypress trees, where it seems to lie in state. Then, there is Frascati, and, on the steep above it, the ruins of Tusculum, where Cicero[75] lived, and wrote, and adorned his favourite house (some fragments of it may yet be seen there), and where Cato[75] was born. We saw its ruined amphitheatre on a grey dull day, when a shrill March wind was blowing, and when the scattered stones of the old city lay strewn about the lonely eminence, as desolate and dead as the ashes of a long extinguished fire.

One day, we walked out, a little party of three, to Albano, fourteen miles distant; possessed by a great desire to go there, by the ancient Appian way, long since ruined and overgrown. We started at half past seven in the morning, and within an hour or so, were out upon the open Campagna. For twelve miles, we went climbing on, over an unbroken succession of mounds, and heaps, and hills, of ruin. Tombs and temples, overthrown and prostrate; small fragments of columns, friezes, pediments; great blocks of granite and marble; mouldering arches, grass-grown and decayed; ruin enough to build a spacious city from; lay strewn about us. Sometimes, loose walls, built up from these fragments by the shepherds, came across our path; sometimes, a ditch between two mounds of broken stones, obstructed our progress; sometimes, the fragments themselves, rolling from beneath our feet, made it a toilsome matter to advance; but it was always ruin. Now, we tracked a piece of the old road, above the ground; now traced it, underneath a grassy covering, as if that were its grave; but all the way was ruin. In the distance, ruined aqueducts went stalking on their giant course along the plain; and every breath of wind that swept towards us, stirred early flowers and grasses, springing up, spontaneously, on miles of ruin. The unseen larks above us, who alone disturbed the awful silence, had their nests in ruin; and the fierce herdsmen, clad in sheepskins, who now and then scowled out upon us from their sleeping nooks, were housed in ruin. The aspect of the desolate Campagna in one direction, where it was most level, reminded me of an American prairie; but what is the solitude of a region where men have never dwelt, to that of a Desert, where a mighty race have left their foot-prints in the earth from which they have vanished; where the resting-places of their Dead, have fallen like their Dead; and the broken hour-glass of Time is but a heap of idle dust! Returning, by the road, at sunset; and looking, from the distance, on the course we had taken in the morning, I almost felt (as I had felt when I first saw it, at that hour) as if the sun would never rise again, but looked its last, that night, upon a ruined world.

To come again on Rome, by moonlight, after such an expedition, is a fitting close to such a day. The narrow streets, devoid of footways, and choked, in every obscure corner, by heaps of dunghill-rubbish, contrast so strongly, in their cramped dimensions, and their filth, and darkness, with the broad square before some haughty church: in the centre of which, a hieroglyphic-covered obelisk, brought from Egypt in the days of the Emperors, looks strangely on the foreign scene about it; or perhaps an ancient pillar, with its honoured statue overthrown, supports a Christian saint: Marcus Aurelius[76] giving place to Paul, and Trajan[76] to St. Peter. Then, there are the ponderous buildings reared from the spoliation of the Coliseum, shutting out the moon, like mountains: while, here and there, are broken arches and rent walls, through which it gushes freely, as the life comes pouring from a wound. The little town of miserable houses, walled, and shut in by barred gates, is the quarter where the Jews are locked up nightly, when the clock strikes eight – a miserable place, densely populated, and reeking with bad odours, but where the people are industrious and money-getting. In the day-time, as you make your way along the narrow streets, you see them all at work: upon the pavement, oftener than

THE VILLA D'ESTE
Samuel Palmer

in their dark and frouzy shops: furbishing old clothes, and driving bargains.

Crossing from these patches of thick darkness, out into the moon once more, the fountain of Trevi, welling from a hundred jets, and rolling over mimic rocks, is silvery to the eye and ear. In the narrow little throat of street, beyond, a booth, dressed out with flaring lamps, and boughs of trees, attracts a group of sulky Romans round its smoking coppers of hot broth, and cauliflower stew; its trays of fried fish, and its flasks of wine. As you rattle round the sharply-twisting corner, a lumbering sound is heard. The coachman stops abruptly, and uncovers, as a van comes slowly by, preceded by a man who bears a large cross; by a torch-bearer; and a priest: the latter chaunting as he goes. It is the Dead Cart, with the bodies of the poor, on their way to burial in the Sacred Field outside the walls, where they will be thrown into the pit that will be covered with a stone to-night, and sealed up for a year.

But whether, in this ride, you pass by obelisks, or columns: ancient temples, theatres, houses, porticoes, or forums: it is strange to see, how every fragment, whenever it is possible, has been blended into some modern structure, and made to serve some modern purpose – a wall, a dwelling-place, a granary, a stable – some use for which it never was designed, and associated with which it cannot otherwise than lamely assort. It is stranger still, to see how many ruins of the old mythology: how many fragments of obsolete legend and observance: have been incorporated into the worship of Christian altars here; and how, in numberless respects, the false faith and the true are fused into a monstrous union.

From one part of the city, looking out beyond the walls, a squat and stunted pyramid (the burial-place of Caius Cestius[77]) makes an opaque triangle in the moonlight. But, to an English traveller, it serves to mark the grave of Shelley[78] too, whose ashes lie beneath a little garden near it. Nearer still, almost within its shadow, lie the bones of Keats, 'whose name was writ in water,' that shines brightly in the landscape of a calm Italian night.

The Holy Week in Rome is supposed to offer great attractions to all visiters; but, saving for the sights of Easter Sunday, I would counsel those who go to Rome for its own interest, to avoid it at that time. The ceremonies, in general, are of the most tedious and wearisome kind; the heat and crowd at every one of them, painfully oppressive; the noise, hubbub, and confusion, quite distracting. We abandoned the pursuit of these shows, very early in the proceedings, and betook ourselves to the Ruins again. But, we plunged into the crowd for a share of the best of the sights; and what we saw, I will describe to you.

At the Sistine chapel, on the Wednesday, we saw very little, for by the time we reached it (though we were early) the besieging crowd had filled it to the door, and overflowed into the adjoining hall, where they were struggling, and squeezing, and mutually expostulating, and making great rushes every time a lady was brought out faint, as if at least fifty people could be accommodated in her vacant standing-room. Hanging in the doorway of the chapel, was a heavy curtain, and this curtain, some twenty people nearest to it, in their anxiety to hear the chaunting of the Miserere, were continually plucking at, in opposition to each other, that it might not fall down and stifle the sound of the voices. The consequence was, that it occasioned the most extraordinary confusion, and seemed to wind itself about the unwary, like a Serpent. Now, a lady was wrapped up in it, and couldn't be unwound. Now, the voice of a stifling gentleman was heard inside it, beseeching to be let out. Now, two muffled arms, no man could say of which sex, struggled in it as in a sack. Now, it was carried by a rush, bodily overhead into the chapel, like an awning. Now, it came out the other way, and blinded one of the Pope's Swiss Guard who had arrived, that moment, to set things to rights.

Being seated at a little distance, among two or three of the Pope's gentlemen, who were very weary and counting the minutes – as perhaps His Holiness was too – we had better opportunities of observing this eccentric entertainment, than of hearing the Miserere. Sometimes, there was a swell of mournful voices that sounded very pathetic and sad, and died away, into a low strain again; but that was all we heard.

At another time, there was the Exhibition of the Relics in Saint Peter's, which took place at between six and seven o'clock in the evening, and was striking from the Cathedral being dark and gloomy, and having a great many people in it. The place into which the relics were brought, one by one, by a party of three priests, was a high balcony near the chief altar. This was the only lighted part of the church. There are always a hundred and twelve lamps burning near the altar, and there were two tall tapers, besides, near the black statue of St. Peter; but these were nothing in such an immense edifice. The gloom, and the general upturning of faces to the balcony, and the prostration of true believers on the pavement, as shining objects, like pictures or looking-glasses, were brought out and shown, had something effective in it, despite the very preposterous manner in which they were held up for the general edification, and the great elevation at which they were displayed; which one would think rather calculated to diminish the comfort derivable from a full conviction of their being genuine.

On the Thursday, we went to see the Pope convey the Sacrament from the Sistine chapel, to deposit it in the Capella Paolina, another chapel in the Vatican; – a ceremony emblematical of the entombment of the Saviour before His Resurrection. We waited in a great gallery with a great crowd of people (three-fourths of them English) for an hour or so, while they were chaunting the Miserere, in the Sistine chapel again. Both chapels opened out of the gallery; and the general attention was concentrated on the occasional opening and shutting of the door of the one for which the Pope was ultimately bound. None of these openings disclosed anything more tremendous than a man on a ladder, lighting a great quantity of candles; but at each and every opening, there was a terrific rush made at this ladder and this man, something like (I should think) a charge of the heavy British cavalry at Waterloo. The man was never brought down, however, nor the ladder; for it performed the strangest antics in the world among the crowd – where it was carried by the man, when the candles were all lighted; and finally it was stuck up against the gallery wall, in a very disorderly manner, just before the opening of the other chapel, and the commencement of a new chaunt, announced the approach of His Holiness. At this crisis, the soldiers of the guard, who had been poking the crowd into all sorts of shapes, formed down the gallery: and the procession came up, between the two lines they made.

There were a few choristers, and then a great many priests, walking two and two, and carrying – the good-looking priests at least – their lighted tapers, so as to throw the light with a good effect upon their faces: for the room was darkened. Those who were not handsome, or who had not long beards, carried *their* tapers anyhow, and abandoned themselves to spiritual contemplation. Meanwhile, the chaunting was very monotonous and dreary. The procession passed on, slowly, into the chapel, and the drone of voices went on, and came on, with it, until the Pope himself appeared, walking under a white satin canopy, and bearing the covered Sacrament in both hands; cardinals and canons clustered round him, making a brilliant show. The soldiers of the guard knelt down as he passed; all the bystanders bowed; and so he passed on into the chapel: the white satin canopy being removed from over him at the door, and a white satin parasol hoisted over his poor old head, in place of it. A few more couples brought up the rear, and passed into the chapel also. Then, the chapel door was shut; and it was all over; and everybody hurried off headlong, as for life or death, to see something else, and say it wasn't worth the trouble.

I think the most popular and most crowded sight (excepting those of Easter Sunday and Monday, which are open to all classes of people) was the Pope washing the feet of Thirteen men, representing the twelve apostles, and Judas Iscariot. The place in which this pious office is performed, is one of the chapels of St. Peter's, which is gaily decorated for the occasion; the thirteen sitting 'all of a row,' on a very high bench, and looking particularly uncomfortable, with the eyes of Heaven knows how many English, French, Americans, Swiss, Germans, Russians, Swedes, Norwegians, and other foreigners, nailed to their faces all the time. They are robed in white; and on their heads they wear a stiff white cap, like a large English porter-pot, without a handle. Each carries in his hand, a nosegay, of the size of a fine cauliflower; and two of them, on this occasion, wore spectacles: which, remembering the characters they sustained, I thought a droll appendage to the costume. There was a great eye to character. St. John was represented by a good-looking young man. St. Peter, by a grave-looking old gentleman, with a flowing brown beard; and Judas Iscariot by such an enormous hypocrite (I could not make out, though, whether the expression of his face was real or assumed) that if he had acted the part to the death and had gone away and hanged himself, he would have left nothing to be desired.

As the two large boxes, appropriated to ladies, at this sight, were full to the throat, and getting near was hopeless, we posted off, along with a great crowd, to be in time at the Table, where the Pope, in person, waits on these Thirteen; and after a prodigious struggle at the Vatican staircase, and several personal conflicts with the Swiss guard, the whole crowd swept into the room. It was a long gallery hung with drapery of white and red, with another great box for ladies (who are obliged to dress in black at these ceremonies, and to wear black veils), a royal box for the King of Naples,[79] and his party; and the table itself, which, set out like a ball supper, and ornamented with golden figures of the real apostles, was arranged on an elevated platform on one side of the gallery. The counterfeit apostles' knives and forks were laid out on that side of the table which was nearest to the wall, so that they might be stared at again, without let or hindrance.

The body of the room was full of male strangers; the crowd immense; the heat very great; and the pressure sometimes frightful. It was at its height when the stream came pouring in, from the feet-washing; and then there were such shrieks and outcries, that a party of Piedmontese dragoons went to the rescue of the Swiss guard, and helped them to calm the tumult.

The ladies were particularly ferocious, in their struggles for places. One lady of my acquaintance was seized round the waist, in the ladies' box, by a strong matron, and hoisted out of her place; and there was another lady (in the back row in the same box) who improved her position by sticking a large pin into the ladies before her.

The gentlemen about me were remarkably anxious to see what was on the table; and one Englishman seemed to have embarked the whole energy of his nature in the determination to discover whether there was any mustard. 'By Jupiter there's vinegar!' I heard him say to his friend, after he had stood on tiptoe an immense time, and had been crushed and beaten on all sides. 'And there's oil!! I saw them distinctly, in cruets! Can any gentleman, in front there, see mustard on the table? Sir, will you oblige me! *Do* you see a Mustard-Pot?'

The apostles and Judas appearing on the platform, after much expectation, were marshalled, in line, in front of the table, with Peter at the top; and a good long stare was taken at them by the company, while twelve of them took a long smell at their nosegays, and Judas – moving his lips very obtrusively – engaged in inward prayer. Then, the Pope, clad in a scarlet robe, and wearing on his head a skull-cap of white satin, appeared in the midst of a crowd of Cardinals and other dignitaries, and took in his hand a little golden ewer, from which he poured a little water over one of Peter's hands, while one attendant held a golden basin; a second, a fine cloth; a third, Peter's nosegay, which was taken from him during the operation. This His Holiness performed, with considerable expedition, on every man in the line (Judas, I observed, to be particularly overcome by his condescension); and then the whole Thirteen sat down to dinner. Grace said by the Pope. Peter in the chair.

There was white wine, and red wine; and the dinner looked very good. The courses appeared in portions, one for each apostle; and these being presented to the Pope, by Cardinals upon their knees, were by him handed to the Thirteen. The manner in which Judas grew more white-livered over his victuals, and languished, with his head on one side, as if he had no appetite, defies all description. Peter was a good, sound, old man, and went in, as the saying is, 'to win;' eating everything that was given him (he got the best: being first in the row) and saying nothing to anybody. The dishes appeared to be chiefly composed of fish and vegetables. The Pope helped the Thirteen to wine also; and, during the whole dinner, somebody read something aloud, out of a large book – the Bible, I presume – which nobody could hear, and to which nobody paid the least attention. The Cardinals, and other attendants, smiled to each other, from time to time, as if the thing were a great farce; and if they thought so, there is little doubt they were perfectly right. His Holiness did what he had to do, as a sensible man gets through a troublesome ceremony, and seemed very glad when it was all over.

The Pilgrims' Suppers: where lords and ladies waited on the Pilgrims, in token of humility, and dried their feet when they had been well washed by deputy: were very attractive. But, of all the many spectacles of dangerous reliance on outward observances, in themselves mere empty forms, none struck me half so much as the Scala Santa, or Holy Staircase, which I saw several times, but to the greatest advantage, or disadvantage, on Good Friday.

This holy staircase is composed of eight-and-twenty steps, said to have belonged to Pontius Pilate's house, and to be the identical stairs on which Our Saviour trod, in coming down from the judgment-seat. Pilgrims ascend it, only on their knees. It is steep; and, at the summit, is a chapel, reported to be full of relics; into which they peep through some iron bars, and then come down again, by one of two side staircases, which are not sacred, and may be walked on.

On Good Friday, there were, on a moderate computation, a hundred people, slowly shuffling up these stairs, on their knees, at one time; while others, who were going up, or had come down – and a few who had done both, and were going up again for the second time – stood loitering in the porch below, where an old gentleman in a sort of watch-box, rattled a tin cannister, with a slit in the top, incessantly, to remind them that he took the money. The majority were country-people, male and female. There were four or five Jesuit priests, however, and some half-dozen well-dressed women. A whole school of boys, twenty at least, were about half-way up – evidently enjoying it very much. They were all wedged together, pretty closely; but the rest of the company gave the boys as wide a berth as possible, in consequence of their betraying some recklessness in the management of their boots.

I never, in my life, saw anything at once so ridiculous, and so unpleasant, as this sight – ridiculous in the absurd incidents inseparable from it; and unpleasant in its senseless and unmeaning degradation. There are two steps to begin with, and then a rather broad landing. The more rigid climbers went along this landing on their knees, as well as up the stairs; and the figures they cut, in their shuffling progress over the level surface, no description can paint. Then, to see them watch their opportunity from the porch, and cut in where there was a place next the wall! And to see one man with an umbrella (brought on purpose, for it was a fine day) hoisting himself, unlawfully, from stair to stair! And to observe a demure lady of fifty-five or so, looking back, every now and then, to assure herself that her legs were properly disposed!

There were such odd differences in the speed of different people too. Some got on as if they were doing a match against time; others stopped to say a prayer on every step. This man touched every stair with his forehead, and kissed it; that man scratched his head all the way. The boys got on brilliantly, and were up and down again before the old lady had accomplished her half dozen stairs. But most of the Penitents came down, very sprightly and fresh, as having done a real good substantial deed which it would take a good deal of sin to counterbalance; and the old gentleman in the watch-box was down upon them with his cannister while they were in this humour, I promise you.

As if such a progress were not in its nature inevitably droll enough, there lay, on the top of the stairs, a wooden figure on a crucifix, resting on a sort of great iron saucer: so ricketty and unsteady, that whenever an enthusiastic person kissed the figure, with more than usual devotion, or threw a coin into the saucer, with more than common readiness (for it served in this respect as a second or supplementary cannister), it gave a great leap and rattle, and nearly shook the attendant lamp out: horribly frightening the people further down, and throwing the guilty party into unspeakable embarrassment.

On Easter Sunday, as well as on the preceding Thursday, the Pope bestows his benediction on the people, from the balcony in front of St. Peter's. This Easter Sunday was a day so bright and blue: so cloudless, balmy, wonderfully bright: that all the previous bad weather vanished from the recollection in a moment. I had seen the Thursday's Benediction dropping damply on some hundreds of umbrellas, but there was not a sparkle then, in all the hundred fountains of Rome – such fountains as they are! – and on this Sunday morning, they were running diamonds. The miles of miserable streets through which we drove (compelled to a certain course by the Pope's dragoons: the Roman police on such occasions) were so full of colour, that nothing in them was capable of wearing a faded aspect. The common people came out in their gayest dresses; the richer people in their smartest vehicles; Cardinals rattled to the church of the Poor Fishermen in their state carriages; shabby magnificence flaunted its thread-bare liveries and tarnished cocked hats, in the sun; and every coach in Rome was put in requisition for the Great Piazza of St. Peter's.

One hundred and fifty thousand people were there, at least! Yet there was ample room. How many carriages were there, I don't know; yet there was room for them too, and to spare. The great steps of the church were densely crowded. There were many of the Contadini, from Albano (who delight in red) in that part of the square; and the mingling of bright colours in the crowd, was beautiful. Below the steps, the troops were ranged. In the magnificent proportions of the place, they looked like a bed of flowers. Sulky Romans, lively peasants from the neighbouring country, groups of pilgrims from distant parts of Italy, sight-seeing foreigners of all nations, made a murmur in the clear air, like so many insects; and high above them all, plashing and bubbling, and making rainbow colours in the light, the two delicious fountains welled and tumbled bountifully.

A kind of bright carpet was hung over the front of the balcony; and the sides of the great window were bedecked with crimson drapery. An awning was stretched too, over the top, to screen the old man from the hot rays of the sun. As noon approached, all eyes were turned up to this window. In due time, the chair was seen approaching to the front, with the gigantic fans of peacock's feathers, close behind. The doll within it (for the balcony is very high) then rose up, and stretched out its tiny arms, while all the male spectators in the square uncovered, and some, but not by any means the greater part, kneeled down. The guns upon the ramparts of the Castle of St. Angelo proclaimed, next moment, that the benediction was given; drums beat; trumpets sounded; arms clashed; and the great mass below, suddenly breaking into smaller heaps, and scattering here and there in rills, was stirred like partycoloured sand.

What a bright noon it was, as we rode away! The Tiber was no longer yellow, but blue. There was a blush on the old bridges, that made them fresh and hale again. The Pantheon, with its majestic front, all seamed and furrowed like an old face, had summer light upon its battered walls. Every squalid and desolate Hut in the Eternal City (bear witness every grim old palace, to the filth and misery of the plebeian neighbour that elbows it, as certainly as Time has laid its grip on its Patrician head!) was fresh and new with some ray of the sun. The very prison in the crowded street, a whirl of carriages and people, had some stray sense of the day, dropping through its chinks and crevices: and dismal prisoners who could not wind their faces round the barricading of the blocked-up windows, stretched out their hands, and clinging to the rusty bars, turned *them* towards the overflowing street: as if it were a cheerful fire, and could be shared in, that way.

But, when the night came on, without a cloud to dim the full moon, what a sight it was to see the Great Square full once more, and the whole church, from the cross to the ground, lighted with innumerable lanterns, tracing out the architecture, and winking and shining all round the colonnade of the piazza! And what a sense of exultation, joy, delight, it was, when the great bell struck half-past seven – on the instant – to behold one bright red mass of fire, soar gallantly from the top of the cupola to the extremest summit of the cross, and the moment it leaped into its place, become the signal of a bursting out of countless lights, as great, and red, and blazing as itself, from every part of the gigantic church; so that every cornice, capital, and smallest ornament of stone, expressed itself in fire: and the black solid ground-work of the enormous dome, seemed to grow transparent as an egg-shell!

A train of gunpowder, an electric chain – nothing could be fired, more suddenly and swiftly, than this second illumination; and when we had got away, and gone upon a distant height, and looked towards it two hours afterwards, there it still stood, shining and glittering in the calm night like a Jewel! Not a line of its proportions wanting; not an angle blunted; not an atom of its radiance lost.

The next night – Easter Monday – there was a great display of fireworks from the Castle of St. Angelo. We hired a room in an opposite house, and made our way to our places, in good time, through a dense mob of people choking up the square in front, and all the avenues leading to it; and so loading the bridge by which the castle is approached, that it seemed ready to sink into the rapid Tiber below. There are statues on this bridge (execrable works) and, among them, great vessels full of burning tow were placed: glaring strangely on the faces of the crowd, and not less strangely on the stone counterfeits above them.

The show began with a tremendous discharge of cannon; and then, for twenty minutes, or half an hour, the whole castle was one incessant sheet of fire, and labyrinth of blazing wheels of every colour, size, and speed: while rockets streamed into the sky, not by ones or twos, or scores, but hundreds at a time. The concluding burst – the Girandola – was like the blowing up into the air, of the whole massive castle, without smoke or dust.

In half an hour afterwards, the immense concourse had dispersed; the moon was looking calmly down upon her wrinkled image in the river; and half a dozen men and boys, with bits of lighted candle in their hands: moving here and there, in search of anything worth having, that might have been dropped in the press: had the whole scene to themselves.

By way of contrast, we rode out into old ruined Rome, after all this firing and booming, to take our leave of the Coliseum. I had seen it by moonlight before (I never could get through a day without going back to it), but its tremendous solitude, that night, is past all telling. The ghostly pillars in the Forum; the triumphal arches of Old Emperors; those enormous masses of ruin which were once their palaces; the grass-grown mounds that mark the graves of ruined temples; the stones of the Via Sacra, smooth with the tread of feet in ancient Rome; even these were dimmed, in their transcendent melancholy, by the dark ghost of its bloody holidays, erect and grim; haunting the old scene; despoiled by pillaging Popes and fighting Princes, but not laid; wringing wild hands of weed, and grass, and bramble; and lamenting to the night in every gap and broken arch – the shadow of its awful self, immovable!

As we lay down on the grass of the Campagna, next day, on our way to Florence, hearing the larks sing, we saw that a little wooden cross had been erected on the spot where the poor Pilgrim Countess was murdered. So, we piled some loose stones about it, as the beginning of a mound to her memory, and wondered if we should ever rest there again, and look back at Rome.

A Rapid Diorama

W E are bound for Naples! And we cross the threshold of the Eternal City at yonder gate, the Gate of San Giovanni Laterano, where the two last objects that attract the notice of a departing visiter, and the two first objects that attract notice of an arriving one, are a proud church and a decaying ruin – good emblems of Rome.

Our way lies over the Campagna, which looks more solemn on a bright blue day like this, than beneath a darker sky; the great extent of ruin being plainer to the eye: and the sunshine through the arches of the broken aqueducts, showing other broken arches shining through them in the melancholy distance. When we have traversed it, and look back from Albano, its dark undulating surface lies below us like a stagnant lake, or like a broad dull Lethe flowing round the walls of Rome, and separating it from all the world! How often have the Legions, in triumphant march, gone glittering across that purple waste, so silent and unpeopled now! How often has the train of captives looked, with sinking hearts, upon the distant city, and beheld its population pouring out, to hail the return of their conqueror! What riot, sensuality and murder, have run mad in the vast Palaces now heaps of brick and shattered marble! What glare of fires, and roar of popular tumult, and wail of pestilence and famine, have come sweeping over the wild plain where nothing is now heard but the wind, and where the solitary lizards gambol unmolested in the sun!

The train of Wine-carts going into Rome, each driven by a shaggy peasant reclining beneath a little gipsy-fashioned canopy of sheepskin, is ended now, and we go toiling up into a higher country where there are trees. The next day brings us on the Pontine Marshes, wearily flat and lonesome, and overgrown with brushwood, and swamped with water, but with a fine road made across them, shaded by a long, long, avenue. Here and there, we pass a solitary guard-house; here and there, a hovel, deserted, and walled up. Some herdsmen loiter on the banks of the stream beside the road, and sometimes a flat-bottomed boat, towed by a man, comes rippling idly along it. A horseman passes occasionally, carrying a long gun cross-wise on the saddle before him, and attended by fierce dogs; but there is nothing else astir save the wind and the shadows, until we come in sight of Terracina.

How blue and bright the sea, rolling below the windows of the Inn so famous in robber stories! How picturesque the great crags and points of rock overhanging to-morrow's narrow road, where galley-slaves are working in the quarries above, and the sentinels who guard them lounge on the sea shore! All night there is the murmur of the sea beneath the stars; and, in the morning, just at daybreak, the prospect suddenly becoming expanded, as if by a miracle, reveals – in the far distance, across the Sea there! – Naples with its Islands, and Vesuvius spouting fire. Within a quarter of an hour, the whole is gone as if it were a vision in the clouds, and there is nothing but the sea and sky.

The Neapolitan Frontier crossed, after two hours' travelling; and the hungriest of soldiers and custom-house officers with difficulty appeased; we enter, by a gateless portal, into the first Neapolitan town – Fondi. Take note of Fondi, in the name of all that is wretched and beggarly.

A filthy channel of mud and refuse meanders down the centre of the miserable street: fed by obscene rivulets that trickle from the abject houses. There is not a door, a window, or a shutter; not a roof, a wall, a post, or a pillar, in all Fondi, but is decayed, and crazy, and rotting away. The wretched history of the town, with all its sieges and pillages by Barbarossa [80] and the rest, might have been acted last year.

How the gaunt dogs that sneak about the miserable street, come to be alive, and undevoured by the people, is one of the enigmas of the world.

A hollow-cheeked and scowling people they are! All beggars; but that's nothing. Look at them as they gather round. Some, are too indolent to come down stairs, or are too wisely mistrustful of the stairs, perhaps, to venture: so stretch out their lean hands from upper windows, and howl; others, come flocking about us, fighting and jostling one another, and demanding, incessantly, charity for the love of God, charity for the love of the Blessed Virgin, charity for the love of all the Saints. A group of miserable children, almost naked, screaming forth the same petition, discover that they can see themselves reflected in the varnish of the carriage, and begin to dance and make grimaces, that they may have the pleasure of seeing their antics repeated in this mirror. A crippled idiot, in the act of striking one of them who drowns his clamorous demand for charity, observes his angry counterpart in the panel, stops short, and thrusting out his tongue, begins to wag his head and chatter. The shrill cry raised at this, awakens half a dozen wild creatures wrapped in frowsy brown cloaks, who are lying on the church-steps with pots and pans for sale. These, scrambling up, approach, and beg defiantly. 'I am hungry. Give me something. Listen to me Signore. I am hungry!' Then, a ghastly old woman, fearful of being too late, comes hobbling down the street, stretching out one hand, and scratching herself all the way with the other, and screaming, long before she can be heard, 'Charity, charity! I'll go and pray for you directly, beautiful lady, if you'll give me charity!' Lastly, the members of a brotherhood for burying the dead: hideously masked, and attired in shabby black robes, white at the skirts, with the splashes of many muddy winters: escorted by a dirty priest, and a congenial Cross-Bearer: come hurrying past. Surrounded by this motley concourse, we move out of Fondi: bad bright eyes glaring at us, out of the darkness of every crazy tenement, like glistening fragments of its filth and putrefaction.

A noble mountain-pass, with the ruins of a fort on a strong eminence, traditionally called the Fort of Fra Diavolo; the old town of Itri, like a device in pastry, built up, almost perpendicularly, on a hill, and approached by long steep flights of steps; beautiful Mola di Gaëta, whose wines, like those of Albano, have degenerated since the days of Horace, or his taste for wine was bad: which is not likely of one who enjoyed it so much, and extolled it so well; another night upon the road at St. Agata; a rest next day at Capua, which is picturesque but hardly so seductive to a traveller now, as the soldiers of Prætorian Rome were wont to find the ancient city of that name; a flat road among vines festooned and looped from tree to tree; and Mount Vesuvius close at hand at last! – its cone and summit whitened with snow; and its smoke hanging over it, in the heavy atmosphere of the day, like a dense cloud. So we go, rattling down-hill, into Naples.

A funeral is coming up the street, towards us. The body, on an open bier, borne on a kind of palanquin, covered with a gay cloth of crimson and gold. The mourners, in white gowns and masks. If there be death abroad, life is well represented too, for all Naples would seem to be out of doors, and tearing to and fro in carriages. Some of these, the common Vetturino vehicles, are drawn by three horses abreast, decked with smart trappings and great abundance of brazen ornament, and always going very fast. Not that their loads are light; for the smallest of them has at least six people inside, four in front, four or five more hanging on behind, and two or three more, in a net or bag below the axle-tree, where they lie half-suffocated with mud and dust. Exhibitors of Punch, buffo singers with guitars, reciters of poetry, reciters of stories, a row of cheap exhibitions with clowns and showmen, drums, and trumpets, painted cloths representing the wonders within, and admiring crowds assembled without, assist the whirl and bustle. Ragged lazzaroni lie asleep in doorways, archways, and kennels; the gentry, gaily dressed, are dashing up and down in carriages on the Chiaja, or walking in the Public Gardens; and quiet letter-writers, perched behind their little desks and inkstands under the Portico of the Great Theatre of San Carlo, in the public street, are waiting for clients.

Here is a Galley-slave in chains, who wants a letter written to a friend. He approaches a clerkly-looking man, sitting under the corner arch, and makes his bargain. He has obtained permission of the Sentinel who guards him: who stands near, leaning against the wall and cracking nuts. The Galley-slave dictates in the ear of the letter-writer, what he desires to say; and as he can't read writing, looks intently in his face, to read there whether he sets down faithfully what he is told. After a time, the Galley-slave becomes discursive – incoherent. The Secretary pauses and rubs his chin. The Galley-slave is voluble and energetic. The Secretary, at length, catches the idea, and with the air of a man who knows how to word it, sets it down; stopping, now and then, to glance back at his text admiringly. The Galley-slave is silent. The Soldier stoically cracks his nuts. Is there anything more to say? inquires the letter-writer. No more. Then listen, friend of mine. He reads it through. The Galley-slave is quite enchanted. It is folded, and addressed, and given to him, and he pays the fee. The Secretary falls back indolently in his chair, and takes a book. The Galley-slave gathers up an empty sack. The Sentinel throws away a handful of nut-shells, shoulders his musket, and away they go together.

Why do the beggars rap their chins constantly, with their right hands, when you look at them? Everything is done in pantomime in Naples, and that is the conventional sign for hunger. A man who is quarrelling with another, yonder, lays the palm of his right hand on the back of his left, and shakes the two thumbs – expressive of a donkey's ears – whereat his adversary is goaded to desperation. Two people bargaining for fish, the buyer empties an imaginary waistcoat pocket

THE FISHMARKET AT NAPLES

J. D. Harding

when he is told the price, and walks away without a word: having thoroughly conveyed to the seller that he considers it too dear. Two people in carriages, meeting, one touches his lips, twice or thrice, holds up the five fingers of his right hand, and gives a horizontal cut in the air with the palm. The other nods briskly, and goes his way. He has been invited to a friendly dinner at half-past five o'clock, and will certainly come.

All over Italy, a peculiar shake of the right hand from the wrist, with the fore-finger stretched out, expresses a negative – the only negative beggars will ever understand. But, in Naples, those five fingers are a copious language.

All this, and every other kind of out-door life and stir, and maccaroni-eating at Sunset, and flower-selling all day long, and begging and stealing everywhere and at all hours, you see upon the bright sea-shore, where the waves of the Bay sparkle merrily. But, lovers and hunters of the picturesque, let us not keep too studiously out of view, the miserable depravity, degradation, and wretchedness, with which this gay Neapolitan life is inseparably associated! It is not well to find Saint Giles's so repulsive, and the Porta Capuana so attractive. A pair of naked legs and a ragged red scarf, do not make *all* the difference between what is interesting and what is coarse and odious? Painting and poetising for ever, if you will, the beauties of this most beautiful and lovely spot of earth, let us, as our duty, try to associate a new picturesque with some faint recognition of man's destiny and capabilities; more hopeful, I believe, among the ice and snow of the North Pole, than in the sun and bloom of Naples.

Capri – once made odious by the deified beast Tiberius[81] – Ischia, Procida, and the thousand distant beauties of the Bay, lie in the blue sea yonder, changing in the mist and sunshine twenty times a day: now close at hand, now far off, now unseen. The fairest country in the world, is spread about us. Whether we turn towards the Miseno shore of the splendid watery amphitheatre, and go by the Grotto of Posilipo to the Grotto del Cane and away to Baiæ: or take the other way, towards Vesuvius and Sorrento, it is one succession of delights. In the last-named direction, where, over doors and archways, there are countless little images of San Gennaro, with his Canute's [82] hand stretched out, to check the fury of the Burning Mountain, we are carried pleasantly, by a railroad on the beautiful Sea Beach, past the town of Torre del Greco, built upon the ashes of the former town destroyed by an eruption of Vesuvius, within a hundred years; and past the flat-roofed houses, granaries, and maccaroni manufactories; to Castel-a-Mare, with its ruined castle, now inhabited by fishermen, standing in the sea upon a heap of rocks. Here, the railroad terminates; but, hence we may ride on, by an un-broken succession of enchanting bays, and beautiful scenery, sloping from the highest summit of Saint Angelo, the highest neighbouring mountain, down to the water's edge – among vineyards, olive trees, gardens of oranges and lemons, orchards, heaped-up rocks, green gorges in the hills – and by the bases of snow-covered heights, and through small towns with handsome, dark-haired women at the doors – and pass delicious summer villas – to Sorrento, where the Poet Tasso drew his inspiration from the beauty surrounding him. Returning, we may climb the heights above Castel-a-Mare, and looking down among the boughs and leaves, see the crisp water glistening in the sun; and clusters of white houses in distant Naples, dwindling, in the great extent of prospect, down to dice. The coming back to the city, by the beach again, at sunset: with the glowing sea on one side, and the darkening mountain, with its smoke and flame, upon the other: is a sublime conclusion to the glory of the day.

That church by the Porta Capuana – near the old fisher-market in the dirtiest quarter of dirty Naples where the revolt of Massaniello [83] began – is memorable for having been the scene of one of his earliest proclamations to the people, and is particularly remarkable for nothing else, unless it be

its waxen and bejewelled Saint in a glass case, with two odd
hands; or the enormous number of beggars who are constantly rapping their chins there, like a battery of castanets.
The Cathedral with the beautiful door, and the columns of
African and Egyptian granite that once ornamented the
temple of Apollo, contains the famous sacred blood of San
Gennaro or Januarius: which is preserved in two phials in a
silver tabernacle, and miraculously liquefies three times a
year, to the great admiration of the people. At the same
moment, the stone (distant some miles) where the Saint
suffered martyrdom, becomes faintly red. It is said that the
officiating priests turn faintly red also, sometimes, when these
miracles occur.

The old, old men who live in hovels at the entrance of
these ancient catacombs, and who, in their age and infirmity,
seem waiting here, to be buried themselves, are members of
a curious body, called the Royal Hospital, who are the official
attendants at funerals. Two of these old spectres totter away,
with lighted tapers, to shew the caverns of death – as un-
concerned as if they were immortal. They were used as
burying-places for three hundred years; and, in one part, is a
large pit full of skulls and bones, said to be the sad remains of
a great mortality occasioned by a plague. In the rest, there is
nothing but dust. They consist, chiefly, of great wide corridors and labyrinths, hewn out of the rock. At the end of
some of these long passages, are unexpected glimpses of the
daylight, shining down from above. It looks as ghastly and
as strange: among the torches, and the dust, and the dark
vaults: as if it, too, were dead and buried.

The present burial-place lies out yonder, on a hill between
the city and Vesuvius. The old Campo Santo with its three
hundred and sixty-five pits, is only used for those who
die in hospitals, and prisons, and are unclaimed by their
friends. The graceful new cemetery, at no great distance
from it, though yet unfinished, has already many graves
among its shrubs and flowers, and airy colonnades. It might

be reasonably objected elsewhere, that some of the tombs are meretricious and too fanciful; but the general brightness seems to justify it here; and Mount Vesuvius separated from them by a lovely slope of ground, exalts and saddens the scene.

If it be solemn to behold from this new City of the Dead, with its dark smoke hanging in the clear sky, how much more awful and impressive is it, viewed from the ghostly ruins of Herculaneum[84] and Pompeii!

Stand at the bottom of the great market-place of Pompeii, and look up the silent streets, through the ruined temples of Jupiter and Isis, over the broken houses with their inmost sanctuaries open to the day, away to Mount Vesuvius, bright and snowy in the peaceful distance; and lose all count of time, and heed of other things, in the strange and melancholy sensation of seeing the Destroyed and the Destroyer making this quiet picture in the sun. Then, ramble on, and see, at every turn, the little familiar tokens of human habitation and every-day pursuits; the chafing of the bucket-rope in the stone rim of the exhausted well; the track of carriage-wheels in the pavement of the street; the marks of drinking-vessels on the stone counter of the wineshop; the Amphoræ in private cellars, stored away so many hundred years ago, and undisturbed to this hour – all rendering the solitude and deadly lonesomeness of the place, ten thousand times more solemn, than if the volcano, in its fury, had swept the city from the earth, and sunk it in the bottom of the sea.

After it was shaken by the earthquake which preceded the eruption, workmen were employed in shaping out, in stone, new ornaments for temples and other buildings that had suffered. Here lies their work, outside the city gate, as if they would return to-morrow.

In the cellar of Diomede's house, where certain skeletons were found huddled together, close to the door, the impression of their bodies on the ashes, hardened with the ashes, and became stamped and fixed there, after they had shrunk, inside, to scanty bones. So, in the theatre of Herculaneum, a comic mask, floating on the stream when it was hot and liquid, stamped its mimic features in it as it hardened into stone; and now, it turns upon the stranger the fantastic look it turned upon the audiences in that same Theatre, two thousand years ago.

Next to the wonder of going up and down the streets, and in and out of the houses, and traversing the secret chambers of the temples of a religion that has vanished from the earth, and finding so many fresh traces of remote antiquity: as if the course of Time had been stopped after this desolation, and there had been no nights and days, months, years, and centuries, since: nothing is more impressive and terrible than the many evidences of the searching nature of the ashes, as bespeaking their irresistible power, and the impossibility of escaping them. In the wine-cellars, they forced their way into the earthen vessels: displacing the wine and choking them, to the brim, with dust. In the tombs, they forced the ashes of the dead from the funeral urns, and rained new ruin even into them. The mouths, and eyes, and skulls of all the skeletons, were stuffed with this terrible hail. In Herculaneum, where the flood was of a different and a heavier kind, it rolled in, like a sea. Imagine a deluge of water turned to marble, at its height – and that is what is called 'the lava' here.

Some workmen were digging the gloomy well on the brink of which we now stand, looking down, when they came on some of the stone benches of the Theatre – those steps (for such they seem) at the bottom of the excavation – and found the buried city of Herculaneum. Presently going down, with lighted torches, we are perplexed by great walls of monstrous thickness, rising up between the benches, shutting out the stage, obtruding their shapeless forms in absurd places, confusing the whole plan, and making it a disordered dream. We cannot, at first, believe, or picture to ourselves, that THIS came rolling in, and drowned the city; and that all that is not here, has been cut away, by the axe, like solid stone. But this perceived and understood, the horror and oppression of its presence are indescribable.

Many of the paintings on the walls in the roofless chambers of both cities, or carefully removed to the museum at Naples, are as fresh and plain, as if they had been executed yesterday. Here, are subjects of still life, as provisions, dead game, bottles, glasses, and the like; familiar classical stories, or mythological fables, always forcibly and plainly told; conceits of cupids, quarrelling, sporting, working at trades; theatrical rehearsals; poets reading their productions to their friends; inscriptions chalked upon the walls; political squibs, advertisements, rough drawings by schoolboys; everything to people and restore the ancient cities, in the fancy of their wondering visiter. Furniture, too, you see, of every kind – lamps, tables, couches; vessels for eating, drinking, and cooking; workmen's tools, surgical instruments, tickets for the theatre, pieces of money, personal ornaments, bunches of keys found clenched in the grasp of skeletons, helmets of guards and warriors; little household bells, yet musical with their old domestic tones.

The least among these objects lends its aid to swell the interest of Vesuvius, and invest it with a perfect fascination. The looking, from either ruined city, into the neighbouring grounds overgrown with beautiful vines and luxuriant trees; and remembering that house upon house, temple on temple, building after building, and street after street, are still lying underneath the roots of all the quiet cultivation, waiting to be turned up to the light of day; is something so wonderful, so full of mystery, so captivating to the imagination, that one would think it would be paramount, and yield to nothing else. To nothing but Vesuvius; but the mountain is the genius of the scene. From every indication of the ruin it has worked, we look, again, with an absorbing interest to where its smoke is rising up into the sky. It is beyond us, as we thread the ruined streets: above us, as we stand upon the

STREET OF THE TOMBS, POMPEII

Samuel Palmer

ruined walls; we follow it through every vista of broken columns, as we wander through the empty court-yards of the houses; and through the garlandings and interlacings of every wanton vine. Turning away to Pæstum yonder, to see the awful structures built, the least aged of them, hundreds of years before the birth of Christ, and standing yet, erect in lonely majesty, upon the wild, malaria-blighted plain – we watch Vesuvius as it disappears from the prospect, and watch for it again, on our return, with the same thrill of interest: as the doom and destiny of all this beautiful country, biding its terrible time.

It is very warm in the sun, on this early spring-day, when we return from Pæstum, but very cold in the shade: insomuch that although we may lunch, pleasantly, at noon, in the open air, by the gate of Pompeii, the neighbouring rivulet supplies thick ice for our wine. But, the sun is shining brightly; there is not a cloud or speck of vapour in the whole blue sky, looking down upon the bay of Naples; and the moon will be at the full to-night. No matter that the snow and ice lie thick upon the summit of Vesuvius, or that we have been on foot all day at Pompeii, or that croakers maintain that strangers should not be on the mountain by night, in such an unusual season. Let us take advantage of the fine weather; make the best of our way to Resina, the little village at the foot of the mountain; prepare ourselves, as well as we can, on so short a notice, at the Guide's house; ascend at once, and have sunset half-way up, moonlight at the top, and midnight to come down in!

At four o'clock in the afternoon, there is a terrible uproar in the little stable-yard of Signor Salvatore the recognised head-guide with the gold band round his cap; and thirty under-guides who are all scuffling and screaming at once, are preparing half a dozen saddled ponies, three litters, and some stout staves, for the journey. Every one of the thirty, quarrels with the other twenty-nine, and frightens the six ponies; and as much of the village as can possibly squeeze itself into the little stable-yard, participates in the tumult, and gets trodden on by the cattle.

After much violent skirmishing, and more noise than would suffice for the storming of Naples, the procession starts. The head-guide, who is liberally paid for all the attendants, rides a little in advance of the party; the other thirty guides proceed by foot. Eight go forward with the litters that are to be used by and by; and the remaining two-and-twenty beg.

We ascend, gradually, by stony lanes like rough broad flights of stairs, for some time. At length, we leave these, and the vineyards on either side of them, and emerge upon a bleak bare region where the lava lies confusedly, in enormous rusty masses: as if the earth had been ploughed up by burning thunderbolts. And now, we halt to see the sun set. The change that falls upon the dreary region, and on the whole mountain, as its red light fades, and the night comes on – and the unutterable solemnity and dreariness that reign around, who that has witnessed it, can ever forget!

It is dark, when after winding, for some time, over the broken ground, we arrive at the foot of the cone: which is extremely steep, and seems to rise, almost perpendicularly, from the spot where we dismount. The only light is reflected from the snow, deep, hard, and white, with which the cone is covered. It is now intensely cold, and the air is piercing. The thirty-one have brought no torches, knowing that the moon will rise before we reach the top. Two of the litters are devoted to the two ladies; the third, to a rather heavy gentleman from Naples, whose hospitality and good-nature have attached him to the expedition, and determined him to assist in doing the honours of the mountain. The rather heavy gentleman is carried by fifteen men; each of the ladies by half a dozen. We who walk, make the best use of our staves; and so the whole party begin to labour upward over the snow, – as if they were toiling to the summit of an ante-diluvian Twelfth-cake.

We are a long time toiling up; and the head-guide looks oddly about him when one of the company – not an Italian, though an habitué of the mountain for many years: whom we will call, for our present purpose, Mr. Pickle of Portici – suggests that, as it is freezing hard, and the usual footing of ashes is covered by the snow and ice, it will surely be difficult to descend. But the sight of the litters above, tilting up, and down, and jerking from this side to that, as the bearers continually slip and stumble, diverts our attention: more especially as the whole length of the rather heavy gentleman is, at that moment, presented to us alarmingly foreshortened, with his head downwards.

The rising of the moon soon afterwards, revives the flagging spirits of the Bearers. Stimulating each other with their usual watchword, 'Courage friend! It is to eat Maccaroni!' they press on, gallantly, for the summit.

From tinging the top of the snow above us, with a band of light, and pouring it in a stream through the valley below, while we have been ascending in the dark, the moon soon lights the whole white mountain side, and the broad sea down below, and tiny Naples in the distance, and every village in the country round. The whole prospect is in this lovely state, when we come upon the platform on the mountain-top – the region of Fire – an exhausted crater formed of great masses of gigantic cinders, like blocks of stone from some tremendous waterfall, burnt up; from every chink and crevice of which, hot, sulphurous smoke is pouring out: while, from another conical-shaped hill, the present crater, rising abruptly from this platform at the end, great sheets of fire are streaming forth: reddening the night with flame, blackening it with smoke, and spotting it with red-hot stones and cinders, that fly up into the air like feathers, and fall down like lead. What words can paint the gloom and grandeur of this scene!

The broken ground; the smoke; the sense of suffocation from the sulphur; the fear of falling down through the crevices in the yawning ground; the stopping, every now and then, for somebody who is missing in the dark (for the dense smoke now obscures the moon); the intolerable noise of the thirty; and the hoarse roaring of the mountain; make it a scene of such confusion, at the same time, that we reel again. But, dragging the ladies through it, and across another exhausted crater to the foot of the present Volcano, we approach close to it on the windy side, and then sit down among the hot ashes at its foot, and look up in silence; faintly estimating the action that is going on within, from its being full a hundred feet higher, at this minute, than it was six weeks ago.

There is something in the fire and roar, that generates an irresistible desire to get nearer to it. We cannot rest long, without starting off, two of us, on our hands and knees, accompanied by the head-guide, to climb to the brim of the flaming crater, and try to look in. Meanwhile, the thirty yell, as with one voice, that it is a dangerous proceeding, and call to us to come back; frightening the rest of the party out of their wits.

What with their noise, and what with the trembling of the thin crust of ground, that seems about to open underneath our feet and plunge us in the burning gulf below (which is the real danger, if there be any); and what with the flashing of the fire in our faces, and the shower of red-hot ashes that is raining down, and the choking smoke and sulphur; we may well feel giddy and irrational, like drunken men. But, we contrive to climb up to the brim, and look down, for a moment, into the Hell of boiling fire below. Then, we all three come rolling down; blackened, and singed, and scorched, and hot, and giddy: and each with his dress alight in half a dozen places.

You have read, a thousand times, that the usual way of descending, is, by sliding down the ashes: which, forming a gradually increasing ledge below the feet, prevent too rapid a descent. But, when we have crossed the two exhausted craters on our way back, and are come to this precipitous place, there is (as Mr. Pickle has foretold) no vestige of ashes to be seen; the whole being a smooth sheet of ice.

In this dilemma, ten or a dozen of the guides cautiously join hands, and make a chain of men; of whom the foremost beat, as well as they can, a rough track with their sticks, down which we prepare to follow. The way being fearfully steep, and none of the party: even of the thirty: being able to keep their feet for six paces together, the ladies are taken out of their litters, and placed, each between two careful persons; while others of the thirty hold by their skirts, to prevent their falling forward – a necessary precaution, tending to the immediate and hopeless dilapidation of their apparel. The rather heavy gentleman is adjured to leave his litter too, and be escorted in a similar manner; but he resolves to be brought down as he was brought up, on the principle that his fifteen bearers are not likely to tumble all at once, and that he is safer so, than trusting to his own legs.

In this order, we begin the descent: sometimes on foot, sometimes shuffling on the ice: always proceeding much more quietly and slowly, than on our upward way: and constantly alarmed by the falling among us of somebody from behind, who endangers the footing of the whole party, and clings pertinaciously to anybody's ankles. It is impossible for the litter to be in advance, too, as the track has to be made; and its appearance behind us, overhead – with some one or other of the bearers always down, and the rather heavy gentleman with his legs always in the air – is very threatening and frightful. We have gone on thus, a very little way, painfully and anxiously, but quite merrily, and regarding it as a great success – and have all fallen several times, and have all been stopped, somehow or other, as we were sliding away – when Mr. Pickle, of Portici, in the act of remarking on these uncommon circumstances as quite beyond his experience, stumbles, falls, disengages himself, with quick presence of mind, from those about him, plunges away head foremost, and rolls, over and over, down the whole surface of the cone!

Sickening as it is to look, and be so powerless to help him, I see him there, in the moonlight – I have had such a dream often – skimming over the white ice, like a cannon-ball. Almost at the same moment, there is a cry from behind; and a man who has carried a light basket of spare cloaks on his head, comes rolling past, at the same frightful speed, closely followed by a boy. At this climax of the chapter of accidents, the remaining eight-and-twenty vociferate to that degree, that a pack of wolves would be music to them!

Giddy, and bloody, and a mere bundle of rags, is Pickle of Portici when we reach the place where we dismounted, and where the horses are waiting; but, thank God, sound in limb! And never are we likely to be more glad to see a man alive and on his feet, than to see him now – making light of it too, though sorely bruised and in great pain. The boy is brought into the Hermitage on the Mountain, while we are at supper, with his head tied up; and the man is heard of, some hours afterwards. He too is bruised and stunned, but has broken no bones; the snow having, fortunately, covered all the larger blocks of rock and stone, and rendered them harmless.

After a cheerful meal, and a good rest before a blazing fire, we again take horse, and continue our descent to Salvatore's house – very slowly, by reason of our bruised friend being hardly able to keep the saddle, or endure the pain of motion. Though it is so late at night, or early in the morning, all the people of the village are waiting about the little stable-yard when we arrive, and looking up the road by which we are expected. Our appearance is hailed with a great clamour of tongues, and a general sensation for which in our modesty we are somewhat at a loss to account, until, turning into the yard, we find that one of a party of French gentlemen who were on the mountain at the same time is lying on some straw in the stable, with a broken limb: looking like Death, and suffering great torture; and that we were confidently supposed to have encountered some worse accident.

So 'well returned, and Heaven be praised!' as the cheerful Vetturíno, who has borne us company all the way from Pisa, says, with all his heart! And away with his ready horses, into sleeping Naples!

It wakes again to Policinelli and pickpockets, buffo singers and beggars, rags, puppets, flowers, brightness, dirt, and universal degradation; airing its Harlequin suit in the sunshine, next day and every day; singing, starving, dancing, gaming, on the sea-shore; and leaving all labour to the burning mountain, which is ever at its work.

Our English dilettanti would be very pathetic on the subject of the national taste, if they could hear an Italian opera half as badly sung in England as we may hear the Foscari performed, to-night, in the splendid theatre of San Carlo. But, for astonishing truth and spirit in seizing and embodying the real life about it, the shabby little San Carlino Theatre – the ricketty house one story high, with a staring picture outside: down among the drums and trumpets, and the tumblers, and the lady conjuror – is without a rival anywhere.

There is one extraordinary feature in the real life of Naples, at which we may take a glance before we go – the Lotteries.

They prevail in most parts of Italy, but are particularly obvious, in their effects and influences, here. They are drawn every Saturday. They bring an immense revenue to the Government; and diffuse a taste for gambling among the poorest of the poor, which is very comfortable to the coffers of the state, and very ruinous to themselves. The lowest stake is one grain; less than a farthing. One hundred numbers – from one to a hundred, inclusive – are put into a box. Five are drawn. Those are the prizes. I buy three numbers. If one of them come up, I win a small prize. If two, some hundreds of times my stake. If three, three thousand five hundred times my stake. I stake (or play as they call it) what I can upon my numbers, and buy what numbers I please. The amount I play,

I pay at the lottery office, where I purchase the ticket; and it is stated on the ticket itself.

Every lottery office keeps a printed book, an Universal Lottery Diviner, where every possible accident and circumstance is provided for, and has a number against it. For instance, let us stake two carlini – about sevenpence. On our way to the lottery office, we run against a black man. When we get there, we say gravely, 'The Diviner.' It is handed over the counter, as a serious matter of business. We look at black man. Such a number. 'Give us that.' We look at running against a person in the street. 'Give us that.' We look at the name of the street itself. 'Give us that.' Now, we have our three numbers.

If the roof of the theatre of San Carlo were to fall in, so many people would play upon the numbers attached to such an accident in the Diviner, that the Government would soon close those numbers, and decline to run the risk of losing any more upon them. This often happens. Not long ago, when there was a fire in the King's Palace, there was such a desperate run on fire, and king, and palace, that further stakes on the numbers attached to those words in the Golden Book were forbidden. Every accident or event, is supposed, by the ignorant populace, to be a revelation to the beholder, or party concerned, in connexion with the lottery. Certain people who have a talent for dreaming fortunately, are much sought after; and there are some priests who are constantly favoured with visions of the lucky numbers.

I heard of a horse running away with a man, and dashing him down, dead, at the corner of a street. Pursuing the horse with incredible speed, was another man, who ran so fast, that he came up, immediately after the accident. He threw himself upon his knees beside the unfortunate rider, and clasped his hand with an expression of the wildest grief. 'If you have life,' he said, 'speak one word to me! If you have one gasp of breath left, mention your age for Heaven's sake, that I may play that number in the lottery.'

It is four o'clock in the afternoon, and we may go to see our lottery drawn. The ceremony takes place, every Saturday, in the Tribunale, or Court of Justice – this singular, earthy-smelling room, or gallery, as mouldy as an old cellar, and as damp as a dungeon. At the upper end, is a platform, with a large horse-shoe table upon it; and a President and Council sitting round – all Judges of the Law. The man on the little stool behind the President, is the Capo Lazzarone, a kind of tribune of the people, appointed on their behalf to see that all is fairly conducted: attended by a few personal friends. A ragged, swarthy fellow he is: with long matted hair hanging down all over his face: and covered, from head to foot, with most unquestionably genuine dirt. All the body of the room is filled with the commonest of the Neapolitan people: and between them and the platform, guarding the steps leading to the latter, is a small body of soldiers.

There is some delay in the arrival of the necessary number of judges; during which, the box, in which the numbers are being placed, is a source of the deepest interest. When the box is full, the boy who is to draw the numbers out of it, becomes the prominent feature of the proceedings. He is already dressed for his part, in a tight brown Holland-coat, with only one (the left) sleeve to it, which leaves his right arm bared to the shoulder, ready for plunging down into the mysterious chest.

During the hush and whisper that pervade the room, all eyes are turned on this young minister of fortune. People begin to inquire his age, with a view to the next lottery; and the number of his brothers and sisters; and the age of his father and mother; and whether he has any moles or pimples upon him; and where, and how many; when the arrival of the last judge but one (a little old man, universally dreaded as possessing the Evil Eye) makes a slight diversion, and would occasion a greater one, but that he is immediately deposed, as a source of interest, by the officiating priest, who advances gravely to his place, followed by a very dirty little boy, carrying his sacred vestments, and a pot of Holy Water.

Here is the last judge come at last, and now he takes his place at the horse-shoe table!

There is a murmur of irrepressible agitation. In the midst of it, the priest puts his head into the sacred vestments, and pulls the same over his shoulders. Then he says a silent prayer; and, dipping a brush into the pot of Holy Water, sprinkles it over the box and over the boy, and gives them·a double-barrelled blessing, which the box and the boy are both hoisted on the table to receive. The boy remaining on the table, the box is now carried round the front of the platform, by an attendant, who holds it up and shakes it lustily all the time; seeming to say, like the conjuror, 'There is no deception, ladies and gentlemen; keep your eyes upon me, if you please!'

At last, the box is set before the boy; and the boy, first holding up his naked arm and open hand, dives down into the hole (it is made like a ballot-box) and pulls out a number, which is rolled up, round something hard, like a bonbon. This he hands to the Judge next him, who unrolls a little bit, and hands it to the President, next to whom he sits. The President unrolls it, very slowly. The Capo Lazzarone leans over his shoulder. The President holds it up, unrolled, to the Capo Lazzarone. The Capo Lazzarone, looking at it eagerly, cries out, in a shrill voice, 'Sessanta-due!' (sixty-two), expressing the two upon his fingers, as he calls it out. Alas! the Capo Lazzarone himself has not staked on sixty-two. His face is very long, and his eyes roll wildly.

As it happens to be a favourite number, however, it is pretty well received, which is not always the case. They are all drawn with the same ceremony, omitting the blessing. One blessing is enough for the whole multiplication-table. The only new incident in the proceedings, is the gradually deepening intensity of the change in the Capo Lazzarone, who has, evidently, speculated to the very utmost extent of

his means; and who, when he sees the last number, and finds
that it is not one of his, clasps his hands, and raises his eyes
to the ceiling before proclaiming it, as though remonstrating,
in a secret agony, with his patron saint, for having committed
so gross a breach of confidence. I hope the Capo Lazzarone
may not desert him for some other member of the Calendar,
but he seems to threaten it.

Where the winners may be, nobody knows. They certainly
are not present; the general disappointment filling one with
pity for the poor people. They look: when we stand aside,
observing them, in their passage through the court-yard
down below: as miserable as the prisoners in the jail (it
forms a part of the building), who are peeping down upon
them, from between their bars; or, as the fragments of
human heads which are still dangling in chains outside, in
memory of the good old times, when their owners were
strung up there, for the popular edification.

Away from Naples in a glorious sunrise, by the road to
Capua, and then on a three days' journey along bye-roads,
that we may see, on the way, the monastery of Monte
Cassino, which is perched on the steep and lofty hill above
the little town of San Germano, and is lost on a misty morning
in the clouds.

So much the better, for the deep sounding of its bell, which,
as we go winding up, on mules, towards the convent, is
heard mysteriously in the still air, while nothing is seen but
the grey mist, moving solemnly and slowly, like a funeral
procession. Behold, at length, the shadowy pile of building
close before us: its grey walls and towers dimly seen, though
so near and so vast: and the raw vapour rolling through its
cloisters heavily.

There are two black shadows walking to and fro in the
quadrangle, near the statues of the Patron Saint and his
sister; and hopping on behind them, in and out of the old
arches, is a raven, croaking in answer to the bell, and uttering,
at intervals, the purest Tuscan. How like a Jesuit he looks!

There never was a sly and stealthy fellow so at home as is this raven, standing now at the refectory door, with his head on one side, and pretending to glance another way, while he is scrutinizing the visiters keenly, and listening with fixed attention. What a dull-headed monk the porter becomes in comparison!

'He speaks like us!' says the porter: 'quite as plainly.' Quite as plainly, Porter. Nothing could be more expressive than his reception of the peasants who are entering the gate with baskets and burdens. There is a roll in his eye, and a chuckle in his throat, which should qualify him to be chosen Superior of an Order of Ravens. He knows all about it. 'It's all right,' he says. 'We know what we know. Come along, good people. Glad to see you!'

How was this extraordinary structure ever built in such a situation, where the labour of conveying the stone, and iron, and marble, so great a height must have been prodigious? 'Caw!' says the raven, welcoming the peasants. How, being despoiled by plunder, fire, and earthquake, has it risen from its ruins, and been again made what we now see it, with its church so sumptuous and magnificent? 'Caw!' says the raven, welcoming the peasants. These people have a miserable appearance, and (as usual) are densely ignorant, and all beg, while the monks are chaunting in the chapel. 'Caw!' says the raven, 'Cuckoo!'

So we leave him, chuckling and rolling his eye at the convent gate, and wind slowly down again, through the cloud. At last emerging from it, we come in sight of the village far below, and the flat green country intersected by rivulets; which is pleasant and fresh to see after the obscurity and haze of the convent – no disrespect to the raven, or the holy friars.

Away we go again, by muddy roads, and through the most shattered and tattered of villages, where there is not a whole window among all the houses, or a whole garment among all the peasants, or the least appearance of anything to eat, in any of the wretched hucksters' shops. The women wear a bright red boddice laced before and behind, a white skirt, and the Neapolitan head-dress of square folds of linen, primitively meant to carry loads on. The men and children wear anything they can get. The soldiers are as dirty and rapacious as the dogs. The inns are such hobgoblin places, that they are infinitely more attractive and amusing than the best hotels in Paris. Here is one near Valmontone (that is Valmontone, the round, walled town on the mount opposite), which is approached by a quagmire almost knee-deep. There is a wild colonnade below, and a dark yard full of empty stables and lofts, and a great long kitchen with a great long bench and a great long form, where a party of travellers, with two priests among them, are crowding round the fire while their supper is cooking. Above the stairs, is a rough brick gallery to sit in, with very little windows with very small patches of knotty glass in them, and all the doors that open from it (a dozen or two) off their hinges, and a bare board on tressels for a table, at which thirty people might dine easily, and a fire-place large enough in itself for a break-fast parlour, where, as the faggots blaze and crackle, they illuminate the ugliest and grimmest of faces, drawn in char-coal on the whitewashed chimney-sides by previous travellers. There is a flaring country lamp on the table; and, hovering about it, scratching her thick black hair continually, a yellow dwarf of a woman, who stands on tiptoe to arrange the hatchet knives, and takes a flying leap to look into the water-jug. The beds in the adjoining rooms are of the liveliest kind. There is not a solitary scrap of looking-glass in the house, and the washing apparatus is identical with the cooking utensils. But the yellow dwarf sets on the table, a good flask of excellent wine, holding a quart at least; and produces, among half-a-dozen other dishes, two-thirds of a roasted kid, smoking hot. She is as good-humoured, too, as dirty, which is saying a great deal. So here's long life to her, in the flask of wine, and prosperity to the establishment!

Rome gained and left behind, and with it the Pilgrims who are now repairing to their own homes again – each with his scallop shell and staff, and soliciting alms for the love of God – we come, by a fair country, to the Falls of Terni, where the whole Velino river dashes, headlong, from a rocky height, amidst shining spray and rainbows. Perugia, strongly fortified by art and nature, on a lofty eminence, rising abruptly from the plain where purple mountains mingle with the distant sky, is glowing, on its market day, with radiant colours. They set off its sombre but rich Gothic buildings admirably. The pavement of its market-place is strewn with country goods. All along the steep hill leading from the town, under the town wall, there is a noisy fair of calves, lambs, pigs, horses, mules, and oxen. Fowls, geese, and turkeys, flutter vigorously among their very hoofs; and buyers, sellers, and spectators, clustering everywhere, block up the road as we come shouting down upon them.

Suddenly, there is a ringing sound among our horses. The driver stops them. Sinking in his saddle, and casting up his eyes to Heaven, he delivers this apostrophe, 'Oh Jove Omnipotent! here is a horse has lost his shoe!'

Notwithstanding the tremendous nature of this accident, and the utterly forlorn look and gesture (impossible in any one but an Italian Vetturíno) with which it is announced, it is not long in being repaired by a mortal Farrier, by whose assistance we reach Castiglione the same night, and Arezzo next day. Mass is, of course, performing in its fine Cathedral, where the sun shines in among the clustered pillars, through rich stained glass windows: half revealing, half concealing, the kneeling figures on the pavement, and striking out paths of spotted light in the long aisles.

But, how much beauty of another kind is here, when, on a fair clear morning, we look, from the summit of a hill, on Florence! See where it lies before us in a sun-lighted valley, bright with the winding Arno, and shut in by swelling hills; its domes, and towers, and palaces, rising from the rich country in a glittering heap, and shining in the sun like gold!

Magnificently stern and sombre are the streets of beautiful Florence; and the strong old piles of building make such heaps of shadow, on the ground and in the river, that there is another and a different city of rich forms and fancies, always lying at our feet. Prodigious palaces, constructed for defence, with small distrustful windows heavily barred, and walls of great thickness formed of huge masses of rough stone, frown, in their old sulky state, on every street. In the midst of the city – in the Piazza of the Grand Duke, adorned with beautiful statues and the Fountain of Neptune – rises the Palazzo Vecchio, with its enormous overhanging battlements, and the Great Tower that watches over the whole town. In its court-yard – worthy of the Castle of Otranto in its ponderous gloom – is a massive staircase that the heaviest waggon and the stoutest team of horses might be driven up. Within it, is a Great Saloon, faded and tarnished in its stately decorations, and mouldering by grains, but recording yet, in pictures on its walls, the triumphs of the Medici and the wars of the old Florentine people. The prison is hard by, in an adjacent court-yard of the building – a foul and dismal place, where some men are shut up close, in small cells like ovens; and where others look through bars and beg; where some are playing draughts, and some are talking to their friends, who smoke, the while, to purify the air; and some are buying wine and fruit of women-vendors; and all are squalid, dirty, and vile to look at. 'They are merry enough, Signore,' says the Jailer. 'They are all blood-stained here,' he adds, indicating, with his hand, three fourths of the whole building. Before the hour is out, an old man, eighty years of age, quarrelling over a bargain with a young girl of seventeen, stabs her dead, in the market-place full of bright flowers; and is brought in prisoner, to swell the number.

Among the four old bridges that span the river, the Ponte Vecchio – that bridge which is covered with the shops of

Jewellers and Goldsmiths – is a most enchanting feature in the scene. The space of one house, in the centre, being left open, the view beyond, is shown as in a frame; and that precious glimpse of sky, and water, and rich buildings, shining so quietly among the huddled roofs and gables on the bridge, is exquisite. Above it, the Gallery of the Grand Duke crosses the river. It was built to connect the two Great Palaces by a secret passage; and it takes its jealous course among the streets and houses, with true despotism: going where it lists, and spurning every obstacle away, before it.

The Grand Duke [85] has a worthier secret passage through the streets, in his black robe and hood, as a member of the Compagnia della Misericordia, which brotherhood includes all ranks of men. If an accident take place, their office is, to raise the sufferer, and bear him tenderly to the Hospital. If a fire break out, it is one of their functions to repair to the spot, and render their assistance and protection. It is, also, among their commonest offices, to attend and console the sick; and they neither receive money, nor eat, nor drink, in any house they visit for this purpose. Those who are on duty for the time, are called together, on a moment's notice, by the tolling of the great bell of the Tower; and it is said that the Grand Duke has been seen, at this sound, to rise from his seat at table, and quietly withdraw to attend the summons.

In this other large Piazza, where an irregular kind of market is held, and stores of old iron and other small merchandise are set out on stalls, or scattered on the pavement, are grouped together, the Cathedral with its great Dome, the beautiful Italian Gothic Tower the Campanile, and the Baptistry with its wrought bronze doors. And here, a small untrodden square in the pavement, is 'the Stone of DANTE,' [86] where (so runs the story) he was used to bring his stool, and sit in contemplation. I wonder was he ever, in his bitter exile, withheld from cursing the very stones in the streets of Florence the ungrateful, by any kind remembrance of this

FLORENCE
Samuel Palmer

old musing-place, and its association with gentle thoughts of little Beatrice!

The chapel of the Medici, the Good and Bad Angels of Florence; the church of Santa Croce where Michael Angelo lies buried, and where every stone in the cloisters is eloquent on great men's deaths; innumerable churches, often masses of unfinished heavy brickwork externally, but solemn and serene within; arrest our lingering steps, in strolling through the city.

In keeping with the tombs among the cloisters, is the Museum of Natural History, famous through the world for its preparations in wax; beginning with models of leaves, seeds, plants, inferior animals; and gradually ascending, through separate organs of the human frame, up to the whole structure of that wonderful creation, exquisitely presented, as in recent death. Few admonitions of our frail mortality can be more solemn, and more sad, or strike so home upon the heart, as the counterfeits of Youth and Beauty that are lying there, upon their beds, in their last sleep.

Beyond the walls, the whole sweet Valley of the Arno, the convent at Fiesole, the Tower of Galileo, Boccaccio's house, old villas and retreats; innumerable spots of interest, all glowing in a landscape of surpassing beauty steeped in the richest light; are spread before us. Returning from so much brightness, how solemn and how grand the streets again, with their great, dark, mournful palaces, and many legends: not of siege, and war, and might, and Iron Hand alone, but of the triumphant growth of peaceful Arts and Sciences.

What light is shed upon the world, at this day, from amidst these rugged Palaces of Florence! Here, open to all comers, in their beautiful and calm retreats, the ancient Sculptors are immortal, side by side with Michael Angelo, Canova, Titian, Rembrandt, Raphael, Poets, Historians, Philosophers – those illustrious men of history, beside whom its crowned heads and harnessed warriors, shew so poor and small, and are so soon forgotten. Here, the imperishable part of noble minds

survives, placid and equal, when strongholds of assault and
defence are overthrown; when the tyranny of the many, or
the few, or both, is but a tale; when Pride and Power are so
much cloistered dust. The fire within the stern streets, and
among the massive Palaces and Towers, kindled by rays from
Heaven, is still burning brightly, when the flickering of war
is extinguished and the household fires of generations have
decayed; as thousands upon thousands of faces, rigid with the
strife and passion of the hour, have faded out of the old
Squares and public haunts, while the nameless Florentine
Lady, preserved from oblivion by a Painter's hand, yet lives
on, in enduring grace and youth.

Let us look back on Florence while we may, and when its
shining Dome is seen no more, go travelling through cheerful Tuscany, with a bright remembrance of it; for Italy will
be the fairer for the recollection. The summer time being
come: and Genoa, and Milan, and the Lake of Como lying
far behind us: and we resting at Faido, a Swiss village, near
the awful rocks and mountains, the everlasting snows and
roaring cataracts, of the Great Saint Gothard: hearing the
Italian tongue for the last time on this journey: let us part
from Italy, with all its miseries and wrongs, affectionately,
in our admiration of the beauties, natural and artificial, of
which it is full to overflowing, and in our tenderness towards
a people, naturally well disposed, and patient, and sweet
tempered. Years of neglect, oppression, and misrule, have
been at work, to change their nature and reduce their spirit;
miserable jealousies, fomented by petty Princes to whom
union was destruction, and division strength, have been a
canker at the root of their nationality, and have barbarized
their language; but the good that was in them ever, is in them
yet, and a noble people may be, one day, raised up from these
ashes. Let us entertain that hope! And let us not remember
Italy the less regardfully, because, in every fragment of her
fallen Temples, and every stone of her deserted palaces and
prisons, she helps to inculcate the lesson that the wheel of

Time is rolling for an end, and
that the world is, in all great
essentials, better, gentler, more
forbearing, and more hopeful,
as it rolls!

THE END

A Note on the Text

PICTURES from Italy was first published as a single
octavo volume in early May 1846 by Bradbury and
Evans. By 30 June, 4911 of the original 6000 copies printed
had been sold and a second edition was prepared for distribu-
tion the same year.[1] Previously, about one third of the book
had appeared in the *Daily News* as 'Travelling Letters
Written on the Road' between January and March 1846:
'The Journey,' January 21; 'Lyons, the Rhone, and the
Goblin of Avignon,' January 24; 'Avignon to Genoa,'
January 31; 'A Retreat at Albaro,' February 9; 'First Sketch
of Genoa. The Streets, Shops, and Houses,' February 16;
'In Genoa,' February 26; 'In Genoa, and out of it,' March
22; and 'Piacenza to Bologna,' March 11. The manuscript
of a fragment of the seventh letter and the entire eighth
'Travelling Letter' are preserved in the Forster Collection
in the Victoria and Albert Museum.

In Dickens's lifetime there were two further important
editions of the complete text: volume XVII of the Library
Edition, advertised as being carefully revised by the author,
and volume XVI of the 1868 Charles Dickens Edition, with
the facsimile of Dickens's signature on the cover indicating
his 'present watchfulness over his own Edition'.

I have selected the 1846 edition of *Pictures from Italy*
as the copy-text for the present edition for two reasons. A
collation of the first edition with the 1859 and 1868 editions
reveals that despite the claims of the advertisements, there is
no evidence, in the case of *Pictures from Italy*, to suggest that
Dickens undertook a systematic revision of the text. There
are no departures from the original text in the actual words,

except for the correction of a few obvious errors, while the alteration of many of Dickens's idiosyncratic colons and semi-colons to commas suggests the work of a compositor. Secondly, when the complete manuscript is no longer extant, as is the case here, the first edition has the advantage of having been set directly from the lost manuscript; and, as Fredson Bowers argues, only this edition is likely to preserve in any authoritative manner such characteristics of the manuscript that have not been normalized by the printing-house style imposed on the copy.[2] The text of 1846, therefore, comes closest to Dickens's original intentions and it is reprinted here with no alterations or emendations. Where errors occur, they have been silently corrected.

Of more general interest are the textual changes Dickens made as he prepared the *Daily News* letters for publication in book form. Working from 'a little paste-board memorandum book with the few printed letters pasted in it' (I,748), Dickens rearranged and revised the letters to form a more coherent whole. Awkward and redundant phrases were eliminated, occasional French or Italian expressions were translated, and the point of view of the letters was systematically altered by dropping the pose of writing them on the road. Five of the letters were significantly expanded: sometimes two or three paragraphs were added, such as the passage describing the Cathedral at Avignon in Chapter Two; on other occasions a whole episode was appended, such as the description of the journey from Genoa to Marseilles and back in Chapter Four. There are only two instances of excisions: a conciliatory footnote in the sixth letter which softened Dickens's generally sharp remarks about the Catholic Church, and a description of a nun taking the black veil in the seventh letter.

Not surprisingly, Dickens's anti-clericalism was strongly censured by the Catholic *Dublin Review* (*see* xxi, September 1846, pp. 184–201). Generally, however, *Pictures from Italy* was free from the bitter animosity occasioned by the publication in 1842 of his first travel book, *American Notes*. The

Italians were not enraged – the book did not appear in Italy until 1879 – nor was there a critic of Macaulay's stature who declined to review the book, as the latter had done in the case of *American Notes*. Critical though Dickens's *Pictures* were, the consensus was that his tolerance for other countries had increased. Writing to Longfellow on June 3, 1845, Forster summed up this feeling when he remarked that Dickens's 'Italian travel has done him good everyway: and I half regret, now, that he had not seen Italy before he went to America'.[3]

1. These figures were kindly supplied to me by Robert L. Patten, who is currently studying the MS account books in the Forster Collection and those in the office of *Punch* Publications.

2. Fredson T. Bowers (ed.), 'A Preface to the Text,' *The Scarlet Letter*, The Centenary Edition of the Works of Nathaniel Hawthorne, 1 (Columbus, Ohio: State Unversity Press, 1962).

3. Forster, MS Letter to Longfellow, 5 June 1845, quoted by Ada C. Nisbet, 'The Mystery of *Martin Chuzzlewit*,' in *Essays Critical and Historical Dedicated to Lily B. Campbell*, University of California Publications English Studies: 1 (Berkeley and Los Angeles: University of California Press, 1950), 212.

Concerning the Original Illustrations

A MONG Dickens's wide circle of friends was the well-known landscape scenic artist Clarkson Stanfield, who had travelled extensively in Italy and illustrated some travel books. By 1846 he and Dickens had become close friends and he would therefore seem to have been the obvious choice as the illustrator of *Pictures from Italy*. Indeed, in a letter dated February 24, 1846 to Frederick Evans, the publisher of the book, which appeared some two months before the works' appearance, Dickens had written: 'I have seen Mr Stanfield on the subject of illustrations for the Travelling Letters; and we purpose having about twelve – "drawn on wood by George Stanfield from designs by Clarkson Stanfield, R.A." the first block to be ready a fortnight hence; the remainder to be furnished, two a week, until they are all done' (I, 737). How, then, did it come about that in spite of this affirmation it was not Stanfield who became the illustrator, but Samuel Palmer, then less well-known than Stanfield and unacquainted with Dickens until the question of the illustrations arose? The reason remains unknown, but there is, I think, one hypothesis which deserves consideration.

Writing of the group of Dickens's friends who were buried, by coincidence, at Kensal Green, Mr Leslie Staples mentions Stanfield 'who lies in the Roman Catholic portion of the cemetery.'[1] That Stanfield was Catholic is not particularly remarkable, but his religion may suggest a reason for the change of illustrators for *Pictures from Italy*. For he was not only a Catholic but also a close friend of Cardinal Wiseman, who was engaged in preparing English opinion for the restoration of the Catholic hierarchy, and this may have caused him to re-examine the consequences of illustrating *Pictures from Italy*. Stanfield was a well-known figure by the 1840s and he may have found himself unwilling to lend his name to a work which many Catholics would find grossly offensive. Furthermore, as an experienced observer of the Italian people, their countryside, and their classical past, Stanfield possibly found Dickens's 'pictures' with their emphasis on superstition, ignorance, and dirt very alien from his own impressions.

Since Dickens's 'shadows in the water' are so obviously anti-Catholic, why did Stanfield agree to illustrate the book in the first place? The answer to this may be found by referring to the genesis of the text. By February 24 only four of the 'Travelling Letters Written on the Road' had appeared in the *Daily News*. Of these, the first three letters were devoted to France, and, if Stanfield's decision to illustrate the book was made on the basis of these, he clearly did not realise what was to follow. Throughout March and April Dickens continued with the final stage of the composition and Stanfield probably did not come to his decision to withdraw until he had read the entire book.

That there was confusion caused by the late change of illustrators and that Palmer's help was sought in a hurry is corroborated by a letter of Palmer's to an anonymous 'Dear Sir' whom he consulted about the price he should charge Dickens:[2]

Mr Dickens has applied to me to draw on wood vignettes of Italian subjects for a work he is about to publish (which it will be better not to mention till he advertises it) as he may not wish it to be known. As the time is very pressing he will (should he decide on seeing my sketches this afternoon) send the publishers to me to settle terms, etc. If they ask me what I charge I shall not know what to ask. Mr Dickens says that besides doing the drawings I shall have to oversee the blocks in their progress. They will be about this size [sketch of building on lakeside, boat and two figures inside, two inches by three inches] and like those in Roger's Italy.

I should wish to do them cheaply but have not a notion about the price. If you could give me a gauge by return of post I should feel obliged and I will come over and speak to you about it as soon as possible but at present cannot leave – expecting Mr. Dickens at 11 o'clock and the publishers in the course of the day or tomorrow. The time when I will call is uncertain.

> I remain Dear Sir
> Yours affec.
> S. Palmer

The small vignettes in Rogers's *Italy* to which Palmer refers became fashionable after the poem's publication in 1822, although the style itself may be traced back to the work of Thomas Bewick.

Palmer executed four drawings for the travel book, for which he received twenty guineas. Two of the drawings, one of the Villa D'Este at Tivoli from the Cypress Avenue and the other of the Vineyard Scene, were designed to allow the text to be dropped in, while the remaining two, the Street of the Tombs, Pompeii and the Colosseum, were sketches measuring about two by three inches.

Since no preliminary sketches by Stanfield survive we cannot know how he intended to illustrate *Pictures from Italy*, but that he felt compromised by the book's marked anti-Catholicism and unsympathetic view of Italy and therefore withdrew from the work does appear likely.

The present edition includes not only the four original illustrations by Palmer, but also two watercolour drawings that he made of two of the same subjects. To these have been added four illustrations by contemporary artists, James Holland, William Callow, J. D. Harding and David Roberts.

1. Leslie C. Staples, 'A Kensal Green Circle, *The Dickensian*, XXXVII (1941), 129.
2. Samual Palmer, letter addressed 'Dear Sir' (1846), Huntington Library, HM, 26326.

Notes

1. *Dr. Wiseman's interpretation.* Nicholas Patrick Stephen Wiseman (1802–65), Cardinal. See J. J. Delaney and J. E. Tobin, *Dictionary of Catholic Biography.*

2. *in Switzerland.* Dickens took his family to Lausanne early in June and stayed there till the end of November 1846. During these months he was busy with his Christmas story, *The Battle of Life,* and with the opening numbers of *Dombey and Son.*

3. *the shady halls of the Pantechnicon.* See *Mechanics Magazine,* 15 (1830), 393, for an article describing the building in Motcomb Street, Belgrave Square, which was originally a bazaar, but afterwards converted into a furniture warehouse.

4. *in the circle at Astley's or Franconi's.* Astley's Amphitheatre was founded in London *c.* 1770 by Philip Astley. Astley's, also known as Davis', specialized in equestrian spectacles, burlettas, and pantomimes.

   In winter, Astley's Circus travelled on the Continent: in 1783 Astley opened a permanent circus in Paris, Amphithéâtre Astley, which in 1793 was taken over by Antonio Franconi, the Italian trainer of birds, who later became an accomplished equestrian himself and whose numerous descendants played a major role in the history of the French circus. In 1807 Franconi opened a new theatre, Cirque Olympique, the first of three successive buildings to bear that name. His circus became equally renowned throughout Europe for its spectacles and equestrian events.

   'The Courier of Saint Petersburgh' was a hippodrama in which Andrew Ducrow (1793–1842), the celebrated English equestrian, starred. Ducrow entered the ring dressed in a dashing military costume, bestriding two horses. As the drama progressed, anywhere from three to seven additional horses galloped between the original two, with Ducrow scooping up their reins as they passed beneath him and managing all the horses at once.

5. *Madame Tussaud.* Marie, née Grosholtz, Tussaud (1760–1850), the Swiss modeller in wax, who came to England in 1800 and

toured the country with her life-size portrait waxworks. In 1835 she set up a permanent exhibition in Baker Street, London.

Mr. Murray's Guide-Book. In 1820 John Murray (1778–1843) published Mariana Starke's *Guide for Travellers on the Continent*; by 1832 the book was in its eighth edition and its success led to a series of guide-books, several of which were written by Murray's son John (1808–92). Dickens is probably referring to the latter's own *Handbook for Travellers in France*, 1843.

6. *Tom Noddy, in the farce.* A foolish or stupid person.

7. *one of the descriptions in the Arabian Nights.* According to Tadao Yamamoto (*Growth and System of the Language of Dickens: An Introduction to a Dickens Lexicon*, Osaka, 1950, p. 67), *Arabian Nights' Entertainments* was the book most frequently referred to by Dickens. The next most frequent was Defoe's *Robinson Crusoe* (1719). See *PI*, p. 41.

8. *the painter of the Primrose family.* Dickens is referring to Oliver Goldsmith's novel *The Vicar of Wakefield* (pub. 1766), about Dr Primrose, the vicar, and his family.

9. *Rienzi.* Cola di Rienzi (1313–54) was a Roman tribune, who in 1347 established a republic, but was obliged to abdicate. He was exiled for seven years, returned to Rome, was made a senator, and assassinated shortly afterwards.

10. *of God's own Image. Genesis*, I, 27.

11. *Ostade.* Adriaen van Ostade (1610–84), Dutch artist and etcher.

12. *this Palace of the Popes.* From 1309–78 Avignon was the residence of seven Popes.

13. *the passages more squalid . . . than any in Saint Giles's.* St Giles', the area bounded by Bainbridge, Dyott and High Streets near Seven Dials, was one of London's most notorious 'rookeries' – the over-crowded courts and alleys where nineteenth-century Irish immigrants settled.

14. *like death and the lady, at the top of the old ballad.* Lenore, the heroine of the ballad by Gottfried August Bürger (1747–94), is carried off on horseback by the spectre of her lover. See also *A Tale of Two Cities*, II, chap. 9.

15. *Vauxhall Gardens.* Vauxhall was the most famous of the eighteenth-century resorts, on the south bank of the Thames, which survived until 1859.

16. Sir Anthony van Dyck (1599–1641) was active in Genoa between 1621 and 1627.

17. *the English Banker*. Dickens's friend, Thomas C. Curry.

18. Samuel Pepys (1633–1703). See *The Diary of Samuel Pepys*, 9 August 1663.

19. Francesco Petrarch (1304–74) and Giovanni Boccaccio (1313–75).

20. *Massena in the time of the terrible Blockade*. André Massena (1758–1817), a French general of the Revolutionary Wars. In 1797 the neutrality of the republic of Genoa was violated by both the French and the British. Under pressure from Napoleon, Genoa was transformed into an 'equalitarian' Ligurian republic, under a French protectorate. In 1800 Massena was besieged in Genoa by the allies; great suffering ensued for the population. Temporary economic relief came in 1805 when France annexed the republic; but the British blockade of the Continental ports, a retaliation against the Berlin and Milan Decrees of 1806, stifled what remained of Genoa's maritime trade. In 1814 Britain and her allies yielded Genoa to the Kingdom of Sardinia.

21. Louis Simond (1767–1831), *A Tour in Italy and Switzerland*, London, 1828. In a letter to Forster, Dickens spoke highly of this book: 'It is a most charming book, and eminently remarkable for its excellent sense, and determination "not to give in to conventional lies".' See Forster, *Life of Charles Dickens* (London, 1872–74), II, 91.

22. Sir Hudson Lowe (1769–1844). British general and governor of St Helena at the time of Napoleon's exile there.

23. Dr. Francesco Antommarchi (1780–1838). Napoleon's physician at St Helena from 1818.

24. *like Mawworm's*. Mawworm, protagonist of *The Hypocrite* (1769), by Isaac Bickerstaffe.

25. *we were declared in quarantine*. Cf. *Little Dorrit*, I, chap. 2, where the travellers are quarantined in Marseilles' harbour because they have 'come from the East.'

26. *invasions of the Barbary Corsairs*. The cruisers of Barbary (the Saracen countries along the north coast of Africa) frequently attacked the ships and coasts of Christian countries.

27. *Hamlet in Ophelia's closet*. *Hamlet*, II, i, 77–80.

28. *like Birnam Wood*. The wood through which the army of Malcom and Macduff passed to attack Macbeth, *Macbeth*, V, iv.

29. *This cathedral is odorous*. The Cupola was decorated with frescoes by Antonio Allegri Correggio (*c*. 1489–1534) between 1522 and 1530.

30. *Mazeppa! To-night!* Byron's *Mazeppa, a Poem* (1819) inspired several dramatic adaptations. *Mazeppa; or, The Wild Horse of the Ukraine* by Henry M. Milner, opened at the Royal Coburg, London, in 1823; *Mazeppa, ou Le Cheval Tartare* by Jean Cuvelier de Trie and Léopold Chandezon, opened in Paris at the Cirque Olympique in 1825.

31. *a mock-heroic poem.* The Rape of the Bucket (1622) by Alessandro Tassoni (1565–1635).

32. *the Deputy Usher of the Black Rod.* Short for 'Gentleman Usher of the Black Rod', so called from his black wand of office, the Chief Gentleman Usher of the Lord Chamberlain's department of the royal household.

33. *as Jeremy Diddler would say.* The chief character in James Kenney's farce *Raising the Wind* (1803).

    like Gulliver in Brobdingnag. See *Gulliver's Travels* (1726), by Jonathan Swift, pt. II.

34. Guido Reni (1575–1642) and Domenichino, properly Domenico Zampieri (1581–1641), were the most proficient followers of the Carracci brothers' school in Bologna. Ludovico Carracci (1555–1619).

35. *Lord Byron.* Byron passed through Bologna twice in 1819, staying at the Ancient Pellegrino inn. Byron owned no property in that area; possibly the waiter was referring to an estate of the Guiccioli family.

36. Ludovico Ariosto (1474–1533), spent the greater part of his life at Ferrara; Torquato Tasso (1544–95) spent many years at the court of Ferrara. He was imprisoned there by Duke Alphonso II of Este from 1579–86.

37. *Parisina and her lover.* 'Parisina' (1816), by Byron, stanza XVIII. The poem deals with the domestic tragedy of the Marquis of Este, who discovered the incestuous loves of his wife Parisina and his bastard son Hugo; both were beheaded.

38. *a staircase, called, I thought, the Giants'.* The Giants' Stairway, with the statues of Mars and Neptune by Jacopo Tatti Sansovino (*c.* 1486–1570), is part of the Doge's Palace.

39. *Yorick's Ghost.* Yorick, the King's former jester, whose skull the gravediggers turn up when digging Ophelia's grave, *Hamlet*, V, i.

40. *shouts of Montagues and Capulets. Romeo and Juliet*, I, i, 89–91.

41. *a Policinello funny.* Policinello < It. *pulcinella.* The name of the principal character in a puppet-show of Italian origin; the prototype of Punch.

42. *the Mysteries of Paris*). Eugène Sue, *Les Mystères de Paris* (1842–43), a sensational novel of the Parisian underworld.

43. *There is no world. Romeo and Juliet,* III, iii, 17–20.

44. *Virgil – our Poet.* Virgil (70–19 BC) was born at Andes, a village near Mantua.

45. *The geese who saved the Capitol.* The geese in the Roman temple of Juno, which by their cackling warned the inhabitants against invading Gauls in the fourth century, BC.

46. Sir Joshua Reynolds (1723–92), 'Fifteen Discourses,' delivered to students between 1769 and 1790 on the history of painting.

47. *The secret of the length of Midas' ears.* Midas, a semi-legendary king of Phrygia, imprudently declared on one occasion that Pan was a superior flute-player to Apollo. In retaliation, the offended god changed his ears to those of an ass, to indicate his stupidity. Midas attempted to conceal this; but his barber saw the length of his ears, and, unable to keep the secret, yet afraid to reveal it, whispered the fact to some reeds, and these, whenever agitated by the wind, passed on the story that Midas had the ears of an ass.

48. *The Palazzo del Te.* The Palazzo was designed in 1525 by Guilio Romano (1499–1546) for the Gonzagas and was decorated with huge frescoes by Romano and his pupils.

49. *Houndsditch, London.* Houndsditch, a street in the City of London between Aldgate and Bishopsgate, was formerly the centre of the old clothes trade; in the nineteenth century it became the headquarters of the ready-made clothing industry.

50. *if I may quote Mrs Primrose.* 'However, Miss Carolina . . . Skeggs has my warm heart,' *Vicar of Wakefield,* chap. 12.

51. *(as Barry shows).* James Barry (1741–1806), 'Lecture III – On Design,' *The Works of James Barry,* 2 vols., London, 1809.

52. *after the opera, under the title of Prometheus.* In 1799 Salvatore Vigano, dancer and composer, devised a ballet 'Die Geschopfe des Prometheus' ('The Creatures of Prometheus'), and commissioned Beethoven in 1800 to write the music (op. 43).

53. Grumio, one of Petruchio's servants, *Taming of the Shrew,* IV, i, 72.

54. *The then reigning Duke of Modena.* Francis IV (1779–1846), a reactionary and despotic sovereign and the penultimate of the Este rulers. Louis Philippe, King of France, 1830–48.

55. 'Norma,' an opera in two acts by Vincenzo Bellini (1801–35), first performed in London, 20 June 1833 at the King's.

56. *Nor is it only distance that lends enchantment to the view.* ''Tis distance lends enchantment to the view, And robes the mountain in its azure hue,' Thomas Campbell (1777–1844), *Pleasures of Hope*, pt. I, 1.7.

57. *Mr Harris, Bookseller.* The book Dickens is referring to is Rev. Isaac Taylor's *Scenes in Europe; for the Amusement and Instruction of Little Tarry-at-Home Travellers* (J. Harris and Son: London, 1819).

58. Andrea del Sarto (1486–1531), Florentine painter.

59. Tobias George Smollett left England in 1769 and died in 1771 at Monte Nero, near Leghorn.

60. Constantine the Great, Roman Emperor (306–37); Septimius Lucius Severus, Roman Emperor (193–211); Titus Flavius Savinus Vespasianus, Roman Emperor (79–81).

61. *the Circus of Romulus.* The Circus of Maxentius or Romulus on the Via Appia, outside Rome, built in 311 AD, is one of the best preserved.

62. Cæcilia Metella was the daughter of Metellus Creticus and wife of Marcus Licinius Crassus, Caesar's legate in Gaul.

63. Gregory XVI (Pope from 1831–46).

64. *Circus Maximus.* The Great Roman circus which occupied the hollow between the Palatine and Aventine hills at Rome.

65. Claudius (Tiberius Claudius Drusus Nero Germanicus), Emperor of Rome from 41–54, who invaded Britain in 43 AD.

66. *the church of the Ara Cœli.* S. Maria d'Aracoeli stands on the spot where the Sybil of the Tiber is said to have announced the coming of Christ to Augustus. The Temple of Jupiter was on the Capitoline Hill.

67. *General Tom Thumb.* This name was given to Charles Sherwood Stratton (1838–83), an American midget exhibited in England by Phineas Taylor Barnum (1810–91), the great American showman, in 1844 and 1857.

68. *poor old Duncan . . . having so much blood in him. Macbeth*, V, i, 35–6.

69. *a Jolly young Waterman.* A man working on a boat or among boats, especially a boatman (as the licensed wherry-man of London) who plied for hire on a river. A drayman was a man who drove a dray (in England, usually a brewer's dray). Barclay, Perkin's brewery in Southwark was one of the largest London breweries in the nineteenth century.

70. Titian (Tiziano Vecello), 1477?–1576; Jacopo Robusti Tintoretto (1518–94); Michaelangelo Buonarroti (1475–1564); Raffaello Santi (1483–1520); Leo IV (Pope from 847–855).

71. Antonio Canova (1757–1822); Lorenzo Bernini (1599–1680).

72. Rembrandt van Rijn (1606–69); Carlo Dolci (1616–88); Bartolomé Esteban Murillo (1618–82); Salvator Rosa (1615–73); Spagnoletto, properly Jusepe de Ribera (1591–1652), the Spanish painter, who settled in Naples *c.* 1616 and remained there for the rest of his life; Beatrice Cenci, one of the daughters of Count Francesco Cenci, towards whom the Count conceived an incestuous passion. After vain attempts to escape her miserable situation, Beatrice plotted with her stepmother and brother to murder the tyrant. Two hired assassins carried out the deed, but the Cenci fell under suspicion, were arrested and executed for parricide in 1599. Cf. Dickens's description of Guido Reni's painting of Beatrice with Shelley's description of the work in his Preface to his play *The Cenci* (1819).

According to Stuart Curran (*Shelley's Cenci: Scorpions Ringed with Fire* (Princeton: Princeton University Press, 1970, p. xi), modern scholars have disproved the ascription of the painting to Reni and that the portrait of the girl is of Beatrice Cenci. A century ago it was one of Rome's most famous pictures, today, writes Curran, it 'hangs modestly in the Palazzo Corsini among the cast-offs of Rome's more august museums.'

73. Pompey (Gnaeus Pompeius, 106–48); Gaius Julius Caesar (102?–44). Caesar fell to a conspiracy led by M. Brutus and C. Cassius, and died at the foot of Pompey's statue.

74. Horace (Quintus Horatius Flaccus, 65–8).

75. Marcus Tullius Cicero (106–43); Marcus Porcius Cato (the Censor), a Roman statesman. He was born at Tusculum, fifteen miles south-east of Rome in 234; he died in BC 149.

76. Marcus Aurelius Antoninus, Roman Emperor from 121–80; Trajan (Marcus Ulpius Traiānus), Roman Emperor from 98–117.

77. Epulo (Gaius) Cestius was from a rich Roman family which had

recently entered public life. He held the tribunate and praetor-ship. He died BC 12 and was buried in a large pyramidal tomb still to be seen in Rome by the Porta S. Paolo.

78. The body of Percy Bysshe Shelley (1792–1822) was cremated near Viareggio; afterwards his ashes were taken to the Protestant cemetery at Rome. John Keats (1795–1821) died at Rome and was buried in the same cemetery, desiring that these words should be engraved on his tomb: 'Here lies one whose name was writ in water.' *Epitaph*. Lord Houghton, *Life of Keats*, ii, 91.

79. Ferdinand II (1810–59), King of the Two Sicilies from 1830.

80. Barbarossa, the nick-name of Frederick I, emperor of the Holy Roman Empire (1152–90). He made five expeditions into Italy in order to subjugate the people.

81. Tiberius Claudius Nero Caesar, Roman Emperor (14–37). Tiberius left Rome in 26 AD for Capri and did not return again, but corresponded by letter with the Senate. While stories of his vice while living there may be discounted, his mind was almost certainly unhinged in the last six years of his life.

82. Canute, King of England (1016–35), who tried to command the advancing tide.

83. *the revolt of Masaniello*. Tommaso Aniello, a Neapolitan fisher-man, who in 1647, led a revolt of the inhabitants against their Spanish rulers. Though the revolt was temporarily successful, he was afterwards assassinated.

84. Herculaneum, the ancient city six miles south-east of Naples; Pompeii was thirteen miles south-east. Both were destroyed by an eruption of Mount Vesuvius in 79 AD.

85. Leopold II (1797–1870), the last grand duke of Tuscany; the Medici, the family that ruled Florence from 1434 and were grand dukes of Tuscany from 1569–1737.

86. Alighieri Dante (1265–1321) was exiled from Florence in 1301 when the Black Guelfs seized power; Dante celebrated his love for Beatrice in the 'Vita Nuova' and the 'Paradiso' of his *Divina Commedia*.

Bibliography

WRITINGS BY DICKENS

Travelling Letters Written on the Road, *Daily News*, January 21, 1846; January 24; January 31; February 9; February 16; February 26; March 2; March 11.

Pictures from Italy. London, 1846.

Travelling Letters Written on the Road, *The Eclectic Magazine*, VII, April 1846, 540–50; VIII, May 1846, 45–56; June 1846, 239–42; July 1846, 397–412; August 1846, 519–33; IX, September 1846, 109–24; October 1846, 190–202.

Travelling Letters Written on the Road. 2 vols., New York, 1846.

L'Italia. Impressioni e descrizioni de Carlo Dickens. Traduzione con note, del Prof. Edoardo Bolchesi. Milano, 1879.

Impressioni d'Italia (*Pictures from Italy*), 1844–1845. Traduzione prefazione, bibliografia e note di Luigi Caneschi. 2 vols., Lanciano, 1911.

REVIEWS OF PICTURES FROM ITALY

Pictures from Italy. Anon. review, *The Athenaeum*, no. 969, May 23, 1846, 519–20; no. 970, May 30, 1846, 546–47.

Pictures from Italy. Anon. review, *The Examiner*, May 30, 1846, pp. 340–41.

Pictures from Italy, by Charles Dickens. Anon. review, *The Times*, June 1, 1846, p. 7.

Dickens's *Pictures from Italy*. Anon. review, *Chambers' Edinburgh Journal*, n.s., V, January–June, 1846, 389–91.

Pictures from Italy. Anon. review, *The Patrician*, I, June, 1846, 182–86.

Dickens' *Pictures from Italy*. Anon. review, *Tait's Edinburgh Magazine*, n.s., XIII, July, 1846, 461–66.

BIBLIOGRAPHY

Dickens's *Pictures from Italy*. Anon. review, *The Dublin Review*, XXI, September, 1846, 184–201.

Pictures from Italy. Anon. review, *The Gentleman's Magazine*, XXVI, July to December, 1846, 3–21.

Pictures from Italy, by Charles Dickens. Anon. review, *The Anglo-American*, VII, June 20, 1846, 193–95.

Fuller, Margaret. Dickens's *Pictures from Italy*. *New York Daily Tribune*, July 24, 1846, p. 1.

PARODIES

Mr. Charles Dickens's Travelling Letters. *Mephystopheles*, I, March 21, 1846, 188.

A Parody. *Mephystopheles*, I, March 28, 1846, 188.

SECONDARY SOURCES

Brand, C. P. *Italy and the English Romantics: The Italianate Fashion in Early Nineteenth-Century England.* Cambridge, 1957.

——. A Bibliography of Travel-Books Describing Italy Published in England 1800–1850, *Italian Studies*, II, 1956, 108–17.

Cannavó, Federico. *Charles Dickens e L'Italia, Nuova Antologia*, 1914, pp. 277–96.

Carlton, William J. Dickens Studies Italian, *Dickensian* LXI, May 1965, 101–8.

Hale, J. R. *England and the Italian Renaissance: The Growth of Interest in its History and Art.* London, 1954.

——. *The Italian Journal of Samuel Rogers, Edited with an Account of Roger's Life and Travel in Italy in 1814–1821.* London, 1956.

Hyatt, Alfred H. (ed.). *The Charm of Venice: an Anthology.* London, 1924.

Massoul, Henri. 'Trois Voyages D'Italie,' *Mercure de France*, vol. 173, 1924, 96–129.

Maugham, H. Neville. *The Book of Italian Travel* (1590–1900). London, 1903.

Morrison, Helen Barber. *The Golden Age of Travel: Literary Impressions of the Grand Tour.* New York, 1951.

Rabizzini, G. 'L'Italia e Dickens,' *Bozzetti de letterature italiana e straniera.* 1914.

Rugoff, Milton. *The Great Travellers.* 2 vols., New York, 1960.

Savanarola, Don Jeremy [Francis S. Mahony]. *Facts and Figures from Italy. Addressed During the Last Two Winters to Charles Dickens, Esq. Being an Appendix to his Pictures.* London, 1847.

Schuyler, Eugene. *Italian Influences.* New York, 1901.

Snyder, Louis and R. B. Morris. *A Treasury of Great Reporting.* New York, 1949.

Index

Index